The Politics of Globalization
in the United States

Edward S. Cohen

Georgetown University Press / Washington, D.C.

Georgetown University Press, Washington, D.C.

© 2001 by Georgetown University Press. All rights reserved.

Printed in the United States of America

10 9 8 7 6 5 4 3 2 1   2001

This volume is printed on acid-free, offset book paper.

Library of Congress Cataloging-in-Publication Data

Cohen, Edward S., 1960–
    The politics of globalization in the United States / by Edward S. Cohen.
        p. cm.— (Essential texts in American government)
    Includes bibliographical references and index.
    ISBN 0-87840-826-6 (cloth : alk. paper) — ISBN 0-87840-827-4 (pbk. : alk. paper)
        1. United States—Economic policy—1993– 2. United States—Politics and
    government—1993– 3. Globalization. I. Title. II. Series.

HC106.82.C64 2001
337.73–dc21   00-061016

Table of Contents

List of Figures   v

List of Tables   v

Preface   vii

Part I: Introduction

Chapter 1: Globalization and the Future of American Politics
and Policymaking   3

Part II: Sovereignty and Globalization

Chapter 2: The Sovereign State, the Nation, and
Popular Sovereignty   33

Chapter 3: Globalization in the Contemporary World:
The End of Sovereignty?   55

Part III: Globalization and the Politics of American Public Policy

Chapter 4: The Politics of Trade and the Clamor for Sovereignty   87

Chapter 5: Immigration and the Politics of Membership   118

Chapter 6: E Pluribus Unum? The Politics of Official English
and Bilingual Education   143

Part IV: Conclusions

Chapter 7: Which Future for the American Polity?   167

Notes   181

Bibliography   201

Index   210

List of Figures

Figure 1-1: Imports and Exports as a Percentage of U.S. Gross Domestic
   Product (GDP), 1950–97   8
Figure 4-1: Growth of World Trade and Economic Output, 1960–95   97
Figure 4-2: Change in Share of Income Received by Each Quintile
   from 1979 to 1995   106
Figure 4-3: Male Full-Time, Year-Round Workers by Real Earnings Range 107
Figure 5-1: Legal Immigration to the United States, Fiscal Years 1901–98 129

List of Tables

Table 3-1: Merchandise Exports as a Percentage of GDP, 1870–1992   70
Table 5-1: Percentage of Immigrants Admitted to the United States
   by Region and Period, Fiscal Years 1955–97   131

Preface

This book is the product of an interest in "globalization" that goes back to the beginning of the 1990s. Indeed, my concern with this issue predates my familiarity with the term and the wide range of research and debate it has generated in academic circles. The real source of this interest was my fascination with and puzzlement over the emergence of widespread popular movements against further immigration and the North American Free Trade Agreement (NAFTA), which coalesced around the presidential primaries of 1992. These were movements that brought together groups and individuals from the left, the center, and the right of the American political spectrum who had always seemed at odds on the fundamental issues of modern political life. But rather than fighting each other, they were cooperating to fight the same political developments and attacking the mainstream political establishment in strikingly similar terms. Moreover, the same kinds of concerns spawned the Reform Party and the presidential candidacy of H. Ross Perot, who seemed to come from nowhere to capture a substantial share of the vote in 1992. Suddenly, the issues of trade, immigration, and language were at the roots of a protest movement that was challenging some of the key pillars of American public policy over the past two or three decades. The research that culminated in this book began as an attempt to figure out why this had happened and what it meant for understanding American politics and policymaking.

It was in the process of pursuing this work that I came across the concept of globalization and the large literature surrounding its meaning, history, and utility as a means to help us understand the direction of contemporary politics. As you will find, I don't use the concept in the same way that many popular commentators and best-selling authors do, and I have some doubts about anyone's ability to salvage the concept from the many simplifications that are often associated with it. Nonetheless, I do believe that globalization is a useful and necessary concept if we are going to come to grips with the changing politics of policymaking in the

United States. As I argue in the book, over the past three decades the relationship between American society and the larger global context has undergone much transformation, as our daily lives have become more and more immersed in and shaped by global developments. Though these changes began during the Cold War, it was only at the end of that period that Americans began to recognize how their lives had changed. When Americans began looking more closely at globalization and its impact on their lives, many found it quite disturbing. During the 1990s, the issue of globalization has come to shape many if not most of the major debates in American politics and has come to be the context in which we figure out the relationship of the United States to the larger globe in a world no longer defined by superpower rivalry. It behooves us, then, to figure out what globalization is about and what it means for the future of the polity.

If this was not clear a couple of years ago, the events surrounding the November 1999 meeting of the World Trade Organization (WTO) in Seattle have ensured that globalization will be a central theme in American politics for a long time to come. The protests outside these meetings raised or illustrated a number of dimensions of the impact of globalization, two of which are especially relevant to the arguments in this book. First, the variety of individuals, groups, and movements that coalesced in Seattle—and the variety of issues they raised or represented—embody the multiple ways in which globalization is shaping the evolution of American society and its relationship with the larger world. These protesters raised a gamut of issues—including trade, income inequality, environmental protection, the rights of migrants, human rights protections, the rights of workers, and the cultural impact of economic change—and found that they all could be tied together by the issue of globalization. In this book, I explore the politics of three areas of policymaking in the United States—trade, immigration, and language—with the same conviction. Rather than being a set of isolated phenomena, the processes of globalization are part of a larger transformation of the role of government in society and of the relationship between states and the global system. Through my analysis of these policy areas, I hope to show the depth of the challenge that globalization poses for our accepted understandings of the shape and purposes of the American political community.

Second, these protests made it clear that any discussion of globalization will have to include a serious consideration of the nature and future of the sovereignty of the modern state. On this issue, my analysis diverges more radically from that of many if not most of the antiglobalization activists in Seattle. I do not believe that globalization has destroyed the sovereignty or relevance of the modern state, nor do I find much sense in the claim that institutions such as the WTO are the vehicle of some emerging "super-sovereign" but unaccountable international powers. Instead, a central theme of my argument in the book is that contemporary globalization is the product of the choices and actions of sovereign states—and especially of the United States—to transform the relationship between the state and the society within its territorial borders. Globalization is the result of, and cannot survive without, a new understanding of the priorities and responsibilities of sovereign states. In my view, globalization emerged from a set of political choices, many of which can be traced back to the 1970s and were driven by domestic political forces and circumstances, to create more market-oriented societies and a more open international economy. Its future, in turn, rests on the success of a new model of the relationship between government and society, one with deep roots in the American political experience.

In the process of presenting this argument, this book also examines the strengths and limitations of existing theories and concepts in political science as tools for understanding globalization. If the contemporary phenomena of global change have political roots, they require a political explanation. This kind of explanation has been lacking in much of the popular discussion of globalization, and one aim of this book is to help provide the tools necessary for a cohesive political understanding of what is happening in our world. While I identify and employ a wide variety of concepts and ideas in political science, the book also suggests important limitations in some of the major approaches of the discipline. This is particularly true in the area of American politics and public policymaking. A final aim of my analysis is to illustrate how students of American politics and policy need to use many of the tools developed in the study of international and comparative politics in their attempts to grapple with the changes facing contemporary American life. Just as globalization is breaking down many of the existing boundaries between "domestic" and "international" politics, so political analysts seeking to understand globalization must break down the boundaries between the concepts and theories that have been developed to explain these different dimensions of modern political life.

Over the years in which I have worked on this project, numerous audiences have heard versions of my argument and provided constructive responses. Panel members and attendees at various meetings of the Midwest Political Science Association and the Northeastern Political Science Association have been attentive and critical readers of my work. I am particularly grateful, though, to two persons. Professor Peter Roman of Duquesne University provided an invitation to present some of my work on trade policy and politics at Duquesne's School of Public and Social Policy, where I received very helpful comments from a well-informed audience. Most important, Professor Graham Wilson of the University of Wisconsin-Madison provided me an invaluable opportunity to present my work on globalization and the politics of immigration to a meeting of the Committee on the Structure and Organization of Governance (SOG) of the International Political Science Association, and provided continuing encouragement to develop my ideas about globalization into a more systematic presentation. The quality of the criticisms and questions asked of my work—and of the discussion of globalization over the whole meeting—was extraordinarily high, and gave me the necessary support and push to complete this project.

At Westminster I owe numerous debts. The Department of Political Science and Sociology has been very supportive of my work, provided an opportunity to present some of it to the department colloquium, and most important, has been a model of academic collegiality that has made all my efforts that much more rewarding. The Faculty Development Committee, the Dean of the College, Dr. John Deegan, and the Faculty Development Director, Dr. Fritz Horn, have helped me pursue my research through grants to fund travel to conferences and research costs, and through a course release that was essential to allow me to finish the manuscript in a respectable time period. All of these persons do much to help make scholarship and research an essential part of life at a small liberal arts college. I also need to give special thanks to Ms. Connie Davis of McGill Library at Westminster, who patiently put up with my never ending and never predictable requests for interlibrary loan materials. Outside Westminster, the staff of the law library at Duquesne University (though unaware of it at the time) helped provide a wonderful context for writing an early draft of much of the book. And I owe a special debt to John Samples of Georgetown University Press, who suggested the idea in the first place and supported the project all along.

Finally, and most important, I owe the greatest debt to Susan Seitz, who constantly reminded me that from the perspective of a law student, the opportunity to work on this book looked like a privilege. For this, and for all the joys of our life together, I dedicate this book to her.

PART I

Introduction

1 ∞

Globalization and the Future of American Politics and Policymaking

As a new century begins, the United States is in a uniquely privileged and powerful position. The decade of the 1990s began with the fall of the Soviet Union and left the United States as the unchallenged global military and political superpower. New or potential aspirants to this status, such as the European Union, Russia, or China, proved too weak or disorganized to pose any significant threat to America's position, a situation confirmed by the Persian Gulf War, the Yugoslavian crises, and many similar events. Economically, the 1990s turned out to be a period of unprecedented and sustained economic growth, which brought new jobs and higher incomes to most Americans while wiping out the annual national budget deficits that had plagued the country since the late 1960s. As Europe and Japan suffered sustained recessions, the United States regained its status as the world's dominant economic power. Meanwhile, America's cultural power, reflected in the spread of its popular culture, the outbreak of democratic revolutions, and its continuing attraction for, and successful integration of, migrants from around the world, continued to grow. If the globe is becoming a more closely interdependent "village," the United States remains its most dominant and leading resident.

Or so it seems. While much of the political, economic, and cultural establishment endorses this vision of a triumphant America, an increasingly vocal and influential group of Americans has voiced a powerful and direct challenge to this account of their country's present and future. From this perspective, the dominant reality of the 1990s has been the globalization of American life. The major result of this phenomenon has been the loss of American sovereignty, the diminished ability of Americans to control their own fates. Whether the challenge comes from the right in the voices of Pat Buchanan and Pat Robertson, from the left in the persons of Jesse Jackson and Ralph Nader, or from the uncertain terrain of Ross Perot and his supporters, the conclusions are the same. The majority of

Americans are now subject to global forces of economic and political power that enrich and benefit a narrow stratum of elite interests at the expense of the larger society. The result has been a decline of the powers of self-government, growing economic insecurity, and an attack on America's values.

Meanwhile, government has proved itself unable to protect Americans from these challenges, as it is rendered powerless and subservient in the face of global changes. Rather than presenting new opportunities, these critics view the new millennium as a source of tangible and weighty threats to American prosperity, self-government, and identity. In November 1999, many of these Americans were marching in the streets of Seattle, protesting a conference of ministers of the World Trade Organization (WTO). For this diverse group of labor union members, economic nationalists, environmentalists, and human rights activists, the WTO was the embodiment of those uncontrollable global forces threatening America's values and our ability to shape our own future.

As a result of this ongoing debate, the term "globalization" has become a staple of public discourse during the 1990s. In the words of Paul Krugman, "Whatever else they might have been, the 90's were the decade of globalization."[1] Newspapers and newsmagazines regularly feature stories or opinion pieces discussing globalization. On the vast array of television programs concerning politics and the economy, discussions regularly return to the themes of a shrinking world and the growing interconnectedness brought about by economic and technological globalization. Meanwhile, over the decade many of the most well-known and widely discussed new books on current affairs have focused on this theme, and all of the major viewpoints on global change have been well represented on the best-seller lists. Some works, such as Kenichi Ohmae's *The End of the Nation State*[2] and Thomas Friedman's *The Lexus and the Olive Tree*,[3] celebrate globalization as the source of new wealth and opportunities for people across the globe. Moreover, they argue that the most successful societies in the coming decades will be those that are most eager to accept and facilitate this process. In Friedman's view, America's current position as the dominant economic and political power in the world can be traced to its willingness and ability to adapt to globalization. Describing its current prominence, Friedman argues the following:

> America is blamed for this [its economic dominance] because, in so many ways, globalization is us. We are not the tiger. Globalization is the tiger. But we are the people most adept at riding the tiger and we're now telling everyone else to get on or get out of the way. The reason we are so good at riding this tiger is that we raised it as a cub.[4]

As long as it continues to accept and adapt to this new global environment, the United States will remain the world's dominant economic power.

But by far the dominant approach in these works has been critical of the pace and direction of global change and its impact on American democracy. From

William Greider's *One World, Ready or Not*[5] to Patrick J. Buchanan's *The Great Betrayal*,[6] writers from across the political spectrum have identified globalization as the source of much of the troubles facing our society. In Greider's representative view, the technological and wealth-creating benefits of globalization have been far outweighed by its costs for American society:

> In broad terms, the accumulated evidence appeared to be negative: the general stagnation of incomes and loss of high-wage jobs, the slower U.S. economic growth, the widening extremes of wealth and poverty, the nation's staggering foreign indebtedness, the general sense of insecurity and social stress. From these facts alone, it would be most difficult to demonstrate that over the last two decades globalization improved economic well-being for most Americans.[7]

In addition to Greider and Buchanan, Benjamin Barber's *Jihad vs. McWorld*,[8] Robert Kuttner's *Everything for Sale*,[9] and *The Case Against the Global Economy*,[10] edited by Jerry Mander and Edward Goldsmith, have added to the chorus of critics claiming that globalization is threatening some of the fundamental values and institutions of American life.

Moreover, many acute observers of American political and social life have contended that the discontent expressed by these critics has deep roots in the larger political culture. At the beginning of the decade, James Davison Hunter argued that a "culture war" was in full swing in American society, and it presaged an increasingly divided and disenchanted society.[11] A few years later, Christopher Lasch described a "revolt of the elites" that he believed had been in process for two decades.[12] In this revolt, the upper classes in American society and politics had abandoned their obligation to the mass of "average Americans," whose fortunes were increasingly divergent from these prosperous and internationally minded elites. More recently, Susan Tolchin's widely noted *The Angry American* described a pervasive sense of anger that many ordinary Americans feel toward the major institutions of their society, and in particular towards government and the political process.[13] According to Tolchin, many Americans share a deep sense that their interests and values have been betrayed by those who are supposed to protect them, and this feeling has only deepened during the supposedly prosperous and contented years of the 1990s. Michael Sandel's more historically oriented *Democracy's Discontent* also attempted to trace the sources of the disaffection many Americans seem to feel from the larger community.[14] He found a real basis for this mood in the evolution of the policies and priorities of the liberal state, which seemed to explicitly distance itself from the interests and outlook of the majority of Americans.

The violent emergence of the right-wing militia groups over the past few years has also spawned a number of accounts attempting to explain what their authors perceive as widespread discontent within American society. In Catherine

McNicol Stock's *Rural Radicals: Righteous Rage in the American Grain,* the current right-wing challenges to the legitimacy of the government are only the most recent examples of a long line of populist protest in American history.[15] Whether this protest takes the form of left-wing or right-wing activism, it shares a common distrust of the elites and large institutions that dominate American life and a belief that the choices made by the powerful inevitably benefit these groups at the expense of the rest of the nation. McNicol suggests that the violent organized wing of antigovernment protest is only the visible surface of a deep current of resentment and sense of powerlessness shared by large sections of the citizenry.

Clearly, then, there are good reasons to believe that the discontent expressed by the critics of globalization is rooted in some deep currents of American life today. If the shared perceptions of these various observers are even partially accurate, the American polity is becoming increasingly divided over some fundamental issues concerning the direction of political, economic, and social change. It is most likely the case, of course, that those who celebrate and those who condemn the direction of American life and politics in the 1990s are both grappling with real aspects of our society as it is developing in the post-Cold War era. But how can such radically differing visions and understandings of our contemporary situation both be accurate? As a recent article in *The Economist* put it:

> The remarkable thing about the debate over globalization is that it is growing more intractable at a time of unprecedented growth. Eight years of boom mean, in conventional wisdom, that voters don't care about economic issues. It is true that the trade deficit is at record highs, though the latest figures are slightly better. It is also true . . . that parts of manufacturing and agriculture are nearer recession than boom. But new jobs have more than made up the losses and the worst-affected regions—the rust belt and corn belt—have the lowest unemployment rates in the country.[16]

How can American society be prosperous and opportunities plentiful while at the same time it is increasingly divided and many citizens feel such a lack of control over their lives and see such little hope for their future?

The aim of this book is to sort out these conflicting visions of American politics and society. I argue that the emergence of such deeply contrasting analyses of the status of the American polity is closely linked to the nature of globalization and its impact upon American society over the past two decades. Global change, I will show, is indeed working to divide the fates of Americans: while some experience enhanced power and prosperity, significant sectors of society are losing much hope of security and control of their own lives. My central argument in this book is that, in contrast to what the critics claim, these developments are *not* the result of a loss of

American sovereignty. Rather, they are the product of a set of political choices designed to transform the role of government in American society, choices intended to promote American power by subjecting larger and larger areas of our lives to the competitive pressures of the market economy. At the same time, U.S. policymakers have been working to transform the global economy into a more dynamic and integrated system that facilitates the growth of American economic power and the spread of this market-oriented vision around the globe. Globalization is to a great degree the product of the continuing power and sovereignty of the American state, not a sign of its failure. Whether they choose to celebrate or condemn the impact of global change on their lives, Americans need to understand that globalization is the product of the choices and priorities of policymakers acting in their name, not of mysterious or malevolent forces beyond their control. The aim of my analysis in this book is to provide the reader with a better understanding of globalization and of the choices and dilemmas it poses for the American polity.

Globalization as a Political Issue

Nations and states, especially large and dynamic ones, always define themselves and their purposes in terms of the threats and opportunities they face in the global arena. For the United States since the end of the Second World War, the threat or challenge was the spread of communism as embodied in the growing power of the Soviet Union. The purpose and mission of the United States, in turn, was the promotion of freedom and democracy around the world to counter this threat. By the early 1990s, however, the communist threat and the Soviet Union itself had disappeared, depriving Americans of the sense of mission and identity upon which they had relied for so long. American politics has been and will continue to be shaped by the attempt to define a new set of purposes and a new understanding of its identity.

The outcome of this search is by no means certain, but it has not been pursued in a vacuum. Well before the collapse of communism, various developments in domestic and global society had begun to pose new challenges and opportunities for the definition of national purpose. Among these, one of the most significant is the phenomenon of globalization. In its most basic sense, globalization refers to the increasing interconnectedness between events and trends around the world. It indicates the sense in which national borders are less and less important in determining the future of the world's people, whose fate is now subject to forces that work simultaneously all over the globe. For some time now, the issues and challenges surrounding globalization have made up an important part of American political life and have worked to promote the emergence of new kinds of political alignments and arguments.

The Politics of Trade and Economic Globalism

The source of the most persistent and visible impact of global change in the United States has been the changing global economy. This issue first manifested itself in the early 1970s, with a recognition of the emerging Japanese and European challenges to American economic power, and was reflected in a variety of trade disputes and in the collapse of the Bretton Woods system for regulating the global financial system.[17] The recessions of the 1970s and the growth of unemployment in many traditional manufacturing industries led to serious pressure for increased government protection of these industries and their jobs against foreign competition. Though many concessions were made in this direction, American policy choices in the 1970s and 1980s continued to favor free trade and the lowering of protectionist barriers around the world. By the early 1990s, the American economy was much more integrated into and dependent upon the global market system than at any point since 1914. Whether one looks at the movement of capital, the trade in goods, or the investment activities of corporations, the American economy is now deeply enmeshed in the dynamics of an increasingly unified global economy.[18] (See figure 1-1.)

During the 1990s, the wisdom of these developments has become an increasingly important subject of public debate and policy choice, and the debate is now

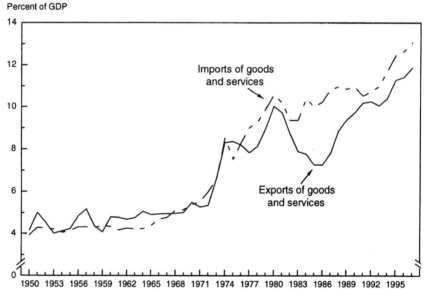

Percent of GDP

Figure 1-1. Imports and Exports as a Percentage of U.S. Gross Domestic Product (GDP), 1950–97. *Source: 1998 Economic Report of the President,* February, 1998, Washington, DC: U.S. Government Printing Office, p. 212

clearly framed in the context of the issue of globalization. The conflicts and controversy surrounding the issue have been clarified in a series of struggles in trade policy, ranging from the North American Free Trade Agreement (NAFTA) treaty ratification in 1993 to the Uruguay Round of the General Agreement on Tariffs and Trade (GATT) agreement to form a World Trade Organization (WTO) in 1995, and from the unsuccessful attempts of the Clinton administration to secure a renewal of "fast-track" negotiating authority in late 1997 to the unexpectedly chaotic demonstrations in Seattle in late 1999. Through the course of these struggles, there has emerged a new and clear set of political arguments and alignments on the question of further immersion of the U.S. economy in the global market system. And most strikingly, what many observers perceived to be a clearly dominant pro-free-trade stance in the early 1990s has turned into a policy arena of increasing uncertainty.[19]

On one side of these conflicts is a coalition that spans the central elements of both the Democratic and Republican parties, the major players in the corporate economy, and most of the established journalistic and academic communities concerned with trade. In their view, the immersion of the American economy in the global marketplace promises to secure continuing benefits of rising standards of living, job creation, consumer choice, and competitiveness. Globalization is portrayed as the wave of the future, an inevitable trend in economic life and a boon to all Americans. Any attempt to resist or reverse this development can only result in declining standards of living and opportunities for the nation as a whole. The following remarks from President Clinton capture this position well:

> History will look back on us and judge how well we responded to this time of intense economic transformation. It is the most intensive period of economic change since the Industrial Revolution. The revolutions in communications and technology, the development of non-stop global markets, the vast currency flows that are now the tides of international business—all these have brought enormous advantages for those who can embrace and succeed in the new global economy. . . . The trend toward globalization, after all, has far surpassed anything the great figures of Bretton Woods could have imagined. Interdependence among nations has grown so deep that literally it is now meaningless to speak of a sharp dividing line between foreign and domestic policy.[20]

Arguments such as these played a central role in securing the approval of the NAFTA and GATT treaties.

A growing chorus of opponents—drawn from the "fringes" of the major parties, from independent political movements on the left and the right, and from a wide variety of citizens dissatisfied with the political process as a whole—challenged this whole analysis. Rather than extolling prosperity, these critics decried what they perceived as a loss of American sovereignty as the fate of Americans was increasingly in the hands of global corporations and international institutions with no responsibility to ordinary citizens. Moreover, globalization had made this sovereignty even more important than ever, as it had created a society in which the ability of citizens to enter into and protect their status and security as part of a broad middle class was diminished by the loss of well-paying manufacturing jobs, widespread corporate downsizing, and increasing inequality of wealth and incomes. As Pat Buchanan has put it recently,

> America's elites are slaves to the ideas of nineteenth-century European scribblers, none of whom ever built a nation. Our industrial base is shrinking and middle America's standard of living is no longer rising, because we forgot how America became a mighty industrial power and we embraced the myth that it was free trade that made us great. To challenge this myth—now an article of faith in both parties— is to be treated as imbecilic or immoral. Yet, the lie must be exposed, for more is being sacrificed on the altar of this Moloch than the jobs of our workers and the standard of living of our people. Our politics are being corrupted, our dependency on unstable foreign regimes is growing, and our survival as a self-reliant and independent republic is at risk.[21]

On the basis of these arguments, this diverse coalition of economic nationalists, reformers, labor unions, and consumer and environmental groups mobilized unexpectedly strong opposition to the major trade agreements and policy choices of the Clinton administration.

The strength of this coalition initially surprised the supporters of free trade. A concerted attempt by these groups to prevent the passage of the NAFTA agreement in Congress, inspired by the success and stature of Ross Perot, had its supporters on the defensive, and only a massive mobilization of effort, money, and political capital secured the passage of the treaty.[22] The much smoother process by which the GATT agreement was negotiated and accepted in Congress seemed to some to indicate that the threat to free trade had passed its height of influence. But the unexpected success of the Pat Buchanan campaign for the 1996 Republican presidential nomination revealed that widespread and continuing worries about free trade were still potent currents in the American political landscape. The revival of tensions surrounding an increasingly fragile global financial system, combined with this widespread political dissatisfaction, proved the confidence of the supporters of open trade increasingly illusory. By the end of 1997, the Clinton administration was forced to drop its attempts to secure a renewal of "fast-track" authority to negotiate further trade agreements, the first major defeat for the proglobalization coalition in the 1990s. Emboldened by this victory, continuing global economic uncertainty, and the ability of protesters to disrupt the WTO ministerial meetings in Seattle, the critics of free trade now occupy a promising position in the policy process.

The Politics of Immigration and Border Control

If economic issues raise some of the largest stakes in globalization, the challenge of immigration presents some of its most tangible effects.[23] Unlike the slow emergence of trade issues, the appearance of immigration on the political agenda in the 1980s was sudden. The quickly rising rates of illegal immigration from the south, the visibility given to the problem of refugees arriving in waves from Southeast Asia and the Caribbean, and the fact that so many of the immigrants were of Asian and Latin American origin all worked to generate public demands for action to regain control over America's borders. These demands, to which Congress responded in a steady stream of legislation from the 1986 Immigration Control Act to the 1990 Immigration Act to the increased commitment of resources to the Border Patrol in the 1990s, asked for an end to illegal immigration and a reconsideration/rewriting of the guidelines for legal immigration. But despite all this pressure and action, the character and levels of immigration did not change drastically over the 1990s. Whereas approximately 7.3 million persons immigrated to the United States in the 1980s, by 1997 about 6.9 million more had arrived. Moreover, the number of Americans who were born in foreign countries continues to grow—from 19.8 million persons in 1990 to 25.8 million in 1997—while their corresponding percentage of the overall American population has also grown—from 7.9% in 1990 to 9.7% in 1997.[24] As in the previous decade, both legal and illegal immigration in the 1990s continued to be dominated by persons arriving from Latin America (especially Mexico), the Caribbean, and Asia.

These patterns have given rise to fundamental disagreements over the impact of global population movement on the character of the political community in the United States. These disagreements and the political alliances to which they give rise are, in turn, strikingly parallel to those concerning trade and economic globalization. On one side of the argument stand the supporters of relatively open immigration policies.[25] Forming a coalition that links employers, human rights activists, and the centers of the major political parties, they emphasize the historic contribution of immigrants to American life and society and indeed to the national mythology. The recent waves of immigrants, they argue, promise to invigorate the economy, the culture, and the polity in similar ways. Immigrants bring crucial economic skills and motivation, along with a commitment to and appreciation of freedom, and they help native-born Americans better understand the larger world with which they are in increasing contact. Indeed, supporters of liberal immigration rules emphasize the connection between these rules and the benefits of economic globalization. Of course, members of this coalition do want to reduce the amount of illegal immigration, but they do not see it as a serious threat to American life, and they tend to worry more about the exclusionary and intolerant impact of anti-immigrant feelings.

On the other side of this issue we see a coalition of unions, cultural and economic nationalists, environmentalists, and some "progressives," sprinkled widely across the political spectrum. These elements are united around a perception that continued immigration is threatening the quality of American economic, political, and social life. The specific arguments vary widely, some emphasizing the role of immigrants in keeping wages down, others their role in bringing new and supposedly unassimilable cultural values into the polity. But all critics come back to the problem of the loss of American sovereignty. The wave of immigration represents the threat that global flows of migration will overwhelm the community's ability to control its own borders, to determine who will be a member of the polity and have access to its benefits. For a nation already facing problems of economic insecurity, environmental damage, and political apathy, large-scale immigration undermines the worth of citizenship for native-born Americans and further threatens their ability to preserve a viable democracy and middle-class society. From this perspective, only drastic measures of immigration reduction and restriction will work to restore the nation's sovereignty.

The 1990s saw a series of ongoing skirmishes as the conflicts over immigration deepened and attempts were made to tinker with immigration and citizenship laws to respond to the critics. On the whole, supporters of the existing policy regime have been successful in defending its basic framework. Proposals to severely curb or totally restrict new immigration, organize mass deportations of illegal workers, and revoke the Constitution's provision of birthright citizenship have received more attention but remain far from enactment. On a variety of lesser issues, however, restrictionists have been able to alter the policy regime to make it more hostile toward migrants. In the case of illegals, a strengthening of the Border Patrol and increasing raids in key industries have had some effect in further reducing whatever sense of security these undocumented migrants may have felt. Most strikingly, the passage of California's Proposition 187, which attempted to deny a whole range of public benefits and services to illegals, marked a major intensification of the attack on current policies. But it has not been only illegals who have been subject to such threats. Since 1994, the Republican-controlled Congress has moved to deny many social services to resident aliens and even naturalized citizens while making it much easier for the Immigration and Naturalization Service (INS) to refuse entry to or summarily deport aliens. These are significant policy changes, which work to sharpen the distinctions between and opportunities of citizens and migrants. Moreover, they have helped to embolden the restrictionist cause and ensure a lively future for this part of the challenge to globalization.

Language and the Politics of Cultural Identity

A third aspect of the impact of global change has been the emergence of a politics of language policy. Though less prominent until recently, the controversy over the role of English in American life illustrates well the dynamics of politics of sovereignty and contains the possibility to spark deep and emotional divisions. In the 1980s, Americans for the first time in decades began to seriously debate the status of English as a national language and especially its role in education. Proposals proliferated at the state and local levels to establish English as the sole official language for the conduct of public business and even for all public displays. Meanwhile, a national movement to challenge the practice of bilingual education in the public schools gained momentum and culminated in the success of California ballot initiative 217, in 1998, prohibiting its use throughout the state. As with trade and immigration, the issue of language had touched deep symbolic and practical questions about the nature of American identity and the priorities of public policymaking.

To this point, the political alliances shaping language policy are less clearly defined than they are in the areas of trade and immigration. The reasons for this can be traced to the more recent emergence of the question, the absence of clear connections to the wider range of interests at stake in policy choices, and especially to the decentralization of education and language policy responsibilities in the American federal system. The clearest continuities, as one would expect, are on the side of those who support the establishment of official protected status for English. Here we see some of the same groups of cultural conservatives and economic nationalists (of the right and the left) that are critical of the other dimensions of the globalization of American society. Language is a crucial symbolic indicator of national identity and culture, and in the modern nation-state "sovereignty" implicates not only the "tangible" questions of goods and persons but also a nation's ability to assert and advance its cultural identity and purposes. The emerging use of new languages (especially Spanish in the United States), we can expect, will be perceived as a threat by those already worried about their status in a new global context, while it will tend to be seen as an advantage for those supporting a greater immersion in the changing world context. To this point, the connections are by no means clear or stable in the controversies over language, but the intensification of such disputes may indeed force political actors to make these linkages, just as they have in the context of trade and immigration conflicts.

Globalization, then, is a multidimensional phenomenon that is working to reshape American society and politics in fundamental ways. As changing global patterns of economic, social, and cultural life increasingly impinge upon the daily lives of Americans, new kinds of divisions, alignments, and issues are emerging in political life. These changes are becoming increasingly central to the structure of

American politics and to the way citizens come to think of their community and nation in relationship to the rest of the world. Globalization has become a key focal point around which Americans define themselves and the purposes of their community. This is a conflicted and dynamic process, which will deeply shape the choices facing American policymaking and political leadership. The outcome of this process is by no means certain, but it is clear that all Americans have a stake in and responsibility for coming to terms with the choices that global change is posing for the polity.

Globalization in American Political Rhetoric

As Americans have become more aware of the impact of global change on the ways they live their lives and the opportunities or constraints they face, political leaders and commentators have attempted to provide interpretations, explanations, and guidance.[26] Since they are actors as well as interpreters, and have policy and political agendas in mind, the arguments they present are oriented to mobilizing support for their positions and ambitions. In this realm of political rhetoric, the emerging divisions concerning globalization and its impact upon American sovereignty are presented and amplified but also clarified. We need to explore the public rhetoric surrounding the impact of global change before we can begin to fully evaluate what it does and does not mean for American public policy and political life.

The first point to notice about this debate is the existence of a common understanding of globalization that seems to be shared by the most prominent commentators on all sides of the issue. This is the contention that globalization is a unified process that is accelerating beyond the control of single nation-states. Global changes on all levels are the product of a growing integration of all elements of social life on a worldwide scale, and governments are increasingly unable to resist them. Crucial imperatives of contemporary life, especially in the economic and technological areas, are pushing aside nation-states and replacing them as the dominant actors in world politics and in shaping the lives of the citizens they rule. William Greider's account captures well this shared understanding:

> The logic of commerce and capital has overpowered the inertia of politics and launched an epoch of great social transformations. Settled facts of material life are being revised for rich and poor nations alike. Social understandings that were formed by the hard political struggles of the twentieth century are put in doubt. Old verities about the rank ordering of nations are revised and a new map of the world is gradually being drawn. These great changes sweep over the affairs of mere

governments and destabilize the established political orders in both advanced and primitive societies.[27]

The alternatives in this debate are two: accept and adjust to global change or resist it by reestablishing tight controls over the borders between the state and the larger world. Either we accept the severe compromise of sovereign power that globalization brings, or we reassert sovereignty by acting to curb the process of global integration.

For the supporters and champions of globalization, the economic and technological imperatives upon which it is based have linked the fates of different states in a manner unprecedented in world history and will only deepen these connections in the coming decades. The costs of any attempt to reverse its course will be so great in terms of the economic and social well-being of all persons that they are prohibitive from any rational perspective. And there is no reason to risk such costs. Focusing especially on the economic effects of trade and investment, these advocates point out the benefits to individuals and consumers of more competition in the production of goods and services brought by global integration. The resulting increases in production efficiency, labor productivity, and technological innovation promise to continue to raise the living standards of all persons involved in the global marketplace. Advocates do recognize some of the costs of economic change, in the form of declining industries and the problems of workers whose skills cannot keep pace with a more competitive and dynamic environment. But these are primarily problems of economic transition; as states and individuals learn how to better thrive in the new environment, unprecedented opportunities and wealth will be available to all.

In this view, it is accepted and indeed essential that global change will reduce the abilities of states to control the economic activities and outcomes within their borders. Such a loss of sovereignty, however, is a welcome benefit or at least a worthwhile trade-off for the benefits of globalization. Political attempts to manipulate economic outcomes in a globalized economy can lead only to inefficiency and a reduction in the overall standard of living, benefiting the chosen few who are able to use the state for their advantage. As these beneficiaries are likely to be unable to compete effectively in the global market, we are all better off as states lose the ability to distort market outcomes. As Thomas Friedman puts it, the key to prosperity in a globalized world is the willingness of states to accept the "golden straightjacket" that constrains policymakers in ways that secure economic and social progress for society as a whole.[28] Moreover, some advocates of these changes point to the growing role of supra-national institutions in replacing individual states as the vehicles for supervision of the global economy. As Robert Wright put it,

> In a way, the "one-world" battle is over. Once you exclude fringe elements on both sides—Ralph Nader and Pat Buchanan, basi-

cally—both Democrats and Republicans accept the reality of NAFTA and the WTO even as they argue about whether these bodies should include environmental and labor laws, a la the EU. Thus, the existence of supranational bodies with significant functions of governance is no longer the issue.[29]

More generally, supporters of globalization tend to see the persistence of unilateral sovereign prerogatives as a major source of conflict and oppression in the modern world. Echoing earlier advocates of free trade, these supporters offer a reduced reliance on the sovereign state as the key to opening a more peaceful and cooperative global community. Extending the argument to the dimension of culture, David Rothkopf presents the case clearly:

> The impact of globalization on culture and the impact of culture on globalization merit discussion. The homogenizing influences of globalization that are most often condemned by the new nationalists and by cultural romantics are actually positive; globalization promotes integration and the removal not only of cultural barriers but of many of the negative dimensions of culture. Globalization is a vital step toward both a more stable world and better lives for the people in it."[30]

A more economically integrated globe may also reduce the ability of states to act independently in defining their priorities and asserting their interests, but it promises a world in which individual liberty, opportunity, and well-being will be greater and more widely distributed than ever before. To be sure, most advocates do not see any imminent disappearance of the state, and for most, international political cooperation is necessary for the success of the global economy. What remains crucial, however, is the restraint on unilateral, absolute exercises of sovereign power. States with limited sovereignty can provide the legal and institutional foundations for a cooperative global economy but cannot interfere with its unmatched ability to provide liberty and opportunity around the globe. Surely, advocates insist, this is a worthwhile compromise.

For the critics of globalization, there is no gainsaying the power and force of the global market economy. Like the advocates, the analyses they present are full of detail concerning the depth and pace of global economic integration, the accelerating technological changes on which it is based, and the limitations faced by all states that attempt to challenge these processes. But there are two essential characteristics that distinguish the accounts presented by these critics. First, they add a distinctly political dimension to the analysis of global change: whatever its current shape, globalization as we know it is the product of certain political choices and actions by states. For most critics, these choices are understood as a result of the dominant power of global interests and institutions in shaping the agendas of contemporary governments. Second and most important, the world they present is one littered by the costs and damages caused by global change, costs that demand a reconsideration and ultimately a rejection of the process as a whole. A reassertion of the sovereignty of the state, not its dilution, is the only road to a worthwhile and prosperous future for the majority of the world's inhabitants.

From this perspective, globalization is not simply the product of inevitable economic or technological forces. Rather, the contemporary global economy was to a great degree the result of political choices traceable to the uses of American power in the years after World War II. Beginning with the Bretton Woods agreements and accelerating through the GATT treaties of the late 1950s onward, the United States worked to create a framework for the emergence of an integrated global system of production, investment, and exchange. This policy was designed to secure the unity of the advanced capitalist world during the Cold War and was put under stress by the recovery of the European and Japanese economies by the 1970s. In this view, American policy helped secure the system in the 1980s by successfully pushing for the dismantling of many of the remaining barriers to global economic exchanges. By the mid-1990s, treaties calling for a stronger European Union, free trade zones in North America, South America, and the Pacific, and the creation of the WTO signified the global adoption of this policy direction, as political elites around the world worked deliberately to weaken the traditional forms of sovereign power and control.

By this time, though, political leaders around the world had little choice. A globalized and integrated world economic system is now working through its own momentum to further drain from the nation-state much of its ability to control the economic destiny of its citizens. Laws and institutions that attempt to secure country-specific standards of living, environmental protection, social security, and cultural identity are falling to the pressures of the global economy. If these pressures continue to mount, all states will be reduced to similar levels of wages and living standards, as the mobility of capital undermines the ability of states to shape economic activity within their borders. In the end, the loss of sovereignty means not the opening of opportunities for individuals but the subjection of whole societies and their members to the dictates of a profit-driven global economy. For Greider,

> The nation-state faces a crisis of relevance. What remains of its pur-
> pose and power if authority over domestic social standards is yielded
> to disinterested market forces? If governments are reduced to bid-
> ding for the favors of multinational enterprises, what basis will citi-
> zens have for determining their own destinies? If commerce and
> finance are free to roam in the borderless world, why should people
> be restricted by the mere geography of their birthplace? Political
> leaders are weak and unstable at present because they lack coherent
> answers to such questions.[31]

As systems of social security and protection fall under the pressures of competitiveness in the famous "race to the bottom," already apparent patterns of increasing economic inequality, growing economic insecurity, and declining powers of self-government will become even more dominant in American society and around the world.

For the critics, then, the real question is how to rebuild sovereignty to mount an effective challenge to globalization and regain citizens' control over their economic fate. Here, there are important divisions. Some of the more "theoretic" commentators believe that, since the problem is of a global dimension, it requires a global solution. For writers like Barber and Greider, at least part of the response is to use global institutions that pool the sovereignty of states to promulgate and enforce a new regime of global rules to govern economic life. But by far the most common approach across the political spectrum, perhaps best articulated by Pat Buchanan, is to call for a unilateral reassertion of American sovereignty. This would be accomplished by a renunciation of many of the commitments and treaties of the last two decades and a return to a more protected national economy and an economic policy more consciously governed by the goal of self-sufficiency. Rather than promising economic doom, this is offered as the only possible strategy, the necessary basis, for a reversal of the declining economic and social fortunes of the American people.[32]

Thus stand the major alternatives in the political rhetoric of global change. In the debates over NAFTA, GATT, immigration, the policies of the International Monetary Fund (IMF), and fast-track authority, commentary on both sides is pulled toward one or the other extreme, praising globalization as the herald of a new millennium or damning it as the destroyer of American independence and prosperity. On both sides, a central question is that of sovereignty and its relevance to the future of American citizens. The trade-off seems clear: we can have globalization or we can have sovereignty. The only question concerns the relative benefits and burdens of the choice we make.

Globalization: The Academic Debate

While politicians and pundits have helped put the problem of globalization on the public agenda, sociologists, economists, and political scientists have struggled to gain a clear purchase on the phenomenon. There is now a vast body of academic work on global change, ranging from specialized historical and conceptual analysis to attempts to bring such analysis to bear on the larger public conversations and policy disputes. In this section, I will review some of the main positions and contributions that have emerged from the latter set of work, focusing on attempts by scholars to use this work to inform public debate on globalization. In particular, I want to emphasize the way that this body of scholarship has raised questions about the trade-off presented in political rhetoric and to lay the foundations for my own attempt to reconstruct the debate about globalization and sovereignty.[33]

The Reich-Kapstein Controversy

In one form or another, the phenomenon now known as "globalization" has been the subject of social scientists since the early 1970s. With the breakdown of the Bretton Woods system, the growth of multinational corporations, the emergence of significant trade frictions among advanced capitalist states, and the crisis of Third World debt, scholars have been forced to come to grips with the ways in which the interconnected global economy has reshaped political conflict around the world. During the 1980s, there was a burgeoning of such work in the areas of international political economy, the history and sociology of the state, the theory of international trade, and the international impact on domestic policymaking, to name the most prominent.[34] By the end of this decade, faced with the growing public discussion of global change, scholars particularly attuned to these currents began attempting to bring this scholarly work to bear on the issues of globalization and sovereignty.

The first major impact of these attempts centered around Robert Reich's *The Work of Nations*.[35] In this book, Reich drew on work in economic theory and business organization to portray an emerging world economy in which corporations were global organizations with no particular national basis or focus. On this basis, he concluded that the idea of a national economy, in which all citizens' economic opportunities were linked and centered around those of the major national corporations, was an anachronism. In the new global economy, those with the particular "symbolic" skills valued by the new organizations prospered, while the rest of the society faced increasing economic instability, if not declining economic fortunes. The further we went down the road of a global economy, he concluded, the more the fates of American citizens would diverge, at least in the absence of corrective government action. Politically, the likely result was the "secession" of the privileged from any obligations to the larger community, on whose economic fortunes they no longer depended. Reich believed that many of the policy choices of the 1980s, choices dismantling many of the institutions and rules limiting market competition and inequality, were signs that such a secession was already beginning with the active help of the state. The challenge was to find a new basis of national unity or to risk deepening division and discord in American life.

Reich's thesis became well known and resonated with many of the concerns of the critics of globalization. But it diverged from the popular arguments in important ways. For one thing, Reich rejected any notion that globalization could or should be reversed, or that the kind of "national economy" that had dominated our political economic visions since the late nineteenth century could be revived. But he also rejected the idea that this left the state powerless and bereft of any sovereign abilities to aid those of its citizens threatened by economic change. Reich did accept the argument that the transformation of corporate structure and activity had rendered obsolete many established approaches to economic regulation. But in place of the old economy, Reich proposed a systematic policy of investment in human capital, a policy regime of education and training to ensure that all citizens could be positioned to prosper in the more competitive global economy. The real challenge, he suggested, was not state capacity but securing the political support for such a program. If immediate economic interest was no longer enough, some other basis would have to be found to force those benefiting from the new global environment to sacrifice so that their fellow citizens would not be left to flounder in the face of the global market.

The first and most important critic of Reich's argument, Ethan Kapstein, accepted the relevance of Reich's questions but disputed many of his conclusions. Kapstein's work focused on both the evolving role of the multinational corporation and the changing international banking system and capital markets. Though he accepted the notion that significant changes had occurred in the way the American and global economies worked, Kapstein contended that Reich had greatly overestimated the radicalness of the changes and misconstrued their impact upon state power and sovereignty. In his view, the state remained central in shaping the dynamics of economic life around the globe, and the notion of national economies with distinct fates and trajectories remained quite relevant for policy choices.

First, Kapstein challenged Reich's view of the corporation.[36] He contended that though all corporate organizations are increasingly global in their spheres of operation, most retain a clear national identity and basis. When one examined their patterns of ownership, the structure and personnel of management, the sources and direction of investment, or the location of production facilities, few of the dominant global economic actors were without a clear national basis of operation and identity. In turn, Kapstein contended, this meant that these corporations were still quite dependent upon the activities, policy choices, and protections of their national governments and thus vulnerable to pressure from the latter. We are far from an era of a unified global productive economy immune to the policy choices of states.

Second, Kapstein's more detailed examination of global capital markets and financial institutions showed that states and politics were by no means rendered powerless in a more integrated world.[37] By all accounts, the world of banking and finance is the most globalized element of contemporary social life. Nonetheless, Kapstein's research suggested that even here governments remained crucial in regulating economic activity and their policies were driven by clear perceptions of national interests and priorities. Not only were the global capital markets established by political action—as some critics of globalization had noted—but their continued existence and the nature of their evolution remained subject to the needs and desire of states operating on very traditional political grounds. The sovereign state, Kapstein concluded, is by no means a passive toy in the hands of global economic forces.

To some degree, this debate reflected the alternatives presented in the political controversies over globalization. While Reich's work embodied many of the concerns of the critics of global change, Kapstein attempted to deflate what he considered the overblown picture of a world in turmoil. But despite their disagreements, Reich and Kapstein both presented arguments that put into question the widely accepted equation of globalization with the decline of sovereignty. Though they disagreed about the degree to which the world economy had become globalized and the implications of such changes for the choices available to the state, both writers clearly emphasized that the use of sovereign power and the world of political choice remain crucial to the form that political and economic life will take over the coming decades. The trends associated with global change may be changing the options open to states as they attempt to pursue their goals. If Reich is correct, they may even be working to transform domestic political alignments and strategies. But the ultimate impact of global changes on American life will remain the product of the ways in which political actors interpret and respond to these changes, and the sovereign state thus remains central to our understanding of the future of globalization. Most important, both writers emphasized the challenge globalization posed for those citizens less able to compete in the world economy, and the need and possibility for positive state action to secure the welfare of all workers in a new kind of economic order.[38]

The State of the Argument Today

By now, these analyses are almost a decade old. How do they stand up in the light of the deepening global interconnections we have witnessed during the 1990s? In the wake of the divisive controversies over the NAFTA and GATT treaties, a new wave of academic commentators has weighed in on the issues of globalization. Like their predecessors, they often disagree about the nature and impact of contemporary global change. But they also share a rejection of many of the extremes of political debate and suggest that the relationships between global change, the patterns of change in American society, and government policy choices are much more complex than daily political arguments suggest. The following sample of three important recent treatments of globalization should make this clear.

In a series of articles, Paul Krugman has attempted to draw on current theory and research in international economics to provide a critical purchase on the debates over the WTO and fast-track authority.[39] His conclusion is that both sides of the debate overemphasize the role of global processes in shaping or determining domestic policy choices and social outcomes. The American economy and polity are still dominated by organizations and policy choices primarily domestic in origin and operation. Focusing especially on the growth in income inequality, Krugman notes that the scholarly consensus is that domestic factors such as technological change, political choices, and the declining power of unions account for by far the majority of this trend. Contrary to the views of both its advocates and opponents, Krugman notes that our reactions and options in dealing with this development remain rooted in domestic political perceptions and alignments. Responsibility for this disturbing development cannot be shifted to "global imperatives," nor does a response require a renunciation of liberal trading policies. In Krugman's words:

> None of the important constraints on American economic and social policy come from abroad. We have the resources to take far better care of our poor and unlucky than we do; if our policies have become increasingly mean-spirited, that is a political choice, not something imposed on us by anonymous forces. We cannot evade responsibility for our actions by claiming that global markets made us do it.[40]

A similar set of conclusions is reached in *Globaphobia*, written by four scholars associated with the Brookings Institution, as an attempt to deflect the growing impact of critics of globalization.[41] Unlike the more common attacks on the critics of globalization, however, this work does not present a picture of unqualified advantages to global change. While emphasizing the aggregate benefits for Americans from the gains in economic efficiency and competitiveness, this work also notes the challenges posed by global change. Echoing Reich's work, the authors emphasize the suffering of those displaced by economic change and advocate an ambitious policy regime to facilitate the adjustment of all citizens to the new economic situation and to counteract its impact in the area of wage and income inequality.

> Those who believe, as we do, that closer economic integration is in America's best interest must address the legitimate concerns that underlie the nation's fear of integration. When open trade policies that benefit the country as a whole also exact a price from certain groups of workers, the country has a responsibility in some way to make amends. In addition, failure to do so would court a growing voter backlash that could reverse the progress already made toward more open markets and unravel the economic gains that the United States has enjoyed as a result of this progress.[42]

This work, then, recognizes the political prerequisites for a well-functioning global economy and the freedom retained by policymakers to manage the impact of global forces on domestic society. In the view of these authors, globalization promises great benefits to Americans, but the preservation of the openness of the American economy will require decisive political action to ensure that these benefits are widely shared by all citizens.

Perhaps the most comprehensive evaluation of these issues, though, is presented in Dani Rodrik's *Has Globalization Gone Too Far?* [43] Rodrik considers a variety of dimensions of globalization, from the specifically economic to the issues of immigration and cultural change. While generally supportive of the further progress of globalization, he is more willing than many others to accept the contention that this process has been quite central to many of the destabilizing social and economic changes faced by advanced capitalist states over the last decade. In his view, the overly optimistic projections of supporters of globalization have been used to justify political choices that neglect the social and political costs of these changes and focus only on its beneficiaries. Rodrik is also candid in acknowledging the real political progress made by critics of global change in Europe and the United States and the need for policymakers to respond more constructively to these challenges. Whatever its analytical weakness, Rodrik argues, the antiglobalization program poses a real threat to the future of current liberal trading and immigration policies.

Most important, Rodrik effectively makes the point that the structure of the global system and the way it shapes domestic society are and will continue to be the products of political choices and action. The sovereign state remains the central vehicle by which political communities define and defend their purposes, and Rodrik calls for more recognition of this fact by those too willing to write off states in the name of a global market economy. Echoing Karl Polanyi, Rodrik argues that only an economic system compatible with the ability of states to protect their larger ideals will be able to succeed and prosper in the long run. Only if advocates and critics of global change recognize the continuing role of the state will we have the possibility of ensuring that global change is secured as a positive element of our futures.

It is clear, then, that contemporary scholarly commentary should make us skeptical of the state of public rhetoric and debate over globalization. The work I have reviewed rejects two of the main arguments shared by both supporters and opponents of globalization. First, from Reich to Rodrik these writers are clear that globalization is not one overwhelming force responsible for all the changes affecting America's economy and society in the past two decades. Second, these analyses are unanimous in suggesting that political action and choice, and particularly the presence of the sovereign state, remain crucial in shaping the global economy and its impact on American society. Rather than marking the irrelevance of domestic political choice, these commentators emphasize that the future of globalization will be shaped by the political response of government to the social changes it brings.

But these treatments leave us with two questions. First, none provides a cohesive *political* analysis of globalization and its relationship to sovereignty.

Much remains to be done in explaining the way state sovereignty interacts with changing economic conditions and the way these interactions are reshaping our politics. Second, these analyses also neglect to clearly explain the reasons for the discrepancy between what scholars know about global change and the very different understandings still dominant in public debate. I will conclude this chapter by presenting a framework for addressing these questions and use the rest of the book to explore its usefulness and implications.

Globalization and Sovereignty:
The Argument and Outline of the Book

In this book I define globalization as the process through which events and actions within the borders of any given state are increasingly shaped by events and actions beyond its borders, and in which actors are increasingly aware of this situation. Thus, the patterns of global change in areas such as trade, migration, language, and culture that I review amount to elements of globalization to the degree that they make choices and outcomes within a given political community more dependent upon choices and actors outside its territorial borders. In this sense, globalization raises questions about the stability and character of the political community by raising uncertainty about accepted notions of the boundaries of the community and role of the state in maintaining these boundaries.

The debates and controversies discussed earlier in this chapter embody this phenomenon. Whether we look at the impact of economic integration, the growth of immigration, or the changing patterns of culture and language, it is clear that American society is increasingly shaped by changes and events from outside its established territorial borders. Many aspects of social life within the United States—such as the choices shaping jobs, investment, and consumption, the ethnic makeup of the population, and patterns of language use and cultural tastes—are increasingly immersed in a global playing field. Choices are not simply affected by actions in other places, but Americans now choose in a context that includes a global range of options. The role of the state's boundaries in shaping these choices is vastly different from what it was only two decades ago, and by definition this raises the problem of sovereignty.

As I have noted, the growing critique of globalization in the United States suggests that all these developments mean that we are losing our sovereignty. *My contention in this book is that this argument is fundamentally misguided and in some respects simply wrong.* Globalization is challenging widely accepted notions of what the state should do, what the proper boundaries of the polity should be, and the relationship between the boundaries of the state and the territorial borders that have traditionally defined these boundaries. It may indeed be working to undermine many of the ways that modern states have gone about defining and enforcing the boundaries for the political communities they represent, the ways we have come to think about the relationship between politics and geography. But sovereignty remains alive and well, especially in the United States. Globalization is in fact better seen as the product of, and a force shaping, new understandings and practices of sovereignty and with them new kinds of relationships between state and society in the contemporary world. One may deplore some of these changes, but they are not beyond our control, nor is the remedy some drastic cutting of our connections to the larger world. The fate of the United States as a political community is still very much in our own hands, and the impact that global change will have on our lives will be the product of political conflicts and policy choices the outcomes of which we still have the power to determine.

Part Two: Sovereignty and Globalization

The book develops this argument and its implications in three parts. I begin, in part two, with an elaboration of the concepts and argument I have just outlined. These two chapters review the evolution of the concept and practice of the modern state and the nation-state, the concepts of sovereignty and popular sovereignty, and the nature of globalization as we know it today, with a focus on the United States. The main theme of this section concerns the relationship between sovereignty and global change. Sovereignty, I emphasize, refers to the authority of the state to set boundaries and the constituency to which it will be responsible, not to any particular set of boundaries, policy priorities, or state capacities. The processes of global change we are experiencing today are connected to a set of policy choices, made by the American state in alliance with a broad network of economic and social interests, to rearrange the relationship between state and society in the United States. The result of these choices has been to encourage the forces of global change as a way of reinforcing a new approach to the policy priorities and political, economic, and social responsibilities of the state. In the United States, the impact of globalization has been primarily the result of a set of policies aimed at expanding the role of market competition in shaping economic and social change at the expense of long-established government responsibilities.

Part Three: Globalization and the Politics of American Public Policy

In part three, I attempt to work out the implications of this approach to governance through more detailed examinations of the politics and policy choices in the areas of trade, immigration, and language and culture in the United States since the 1960s. The analysis in each area emphasizes the ways in which key policy decisions made over the last three decades have encouraged the immersion of American society in a global environment that is changing more rapidly with every decade and is increasingly organized around global market relationships. I emphasize the ways in which globalization is thus a response to policy choices, to decisions to mobilize the power of government to refashion the boundaries of the political community, and ultimately the purposes of that community itself. These choices, in turn, are linked to the priorities and interests of certain groups in American society, those who perceive great opportunities to benefit from a global range of choices. The contemporary politics of globalization, which I explore in each policy context, involves challenges to these policy choices by groups that are—or believe themselves to be—less able to compete well in such an environment and/or those who believe that the impact of globalization will destroy the proper relationship between government and the American people. Though expressed in terms of the defense of American sovereignty, these challenges are actually attempts to preserve or reassert a long-established pattern of policy priorities and a fast-receding understanding of the political community.

The chapters in part three work out this argument in more detail. In chapter 4 I analyze the emerging politics of trade, focusing especially on the debates over NAFTA. Here I explore the ways in which the new relationship of the United States and global economy has brought the issue of sovereignty to the forefront of contemporary political argument. In chapter 5, the focus turns to the recent history and politics of immigration and its impact on the nature of the American political community. The specific pattern of immigration over the past three decades, and the policy choices that have promoted the influx of new migrants to the United States have led to the revival of a debate over the meaning of American "citizenship" in the post-Cold War world. Chapter 6 turns to the emergence of a politics of language in the United States, emphasizing the movement for "Official English" and against bilingual education over the past two decades. Responding to the growing impact of new cultural trends and practices in American life, these controversies have crystallized into a debate over the nature of American national "identity" and its relationship to the role of government in American life.

My decision to explore the politics of globalization through a focus on the three policy areas of trade, immigration, and language may strike some readers as unusual. For one thing, my choice of policy areas does not follow the standard categories in the study of public policy, such as Theodore Lowi's influential typology of "distributive," "redistributive," and "regulatory" policies.[44] Though there are aspects of policymaking and politics in each area that may fall under one or more of these categories, my choices do not represent an attempt to select cases to illustrate the impact of global change on these types of policy. At the same time, my selection of policy areas will seem to many to ignore some of the central contexts for contemporary political conflict over globalization. Over the past two or three years, for instance, the controversies over the instability of the global financial system, the fear that the WTO will undermine the ability of the United States and other countries to enforce laws that protect the environment, and the debate over wages and working conditions in emerging industrial countries have been central in spreading interest and political engagement in the issues surrounding globalization. In the scholarly literature, moreover, controversies over globalization rage in such areas as the taxation policies of advanced industrial states, the future of the welfare state, and the efficacy of attempts to manage the level of economic activity. Any careful observer of the events in Seattle would have found many instances in which all these issues came to the fore, both inside and outside the WTO meetings. On the other hand, though trade policy has indeed been a major issue of concern, the debates over immigration and language seem to have faded from the headlines over the past five years.

I have chosen this particular combination of policy areas, though, because my approach to the politics of globalization asks a set of questions that are rarely explored in the area of public policy scholarship or in most treatments of global change. Most fundamentally, I contend that globalization operates to challenge long-established understandings of the boundaries of the political community, the purposes that bind it together, and the role of government in promoting these goals. These understandings and expectations, it seems to me, involve a complex set of questions that include not only "material" issues surrounding the structure of the economy but also the political and cultural identity of the polity. The modern nation-state provides a fundamental sense of identity and place for its citizens, and the real significance of globalization lies in its challenge to the structure and meaning of the political community that makes up the nation-state, in the United States and throughout the world. To a great extent, this sense of identity and place is embodied in the way a government goes about taxing its citizens, providing security from economic change, and asserting the value of its natural environment. But the character and aims of the political community are also asserted and promoted through the choices and rules that determine the membership and the cultural understandings of the polity. An approach to the politics of globalization that ignores these areas of policymaking will, I believe, miss some of the most fundamental challenges globalization poses for the American political community today.

In these three chapters, then, I begin with an analysis of trade policy, an area of conflict familiar to observers of globalization, where politics seems to clearly focus on the distribution of benefits and burdens resulting from the reduction of barriers to trade. I then turn to the question of immigration, where political conflict involves the question of benefits and costs but also raises important questions concerning the purposes and character of the American polity. The politics of immigration reveals the ways in which the distributive or redistributive aspects of policy choice are closely linked to their role in shaping the symbolic and even mythical elements of national identity, and it helps us reflect upon the ways this same linkage may be present in the politics of trade. The analysis of the politics of language, finally, provides a more in-depth discussion of the ways in which national identity is partially constituted through the policy choices of governments, especially those that determine the boundaries of the polity. My own approach is based on the notion that "material" and "symbolic" dimensions of politics are closely linked in all three areas, and in the politics of policymaking more generally. I use a close analysis of these three areas to offer a narrative of contemporary political conflict in which the political responses to globalization embody alternative visions of American life, visions that combine views of the proper distribution of rights, privileges, and obligations with ideal images of the nature and purposes of the national community. Had I chosen to focus only on the more obvious and prominent current controversies discussed above, I would not have been able to illustrate the depth and multifaceted nature of the challenges posed by globalization for the way Americans understand their political identity and the role of their polity in the changing global system.

I want to make clear that in these chapters on trade, immigration, and language, it is not my intention to assert that *all* the dimensions of political conflict and policy choice are now determined by the impact of globalization. In particular, conflicts over immigration and language have deep roots in American history, and the positions and coalitions that shape politics in these areas draw on complex legacies and traditions that have little directly to do with contemporary global change. What I am suggesting, though, is that the processes of globalization are now increasingly important in shaping the context in which these ideas and conflicts are played out. Intense movements of support or opposition to increased trade or immigration, for instance, have emerged at many different points in American political history. Today, however, the direction and outcome of these struggles are shaped by the new political, social, and economic context created by globalization. Their outcomes will be determined by the ways in which Americans decide to grapple with this new set of realities.

Part Four: The Politics of Globalization

The analysis is summed up in the conclusion, which makes up part four of the book. Here I suggest that the deepening immersion of American society in a changing global system has had dramatic effects on the structure of authority and legitimacy in the American polity. From the 1940s onward, most Americans had been included in a new social compact. In return for the support of citizens, the government would manage the economy to promote the ability of most citizens to achieve a stable middle-class standard of living while it pursued a global policy that would assert the superiority of American political and social ideals. The national community would be one of shared economic and political fate, held together by a degree of mutual sacrifice and an equitable sharing of the gains of economic prosperity. All of this would be secured by establishing relatively closed borders within which the unity of the national identity and culture would be protected from external disruptions.

For students of contemporary politics, it is no great news that this bargain has fallen apart. But what is insufficiently recognized is the important role that the globalization of American life has played and is continuing to play in this situation. Drawing on the work of Reich, Rodrik, and others, I will emphasize that the policies promoting global change have been central in dividing the nation between those benefiting from the collapse of this bargain and those who see their lives made more insecure and difficult as a result of these changes. The campaign to restore American sovereignty is driven by those Americans who have come to believe that they have been abandoned by a state that is supposed to protect their interests and values. Because they see themselves increasingly ignored in the setting of public priorities and purposes and believe that the state is not responsive to their interests, it is easy to conclude that the state is either unable or unwilling to carry out what many still accept as the duties of sovereign authority.

As I will try to show, these perceptions are not totally unfounded and promise to play an increasing role in shaping the politics of American public policy. The policy choices that have helped to globalize American society have worked to divide the nation over fundamental questions of interest and identity. My aim in this book is to provide readers with a framework for understanding this situation, to explain the ways it is likely to continue to transform American politics, and to suggest alternative approaches to dealing with global change in the hope that these divisions can be prevented from severely threatening the foundations of American democracy.

PART II ❧

Sovereignty and Globalization

2 ∽

The Sovereign State, the Nation, and Popular Sovereignty

The contemporary debates over sovereignty and globalization involve concepts and ideas with long historical legacies. This is not surprising; after all, the sovereign state has been the leading actor in world politics for at least the past two centuries. Claims of the decline or end of sovereignty, then, ask us to reconsider the meaning and value of some of the central institutions and norms that shape the ways we are used to organizing political life. Nonetheless, a close examination of many contemporary arguments reveals little clear understanding of the sources and evolution of some of the central issues at stake—including sovereignty, the nation-state, nationalism, and globalization. Too often, participants in these debates seem to be using a vocabulary whose words they know how to pronounce but about the meaning of which they seem uncertain. Moreover, this lack of clarity with key concepts is part of a broader absence of solid historical background to most current discussions of globalization. Too often, conclusions about the direction of political and economic change in the world are based on discussions that rarely step beyond the past two or three decades of history. But the modern state and the capitalist economy have been central parts of Western history for at least three centuries, and arguments about their destiny that fail to take this history seriously can only be misleading guides to what globalization may mean today.

Thus, before we can really engage the current debates over contentious policy choices in trade, immigration, and language, we need to step back and review the origins and meaning of the political concepts and institutions central to the debates over globalization. The two chapters in this part of the book aim to do just this. In this chapter, I focus on the origins, evolution, and meaning of the concept of sovereignty and the sovereign state. I argue that, though this concept is today often reduced simply to the power or control a state has over its physical territory, sovereignty is actually a way of talking about a much more complex set of relationships between political power, authority, territory, representation, and responsibility. As part of this exploration, I trace the way the idea and practice of the sovereign state have evolved over time under the impact of nationalism and democracy, focusing on the notion of "boundary-setting" as central to the practice of sovereignty. The first part of this chapter is more theoretical in focus, while the second and third look at the evolution of the meaning and practice of sovereignty over the past two centuries, first in Europe and then in the United States. In the following chapter, I turn to an analysis of globalization and employ the discussion of sovereignty to develop my framework for analyzing and understanding the conflicts surrounding policy choices in the United States over the past two decades.

Defining Sovereignty

Political Authority and Political Capacity

The history of the concept of sovereignty is in many ways the history of the modern system of states, by which all territory was politically organized in the late twentieth century.[1] This system of states emerged first in western and central Europe in the fifteenth and sixteenth centuries, a product of the collapse of the complex feudal patterns of rule. In the context of new military technologies, a revival of the market economy, and the crisis in Christianity, intrepid regional power holders in Europe began attempting to centralize all political power and authority in their own hands. In a major departure from the medieval pattern of overlapping jurisdictions, these new rulers attempted to create a new kind of political system within the territories they controlled, in which all exercise of power was ultimately subject to one source of authority. All the subjects of this authority, in turn, would be dependent upon the one central power in the state for whatever rights or privileges they could claim. No longer would persons and institutions occupying the same territory—be they lords, knights, or a universal church—be able to claim independent and overlapping authority over the persons and wealth in that territory. As Wolfgang Reinicke has noted, this claim to ultimate authority has both "internal" and "external" dimensions; the state is the final authority over what happens within its borders and by extension must have the final say over what and who is allowed to move into and out of its territory.[2]

    As a result of an uncertain and violent process that extended over a number of centuries, Europe was indeed finally divided into a set of separate states, each claiming absolute and final authority within its borders. At the center of these states was an institution in which all power and authority was consolidated. This was usually a monarchy but, as in the case of Britain, could also be a legislative body. By the late seventeenth century, this institution would be referred to as the "sovereign," and in the new international law that emerged during this era each sovereign would recognize the final authority and independence of the other. Although the system of sovereign states would continue to be challenged into this century, by the middle of the nineteenth century European politics was the politics of sovereign states. Meanwhile, this model of political organization had already spread to the Western Hemisphere, and over the next century the spread of colonialism and then the collapse of the colonial empires led to the universal acceptance and/or imposition of this model of political life throughout the globe.

But what exactly does "sovereignty" mean, and how does understanding it help us understand the modern state? In his classic treatment, F.H. Hinsley offered the following definition:

> The idea of sovereignty was the idea that there is a final and absolute political authority in the political community; and everything that needs to be added to complete the definition is added if this statement is continued in the following words: "*and no final and absolute authority exists elsewhere.*"[3]

It is important that we look closely at this definition and consider it in light of some of the contemporary scholarship on sovereignty, as well as the popular debates surrounding the term. Although its meaning often seems obvious, "sovereignty" is actually a very complex term that leads us to consider some of the fundamental elements of contemporary political life.

The first thing to notice about this definition is that it focuses on the *authority*, and not the power or capacity, of the state. In most of the contemporary debate discussed in the first chapter, sovereignty is implicitly associated with the state's ability to stop what are supposedly unwanted intrusions into its territory. If such intrusions, whether of capital, persons, or ideas, continue in spite of the state's opposition, it has by definition lost (at least some degree of) its sovereignty. But Hinsley's definition focuses first on the state's legal authority, its right to have the ultimate say over what will and will not be allowed to cross its borders and what will and will not be done within its borders or territory.[4] Any viable state must be able to enforce its decisions on such issues, but Hinsley asks us first to look at the overall structure of the political community and its purposes to understand what sovereignty is about. The more recent treatment of the question by Janice Thomson comes to the same conclusion. Sovereignty, she writes, is not first of all a reference to specific powers of the state but to the fact that a state is "empowered or authorized to decide what is political in the first place."[5] The decision as to what is political is a decision about the priorities of the political community the state is representing; it determines the activities and outcomes that will and will not be a focus of the concern and activity of the state. Any discussions concerning the "decline" of sovereignty, she argues, must take this into account. "Sovereignty is not about state control but about state authority. The question is whether or not the state's ability to make authoritative political decisions has eroded; that is, whether ultimate political authority has shifted from the state to nonstate actors or institutions."[6]

Historically, states have come to very different conclusions about the purposes their efforts and powers should promote. As these purposes change, so do the relevant powers or capacities a state requires to achieve its aims; some activities may be monopolized or regulated by the state in certain periods and not in others. For example, when a state is determined to control the religious beliefs and practices of its subjects, as most absolutist states were determined to do, it needs very different capacities than liberal states that leave such beliefs to the choices of individuals. In the same way, states have pursued mercantilist goals of protecting their balance of trade, liberal approaches that emphasize the protection of free markets and free trade, and the Keynesian purposes of economic stabilization and the provision of economic and social security. Institutional and legal capacities and powers necessary for one of these programs may be unnecessary and even harmful to the pursuit of other programs. Enforcing a gold standard, for instance, requires a whole set of institutions that are redundant in a state concerned with managing a floating currency; encouraging immigration to support a labor-scarce economy requires capacities and rules different from those necessary for limiting immigration to protect high wages and living standards.

A key problem in making this distinction between sovereign authority and state capacity is that popular discussions of the issue tend to blend them into one idea, and in fact are usually concerned with the latter. Critics who claim that the United States has lost some of its sovereignty are usually claiming that government no longer has the capacity to carry out certain aims, such as limiting imports or immigration. Another way to accommodate the tendency to confuse these two dimensions of sovereignty, suggested by Wolfgang Reinicke, is to distinguish between "legal" or de jure, sovereignty—the right to have the ultimate say over the nature of the polity and the priorities of government policy—and "operational" sovereignty—the capacity necessary for government to ensure its policy aims are achieved.[7] Reinicke's distinction closely parallels mine, but in the book I will stick with the distinction between sovereignty and capacity because I believe it is essential to remember that states (or the same state at different periods of history) can be equally sovereign while pursuing very different aims and thus using very different capacities. The rapid influx and exit of capital or the easy entry of persons into a state's territory may be exactly what a state wants to happen, not a failure to control its borders. A state is sovereign so long as it can independently and effectively decide what its purposes will be and then find appropriate means to attain its goals. The means it chooses to use—whether in the form of legal rules, taxation capacity, military force, regulatory enforcement, etc.—are relevant only in light of the purposes it aims to promote.

Of course, a state can no longer be considered sovereign if it lacks any effective means of enforcing its rule over a given territory or population. The diplomatic history of the past two centuries is replete with controversies over whether a particular government's claim to sovereignty over a territory should be recognized by other states, controversies in which the issue often comes down to the degree of effective control that government has over its territory.[8] As Robert Jackson has emphasized, there are areas of the world today where existing states have effectively lost any real control over their societies, to the point that any remaining sense of sovereignty is a fiction.[9] But these are extreme cases, which few would consider relevant to the situation of the United States today. The real problem for us will be to distinguish a government's loss of any capacity to control its territory from the choice of different capacities in the pursuit of different policy priorities. These are two very different situations and require that we take care not to confuse the sovereignty of the state with any specific set of powers or institutions it may have or lose. As we examine the current debates on the impact of global change on American sovereignty, we will find this distinction between sovereign authority and specific state capacities central to understanding both the arguments being offered and the actual developments in the relationship between government and society in the United States.

The next aspect of Hinsley's definition brings us to an equally complicated element of sovereignty. As he points out, the existence of a sovereign state implies the existence of other states; sovereignty signifies a relationship between states, in which the limit of each state's authority is clearly identified. This raises two central dimensions of sovereignty. First, as Hinsley makes clear throughout his book, the way in which sovereignty is understood at any particular point in history is determined internationally. States exist in a larger community that is the final arbiter of what sovereignty means and of who can legitimately claim to be sovereign. Usually it is the most powerful states that shape this definition, and it is embodied in the practices and agreements through which states manage their relationships. It follows that significant shifts in the practice of sovereignty will develop in the interactions and policy choices of states and will involve the process of mutual accommodation to changing global situations. As we will see, the emergence of globalization in the contemporary world is linked to the spread of new ways of thinking about the sovereignty of the state and the acceptance of these new approaches by most of the major governments in the major capitalist economies.[10] As Hinsley sums up this point:

> To argue in this way is to associate the attribute of sovereignty with the possession by the state of the freedom to act as it chooses instead of with the absence over and above the state of a superior authority. To do that is to confuse the situation to which states may often have aspired, but have never in fact enjoyed, with the opposite condition

from which the concept of sovereignty in its international version historically obtained its relevance and from which it continues to derive it—that condition in which a collection of states, all insisting on their independence, were brought to recognize that they do not exist in isolation but are forced to live with other states.[11]

The Borders and Boundaries of the Sovereign State

The second dimension of our definition of sovereignty concerns the nature of the borders that divide states and indicate the limits of each state's sovereign authority. Traditionally, in both scholarship and public discussion, the issue of the extent and limits of a state's sovereignty has been linked to the territorial borders of modern political communities. The authority of any state extends uniformly within its territorial borders and, with very few exceptions,[12] is nonexistent outside these borders. These borders, lines on the maps of the globe, are the basic guidelines through which states assert their authority and recognize the existence and legitimacy of other states. They are also indications of the source and limits of the responsibility of any state in the exercise of its power. Since authority exists only within the borders of the territory, the state is responsible only or mostly to forces and groups within that territory for the way it uses its power. It is the interests and security (however defined) of the residents of that territory, and none beyond them, that the state is responsible for protecting and promoting. In this sense, sovereignty works to indicate the nature of the responsibility that is the flip side of any arrangement of political authority.

In this study, however, I will use the term "boundaries" rather than "borders" to indicate the limits of the state's authority and responsibility.[13] What is the difference, and why choose one term over the other? For most of the history of the modern state the identification between a state's territorial borders and the boundaries or limits of its authority was adequate, as the territorial limitations on a state's authority were the most significant ones, at least regarding the state's relationship to other states and larger global developments. A central part of the story of globalization, however, concerns the ways in which the sovereignty of the contemporary state is increasingly uncoupled from its territorial borders. Analysts who explore the exercise of the contemporary state's authority—especially that of the United States—and the nature of the constituencies to which it is held responsible in the exercise of its power find that territorial borders no longer adequately suffice for understanding sovereignty. Increasingly, the United States claims sovereign authority to govern activities taking place outside its borders but deeply affecting its interests—the U.S. role in trying to control the drug trade is an excellent example of this.[14] At the same time, the U.S. government often shares authority to govern activities taking place within its territory. In many controversies surrounding the regulation of trade practices or environmental protection, American policymakers are now constrained by international organizations and agreements that limit the freedom of individual states. Placing too much emphasis on "borders" as they have traditionally been known can lead us astray in understanding sovereignty in the contemporary world.

As I will use the term in this study, then, "boundaries" refers to the extent and limits of the individuals and activities over which any state claims sovereign authority. In essence, the boundaries of the state constitute the political community that the state claims to represent and to which its leaders are responsible. At certain times, the territorial borders of the state may indeed be the most essential part of these boundaries, but as we have seen, they need not be. Moreover, the concept of boundaries helps us understand the relationship of the state's political community or constituency to the persons and activities that occur within its territorial borders. One legacy of the ideal of the nation-state is that it leads us to automatically identify the political community in whose name a state acts with all those persons inside its territory. Thus, the U.S. government has often been assumed to be responsible for "American" economic interests. In a more globalized world, though, we will find many cases where government is responsive to economic actors whose interests and operations are global and not bound by the territory of the state. The interests and claims of international institutions will also play an important role in shaping the policy choices of the state, even when many domestic interests and organizations are opposed to these claims. We will need to be careful, then, not to assume that a sovereign state is always limited to the promotion of the goals and interests of those groups living within its borders.

Not only does the concept of "boundaries" identify the constituency of the state, but it also helps point us to the relationship between the state and other institutions subject to its authority. As it defines its purposes and aims, the state identifies the attitude it will take toward the major institutions and activities in society; in Thomson's phrase, it defines the boundaries of the political in that society. For instance, a state in which the promotion of free markets is a central purpose will have a different relationship to the economy than one that identifies equality and security as central aims. The promotion of a uniform national identity will lead to different relationships with various cultural institutions than will a relaxed acceptance of cultural pluralism. This is an aspect of the exercise of state power closely related to the question of capacity and somewhat different from the boundaries of the political community itself. But these dimensions of the practice of sovereignty are inseparable. As a state acts to further the interests of the community it serves, it works to secure the dominant values of that community; as these change over time, so does the relationship between the state and the other major social institutions. Most observers of the modern state recognize these connections, but a reliance on the notion of territoriality obscures the complex interconnections between these various dimensions through which sovereignty operates to shape political life.

The picture of sovereignty that I have presented in this discussion takes us far from the simplistic notions that usually prevail in public debate. Rather than a fixed property of the state that is more or less present, sovereignty points us to the relationship between a state and the political community in whose name it acts and embodies the complex relationship between the authority of that state and its responsibility toward its constituencies. This account also emphasizes the dynamic nature of sovereignty over time; as the state's constituency and its purposes change, so do the meaning and practice of sovereignty. Indeed, in its most fundamental sense, sovereignty indicates the central role of boundary setting and maintenance in the politics of the modern state. In articulating their purposes and pursuing policy choices that promote these purposes, states establish and reestablish their boundaries in relation to other states, to the community they represent, and to other institutions and activities within this community.[15]

Most important for this study is the idea that the interaction between states and their larger international or global environments often determines the pressure and direction of change. Periods of intense change in the state's environment usually coincide with transformations in the boundaries, purposes, and policy choices that determine how it exercises sovereignty. This book contends that we are experiencing exactly such a period now. The processes we know as globalization have created a very different context in which the American state has to act and pursue its interests. Though it is common to view these changes as undermining sovereignty, what we are in fact observing is a process in which the state is redefining its boundaries and purposes. The startling increase in the degree to which global developments are impinging on American life is both the cause and the result of a transformation in the relationship of the state and the larger society. It indicates the vigorous operation of a new mode of exercising sovereignty, not its disappearance.

My discussion has gone far from Hinsley's seemingly clear and simple statement, and over the coming chapters I will add more to this account. To round out this approach, we will need to look more closely at the ways in which globalization has reshaped American society (see chapter 3), the subtle ways in which the boundaries of the state are simultaneously linked to the material and symbolic dimensions of policy choice, and the political processes through which these boundaries are defined and redefined. But a solid grasp of what is happening today requires that we look first at how we have come to our current situation. The rest of this chapter discusses the evolution of the practice of sovereignty in the world generally and in the United States. By reviewing the ways in which this practice has evolved through time, we will be better prepared to analyze the way it is changing today.

The Evolution of the Modern Sovereign State

From Sovereignty to Popular Sovereignty

The earliest concepts of sovereignty, developed by such writers as Jean Bodin and Thomas Hobbes and elaborated by the natural lawyers Grotius and Pufendorf, saw it as a way of explaining and justifying the newly emergent form of political community we know as the absolutist state. In its contention that there could be only one source of power and authority in any society, and its insistence that the existence of such a source was essential to social order, sovereignty worked well to justify the new kinds of uniform political spaces that the new states were creating within their boundaries. But the concept also seemed to provide a grounding or direction for the exercise of this power and authority. Unlike earlier approaches, such as Machiavelli's, which seemed to refer only to the personal interests and future of the "prince," sovereignty in principle separated the institutions of the state from the personal whims of any particular sovereign. As Hobbes made clear, the sovereign power of the state embodied the common interests and will of all the members of the political community and thus was a power beyond the personal capacities of any given ruler. The purpose of the sovereign state was to promote the interests of that community as a whole, especially its interests in peace, security, and order.[16]

To be sure, these constraints often carried little weight in the practices of the new states. Indeed, under most of the early views of sovereignty, it was up to the sovereign to define the interests of the state—thus Louis XIV's famous "L'état c'est moi." But it is important to note the ambiguity of this phrase. If it can mean that the state is simply what the sovereign wills, it can also mean that the sovereign's identity becomes submerged by that of the state he or she is ruling; the ruler is absorbed by the state's interests and purposes. The concept of sovereignty, then, was full of potential implications for the way political actors could and should understand the modern state as a political community. It defined the power and authority of the state as rooted in the interests, purposes, and needs of the political community for which it was responsible, and that it indeed represented. The earliest formulations linked sovereignty to the absolutist state, but it soon became clear that the concept was amenable to very different understandings.

This discovery, as it turned out, was linked to the combination of social forces known as "democracy" and "nationalism," which started to reshape the modern state in the late eighteenth century. Already in the English Civil Wars of the seventeenth century, radical critics of absolutism had begun articulating the notion of "popular sovereignty."[17] In a crucial development, these critics came to accept the modern state as the proper form for the organization of political life, but they challenged the dominant understanding of where the sovereignty of the polity was ultimately located. According to this formulation, presented most famously by John Locke, "the people" were the sources of sovereign power, and its exercise must be subordinated to their will and judgement. Unlike Bodin's or Hobbes's version of sovereignty, Locke's rejected the notion that only the ruler could act in the name of the sovereign will of the community.[18] Rather, sovereignty existed, emerged, and remained lodged in the activity of the people, and those exercising the power of the state could do it only on the basis of a regularly renewed consent of the people.

"Popular sovereignty" presented a fundamental and ultimately successful challenge to absolutism. By emphasizing that the community, rather than being conjured up by the state, had a role in creating the state's authority, it required a new kind of practice for the exercise of power. The democratic revolutions of the late eighteenth century in the United States and Europe began the process whereby this practice would emerge. But as it turned out, democracy was only part of the story. The consolidation of a norm of popular sovereignty in world politics required the emergence and triumph of nationalism as the ultimate form of political identity. Though democratic notions may have left the identity and interests of "the people" somewhat vague, nationalism clearly defined "the nation"—as a historical and cultural force—as the source of sovereignty. As Benedict Anderson has emphasized, the idea of the nation provided a powerful tool for unifying and indeed creating a political community within the boundaries of the state.[19] Nationalism gave the state a clear purpose and direction and set the stage for the spread of the idea of the "nation-state" in international law and popular political imagination. For practical purposes, popular sovereignty in the past two centuries has meant the creation of a state that represents a nation and exercises power to promote its purposes.

The role of nationalism in shaping the practice and culture of sovereignty in the modern world cannot be overemphasized. Though democratic movements were often easily sidetracked in nineteenth-century Europe, every state was forced to grapple with nationalism. In some states, most particularly Britain and France during the Third Republic, nationalism worked to direct democratic impulses away from radical change. In more authoritarian contexts, such as Prussia/Germany, nationalism was the preferred tool for counteracting democratic pressures. In the remaining European multinational empires, nationalist movements provided the main challenge to the central state, eventually succeeding in dismembering all these empires. The lesson of this century was that, in the long run, state authority could be legitimated only on the basis that it claimed to embody the purposes of a cohesive national community.

World War I proved crucial to the consolidation of the ideal of the nation-state. During the war, the major participants mobilized resources and populations to an unprecedented extent. To cement the loyalty of those they governed, states engaged in massive efforts of propaganda and persuasion that linked the state's military efforts to the promotion and protection of the interests, ideals, and purposes of the unified national community. These efforts solidified the "imagined communities" of the nation and the notion that state authority derived from that community. Furthermore, states were forced to take the major practical steps toward the full inclusion of all citizens in the political and social life of the nation. The democratic practices of near universal franchise and the extension of welfare state protections were justified in the name of, and probably only possible on the basis of, the coherence and sacrifices demanded by the national community.

The aftermath of the Great War saw the final consolidation of the nation-state as the norm governing the organization of world politics. Woodrow Wilson's "Fourteen Points," the League of Nations charter, and the creation of new states in eastern Europe were crucial steps in the transformation of international law and public opinion into bulwarks for the nation-state. Even the rearrangement of colonial claims, with its promise of eventual independence, worked to further the spread of nationalist ideals. Indeed, the combination of the wartime propaganda for "national self-determination" with the failure of its realization for so much of the colonial world sparked the consolidation of movements for national independence from China and India to the Middle East and Africa. By this point, few contested the notion that at some point in the future the entire globe would be organized as a system of independent, sovereign nation-states.

The Sovereign Nation-State since World War II

Of course, the expansionist projects of Nazi Germany and Japan did bring the world to the brink of rejecting the nation-state, and the emergence of a reinvigorated Soviet Union after the war served to prolong for decades the model of the multinational empire. But the dominant fact of global political life since 1945 has been the spread of the sovereign nation-state. From the reconstitution of international law in the United Nations charter to the final breakup of the European colonial empires and the continuing national conflicts following the collapse of the Soviet Union, we have seen the triumph of national sovereignty in the practice, as well as the theory, of the political organization of the globe.

It is important to take stock of what this ideal had come to mean in the decades after 1945, especially in the more industrialized areas of the world.[20] A political creation that was originally aimed at securing the boundaries of rule among a group of individual sovereigns had been redefined into a framework in which a project of collective political definition could be pursued. Protected (at least in theory) from outside interference, the nation-state would be able to secure a coherent, relatively closed and stable community in which all members would share a common national identity and the shared common purposes that would come with this identity. As in earlier eras, a new definition of the general outlines of such purposes emerged among all the major states. In addition to offering security from outside threats, the sovereign state would now be responsible for protecting human rights and providing a basic level of economic and social security and opportunity for all members of the national community. The government of the state would be expected to be responsible to the will of the nation as expressed in democratic procedures. And, finally, the state would protect and promote the cultural ideals and practices that defined the nation in whose name it acted.

To facilitate the accomplishment of these ends, a set of international norms and institutions was created in the decades following 1945. The United Nations charter and institutions, along with the body of international law they maintained, firmly enshrined the principle of national self-determination and played a central role in overseeing and legitimizing the dismantling of the European colonial empires. Through its various programs of economic development assistance, the provision of administrative expertise, and the promotion of the cultural traditions of the "emerging" nations, the United Nations worked to try to secure for the new states the infrastructures necessary for operating a state along the lines of the new international norms. The United States played a similar role in regard to Western Europe and Japan. Its programs of economic assistance, the exercise of political oversight over the rebuilding of the political infrastructures of these states, and eventually the creation of an anticommunist Western alliance all worked to rebuild these devastated areas in ways consonant with global expectations.

If the international institutions of the U.N. system secured the political context for the sovereign nation-state, a new set of rules and institutions governing the global capitalist economy helped to secure its social and economic foundations. As J. G. Ruggie has explained, the "Bretton Woods" system created an international economic system designed to combine the growth-promoting effects of freer trade with enough autonomy and insulation of national economies to allow the most advanced states to provide an unprecedented degree of wealth and security to a wide range of their citizenry.[21] Such key practices as the stabilization of currency values, the provision of investment capital, the opening of the American market to imports while allowing the protection of the European and Japanese markets, and the exemption of agriculture and the service sector from free trading rules helped to ensure economic growth around the world while minimizing the social dislocations previously associated with rapid growth and open markets. In this world of "embedded liberalism," it was expected that states would use their economic autonomy to secure a new element of sovereign responsibility—providing for the basic economic security and well-being of their national communities.

As the term indicates, embedded liberalism was itself based upon a new kind of social compact with the democratic capitalist states. In this compact, governments and elites agreed to provide for the security and opportunity of all citizens in return for the majority's acceptance of the institutions of the market economy. This compact, usually referred to as the "welfare state," grew out of the deep social conflicts of the interwar period followed by the experiences of national trauma during the Second World War. Political and social elites traded limitations on marketplace freedoms and inequality for a commitment to the authority of the state to guarantee the basic rules of capitalism and preserve social order. This compact was central to the redefinition of sovereignty in the post-1945 era. By accepting an obligation to promote the security and well-being of the entire population of citizens, states accepted a new set of responsibilities as part of their claims to sovereign authority. The international agreements and principles that articulated these responsibilities and the institutions built to promote their fulfillment were all based upon this new understanding of sovereignty.

But these arrangements marked more than the emergence of a new practice of sovereign authority among states. In the post-1945 world, a new architecture of politics was created, in which the very means by which any particular state secured its sovereign authority was transformed. This architecture was based on a kind of deal, in which states accepted greater international constraints on their policymaking autonomy—in such areas as civil rights, refugee and migrant policy, and economic management—in return for an international guarantee of their authority to control a particular territory and population and pursue a certain program of domestic policies. The framework of United Nations treaties and organizations, international economic regulatory bodies, and other multilateral treaties marked a major historical step in the "unbundling" of the classic powers and claims of sovereign authority. After three decades of some of the most intensive closing of borders and assertions of unilateral sovereign prerogatives, this new era ushered in a gradual acceptance of a need for states to share some control over their boundaries and facilitate the intrusion of international or global processes into the sphere of their authority.

These developments are quite striking in retrospect because they amount to the first steps toward the kinds of practices now identified with globalization. Though they were not driven by a market-oriented paradigm that celebrated competition and the loosening of restraints on economic activity— indeed, as we have seen, the intention was to ensure that economic activity was subject to close political management—institutions such as the International Monetary Fund (IMF) and the General Agreement on Tariffs and Trade (GATT) treaties did play a decisive role in the revival of international trade and investment in the post-1945 era. Moreover, the larger process of multilateral and international cooperation in key areas of policy responsibilities set the groundwork for the kind of political practices essential to a more interdependent global system. In effect, many of the crucial prerequisites for the current process of globalization were set in the gradual evolution of the international political order begun in the late 1940s. By breaking with long-held understandings of the unilateral rights of sovereign states and recognizing the need to share key aspects of sovereignty to pursue common ends, states during this period began developing the tools that would play a central role in facilitating the more intensive and divisive process of globalization at the end of the twentieth century.

These developments did not occur without the forceful leadership of the United States. In the aftermath of the Second World War and for the subsequent two and a half decades, the United States was the most dominant economic, military, and political power in the noncommunist world. In its role as a hegemonic power, the country used its influence to initiate and support the growth of the institutions and practices that sustained the system of embedded liberalism and the new approach to sovereignty upon which it depended, in both domestic and international politics.[22] Through policies such as the Marshall Plan, the use of the dollar as the reserve currency of the world economy, and the initiation of the GATT rounds of tariff reductions, U.S. policymakers were crucial to the creation of this new architecture of political life around the world. Moreover, this policy approach required important changes in the position of American life in relation to the larger globe. To sustain the new global system, the U.S. economy and society gradually experienced a greater interaction with the larger world through such policies and the opening of American markets to foreign imports, a transformation of immigration policy through the elimination of racial and ethnic quotas on legal immigration, and support for greater foreign investment by American multinational firms.[23] Not only were the roots of globalization planted in the post-1945 era, but American political leadership was central to their growth.

What does this mean for our understanding of the politics of globalization today? First, as I will discuss in more depth in chapter 3, we must be careful not to ignore the political roots and context that support the process by which any state's boundaries within the global system are sustained or changed. The post-1945 era saw the creation of a new practice of sovereignty both within and between states. This practice emerged from the exercise of political will and choice, and it is safe to assume that any such transformations in the global order will always depend to some degree on political action. Second, we must remember that some of the developments in American society associated with globalization as a unique process may in fact have resulted from the efforts of policymakers to create or preserve the United States' hegemonic role in world politics. Since the United States continues to play this role in the world, it is imperative that we consider how such factors have operated to reshape American life. Indeed, as I will try to show, the process of globalization today is closely tied with the exercise of American power and depends upon the same kinds of shifts in the practice of sovereignty that began fifty years ago. But before we go too far in this direction, we need to look a little more closely at how the new kind of social compact that emerged in this earlier period affected political life within the major advanced industrial states.

Sovereignty and the New Social Compact

The outlines of the new social compact emerged relatively quickly after 1945, and many of its roots can be found in the interwar period or even at the turn of this century. But it is important to emphasize two essential aspects of this new approach to sovereignty. First, we must remember how sharply these new institutions and priorities broke from the politics of earlier decades. Before the Second World War, most states were in economic chaos, torn by deep divisions over the structure of the polity and society. In some, the very legitimacy of the democratic-capitalist state had collapsed. The views and practices adopted after the war marked a fundamental turning point in the future of advanced capitalist states and succeeded beyond most expectations in rebuilding political legitimacy in these states.

Second, it is even more important to recognize the depth to which the new expectations and arrangements of sovereignty penetrated the level of popular political opinion about the role of the state and its responsibilities toward the national community. The new sovereignty consolidated a vision of the political world in which states existed to secure the well-being and cultural legacies of cohesive and clearly bounded national communities. Membership in these communities entailed a system of mutual sacrifice for the good of all, and popular majorities were especially concerned to ensure that such political bargains were enforced on social and political elites. In turn, the success of such bargains would be felt in the worth and dignity that citizenship in such a polity conferred on all its members. The responsibility for keeping these bargains, enforcing mutual sacrifice, equitably distributing the benefits it yielded, and preserving the distinctiveness and worth of citizenship was laid at the door of the state and understood to be the essence of its policy priorities.

How would these priorities be manifested? Most crucial to the expectations of the new sovereignty were the system of economic management and the provision of social welfare. On the basis of the protections provided by the international system, states would work to promote economic environments that combined rapid growth with low inflation, although the exact combination and emphasis would vary among states. Substantial guarantees of security and opportunity, which again varied in nature and degree from state to state, would ensure that all members of the national community would be protected from economic instability. (Indeed, as Rodrik has pointed out, these benefits were the most comprehensive in those states where exposure to the fluctuations of international trade was the highest.)[24] Meanwhile, the overall system of governance would be characterized by the active participation and representation of all the major sectors of society. Again, the nature of this participation varied across countries and over time, but the expectation was firmly established that all elements of the community shared its economic fate, and none of them should be isolated from the policymaking process.

To make these arrangements work, the community's borders had to be clearly defined and enforced. If the distinction between member and outsider was not clear, the motivation to share in the sacrifices the community needed, and the state's ability to enforce such sacrifices, would be weakened.[25] The first element of defining these borders was to provide autonomy for economic management and for the control of the flow of goods and capital into and out of each state. We have already seen how this worked. The second part of the formula was the control over population migration.[26] Throughout the advanced capitalist world, the two to three decades after 1945 were characterized by very restrictive national policies over immigration and naturalization, policies that reinforced the patterns of closure already apparent during the 1930s. Where migration did occur, it was strictly controlled, with the main goals being national (re-)unification or the filling of specific labor supply needs. In the latter case, the typical arrangements in this period allowed for temporary migration and denied such migrants access to most of the benefits of citizenship and usually to the very possibility of becoming citizens of the political communities in which they resided. Through these arrangements the borders of the community would be clear, the special status and identity of its members would be assured, and thus the political bargains that sustained its legitimacy could be preserved.

A third element of the new sovereignty was the state's role in promoting and disseminating the identity and purposes of the national community and its culture. With its boundaries defined and political and economic bases secured, the nation-state ideal could flourish in a manner unprecedented to this point. To support this ideal, states used their educational, cultural, and communication policies to strengthen the cultural bonds of nationalism and national identity within their boundaries. This meant the support of the dominant language in the community, the elaboration of a national myth, and the subsidizing of cultural productions—in literature, film, television, etc.—that would help reinforce the emerging national political bargains. Of course, different states faced different challenges and were more or less successful in achieving these goals. But the project of securing a common national identity and outlook and supporting the purposes it embodied also emerged as a central expectation among citizens and elites alike, an intrinsic part of the state's responsibility to the political community.

The new sovereignty, then, combined some of the traditional aims of sovereign states and nationalism with a new and distinctive set of practices, institutions, and expectations to create a new standard of legitimacy for advanced capitalist states. Based on a domestic social compact, this standard was reinforced by a set of international institutions and understandings that reinforced its authority while providing the kinds of external supports that individual states needed to meet their new obligations. As with earlier forms of sovereignty, this was a political formula constructed through the mobilization of political power and choice by the major players in the international arena, in this case the power of the United States and the protection it provided with military alliances and economic supports. More than most earlier constructions, however, this formula was tremendously successful in gaining widespread acceptance for a specific set of norms and expectations concerning the use of political power and authority. Indeed, the practical disappearance of serious discussion about the meaning of sovereignty in the political life of the advanced capitalist states indicated the depth of the consensus forged around these new understandings.

In the late 1990s, of course, conflict and debate over sovereignty returned with a vengeance. The post-World War II reconstruction of the responsibilities and purposes of the state became a subject of major dispute and, in some areas, radical change. This study focuses on the ways in which this conflict and debate are playing out in American political life and thus requires a closer look at the meaning of the new sovereignty in the United States. The institutions, practices, and expectations of the post-1945 era took distinctive forms in American politics, and we must understand these in some depth before we can appreciate the nature and significance of the current debates over globalization and sovereignty in American public policymaking.

Sovereignty and the Nation-State in the United States

Historical Background

Although the American Revolution was a central event in the emergence of modern notions of popular sovereignty and nationalism, the United States has been engulfed in conflict over the meaning of these ideas throughout its history. The new republic fairly quickly instituted universal suffrage and political equality for its citizens, but during its first eight decades the questions of exactly who would be citizens and the rights that would come with this status remained unresolved. At the same time, the meaning of sovereignty in a federal system and the question of ultimate political loyalty haunted the polity, only to lead to a bloody civil war. The resolution of this conflict, though, would set the stage for the specific manner in which the American nation-state would develop into the twentieth century.

As James McPherson has emphasized, the Civil War was central to the emerging sense of an American national identity.[27] The North's victory resolved once and for all the conflict between national and state-based visions of citizenship and loyalty in the republic. By ending slavery, establishing a national basis for citizenship, and firmly establishing national supremacy under the Constitution, the war consolidated a widespread sense of national identity and purpose. In Lincoln's political rhetoric, the nation gained a clear voice and definition along with a coherent historical mythology and rationale. Through the war mobilization and the policy choices that supported it, such as a protective tariff and support for creation of a national transportation infrastructure, the basic building blocks of a nationally integrated system of production and marketing were securely put into place. The United States emerged from its Civil War seemingly ready to assert and pursue its national purposes domestically and in the larger global arena.

At just this point, however, the American polity began to face the same rapid transformations that were shaking up political and social life in Europe and around the world. Having abandoned Reconstruction for the pursuit of economic opportunities, Americans were now forced to face the manifold impact of a corporate-dominated industrial economy. Monopolization, urbanization, inequality, and the booms and busts to which the system was prone all challenged the relatively egalitarian and predominantly agricultural and locally or regionally organized economy that had been the central aspiration of the Jacksonian era. The rapid growth of immigration from southern and eastern Europe, in turn, challenged Americans' sense of themselves as a primarily Protestant and Anglo people and raised all the practical problems of dealing with an increasingly diverse population and cultural climate. In addition to these changes, a historically inward-looking republic emerged as a more important and active player in the world of power politics. By the turn of the century, the United States would become a colonial power in Latin America and Asia, increasingly embroiled in the pull of European conflicts. Such a fundamentally transformed society with an unprecedented relationship to the larger world would force Americans to rethink their understanding of themselves and of the purposes of their political community.

The Emergence of the Modern American State

The particular American approach to the consolidation of a relatively unified and closed national community grew out of these challenges. Over time, political and economic elites refashioned the boundaries of the state and polity into a more successfully unified nation-state able to dominate world politics. To simplify greatly, condensing the many unresolved political struggles and policy ambiguities into a clear account, we can identify two broad stages in the building of the American nation-state.

The first stage spans the 1880s to the 1920s, and is centered around the Progressive Era.[28] The dominant themes of this stage are the consolidation of a national economy and the re-creation of a cultural identity for the nation. In economic policy, the United States committed itself to a high protective tariff as a means to secure the growing industrial economy, and it encouraged the spread of national transportation and communication systems. By the early twentieth century, a national bureaucracy, designed to stabilize and oversee the agricultural, industrial and financial systems, had been erected, one that survived the cycle of expansion and retrenchment of government power during and after the First World War. Despite attempts at the state and local level to move further in the provision of public services and social security, there remained no national commitment to these responsibilities. But the combination of external protection and internal promotion had worked to help create a decidedly recognizable national industrial economy, marking a fundamental shift in the nature of American economic life and in the responsibilities of the national state.

Meanwhile, this era also saw sustained efforts of protection and promotion in the creation of a more clear and uniform national identity. In the area of protection, long-standing pressures for immigration control had increasing success and culminated in the Immigration Act of 1924, which significantly closed the doors to future population flows. In addition, the legislation clearly enunciated and embodied the desire to limit the impact of Catholic and eastern and southern European immigration, preserving for the moment the clear Anglo-Protestant flavor of the polity. (Of course, this legislation followed on the earlier closing of the doors to Asian immigration, accomplished before 1914.) These moves were accompanied by sustained efforts, especially prominent in education, naturalization, and language policies, to assimilate immigrants into the dominant culture. The especially potent experience of nationalism and nativism during the First World War was crucial to the success of this program, as was the full enforcement of legal segregation throughout the south and similar informal practices in the rest of the country. Together, these policies created a clearly bounded polity, secured by the practical exclusion of nonwhite citizens from political power and the assimilation of immigrants into the dominant political and national culture.

The second stage in the consolidation of the American nation-state occurred in the 1930s and 1940s, in particular with the Roosevelt administration's New Deal programs and the subsequent involvement in the Second World War.[29] The New Deal transformed the scope of national responsibilities through a major realignment of political parties and loyalties. Drawing on the support of urban ethnics, the union movement, and key elements of the business community, the New Deal established a national commitment to protecting the economic security of and promoting economic opportunity for the working and middle classes. The Roosevelt administration would pay for these priorities with greater taxes and regulation on the business community, providing in return a program to promote economic stability and growth while securing the basic institutions of corporate industrial capitalism. Together, these programs transformed the status of national citizenship. They created a real national community of economic fate, secured through sacrifice by the powerful and activism by the state to ensure that all could share in some of the benefits of a growing economy. As in the case of the European welfare states, this combination renegotiated and deepened the ties binding the members of the nation-state.

The Roosevelt administration's impact on the cultural aspects of national identity was more subtle but just as important. By linking urbanized ethnic groups to the state, the policies and politics of the New Deal deemphasized the forced Americanization of an earlier era and created a new national mythology in which the immigrant experience played a more central role. American identity, while still one that generally excluded nonwhites, was now decidedly less Anglo-Protestant in its official manifestations and rhetoric. As some writers have noted, the increasingly closed international environment of the era worked to support these efforts. With increased national economic self-sufficiency imposed by the breakdown of the global trading and financial system and with the continued strict limitations on immigration, the borders between the national community and the larger world were drawn more clearly and tightly than ever. If Michael Walzer's insight is correct, and inclusiveness within a community depends upon clear boundaries between that community and its larger context,[30] it is likely that the transformations in the internal boundaries of the American political community in this period were made possible by the closing of external boundaries, a process common throughout the world during the 1930s and 1940s.

All these developments, of course, were heightened and probably secured by the national mobilization during the Second World War and the subsequent Cold War confrontation with Soviet communism. Together, these experiences consolidated the sense of shared national sacrifice and linked a distinct sense of world mission and responsibility to the new and more inclusive elements of the democratic national mythology developed during the 1930s.[31] Historically, then, the experiences and policy choices of the Roosevelt era served to complete the sovereign nation-state ideal in the American context. While the Progressive Era secured the boundaries of the national community in relation to other states, the New Deal period transformed and deepened the shared commitments and worth of citizenship to the members of the community. In doing so, it also significantly transformed the boundaries between the state and other institutions in society and thus promoted a new set of expectations concerning the responsibilities of the state toward its citizens.

In the decades after 1945, these expectations quickly permeated American political culture and transformed our understanding of sovereignty. The national state would be a highly unified and insulated polity and society in which all (white, initially) citizens could expect to attain a middle-class status in return for a commitment to hard work and the dominant cultural and historical mythology of the society. The role of the state was to ensure these outcomes by protecting the state from external threats and promoting the mutual sacrifice and compromise necessary for economic stabilization, social security, and middle-class entitlements. Politically, this arrangement would validate the worth and value of the average middle-class citizenry and assert the nation's priorities in the larger world context. The material and symbolic elements were closely linked: the value of all

Americans was embodied not only in cultural politics but in the policies that ensured widespread economic opportunity and security for all (recognized) members of the national community.

Thus, in their own way, Americans came to share with the rest of the world an unquestioned model of what the nation-state was and what the responsibilities of sovereign power entailed. As a closely bounded community, the nation-state would be culturally unified, and its power and will embodied in a state whose borders matched those of the national-political community. The responsibility of that state—the source of its authority to represent the sovereign community—was to protect and secure the collective interests of its members, but now this commitment had expanded far beyond national defense. The common interests of the polity now included providing economic security and opportunity for its members by actively promoting the growth and stability of the national economy and assuring a relatively egalitarian distribution of its benefits. Indeed, as Robert Reich has pointed out, this approach to policy both created and required the existence of an economy that was predominantly national in organization.[32] To a great degree, American purpose and identity came to be defined by a polity in which these kinds of outcomes were guaranteed, and this definition would dominate American political life in the decades following 1945.

But this account of the transformation of American politics in the 1930s and 1940s would not be complete without important qualifications. As historians and political scientists often emphasize, the emergence of the activist or positive state in the United States was shaped and limited by the unique elements of American history. In particular, a deep-seated suspicion of the national government, a relatively widespread belief in the virtues of private ownership and capitalist competition, and an unwillingness to become too dependent upon the state meant that the welfare state in the United States would not be nearly as all-encompassing and pervasive in its guarantees as it was in Europe. Moreover, America's deeply individualistic political culture would prove much more resistant than the cultures of other advanced capitalist states to a collectivist. Once the unique pressures of the Depression and the Second World War diminished, there were clear signs that the deep sense of a community of shared fate was already beginning to fray. Although the fear of communism and the Soviet Union would preserve some of the same sense of community over the succeeding decades, this could not totally replace the more positive sense of communal engagement of the 1930s and especially the 1940s.

What did this mean for the new social compact and role of government in the United States? In the terminology of political scientists, America's welfare state and political economy took on a distinctly "liberal" cast.[33] As Alan Brinkley has noted, by the late 1940s it had become clear that the new American state would not present any significant challenge to the overall structure of the capitalist economy. Rather, it would focus on smoothing out the economy's instabilities while using social policy to create a large, prosperous, and property-owning middle class that would exist within the confines of the larger social and economic structure.[34] Instead of consolidating a cohesive national community on the social democratic model, the American version of the new social compact focused on enabling citizens to pursue their own paths to prosperity in a relatively secure environment. Institutionally, this meant much less political direction over the economy and the absence of the egalitarian social provisions common in Western Europe.

Over time, the impact of this particular approach was clear. Although Americans came to expect a historically unprecedented number of protections from their government, American political culture remained much more liberal and individualistic than the cultures of other advanced industrial states. Citizens did come to rely on the state to secure economic prosperity and opportunity, especially for the middle classes, but remained much more resistant to the kinds of obligations and regulation that would have been required of a more cohesive national community. As a result, when the policy structure created in the 1930s and 1940s began to run into real difficulty, Americans would be less willing to accept more extensive control over their lives and more willing to consider political alternatives that promised to reduce the role of government and to provide citizens with more freedom to pursue their opportunities and fortunes. In the end, deconstructing the framework of the postwar social and political order, and thus creating the conditions necessary for a new round of globalization, would prove easier in the United States than anywhere else.

But we are jumping ahead. For the moment, it is crucial to remember the real transformation that the new social compact did bring in American politics, particularly in expectations that citizens came to have about the responsibilities of government. Though Americans may have been less willing than most Europeans to accept ambitious programs of social and economic planning, from the 1940s onward the expectation that government would secure economic opportunity and prosperity to its citizens laid deep roots in the political culture. To be sure, these responsibilities and the proper ways of achieving them were often deeply controversial and contested, and some of the strains beneath the surface were very deep and apparent early on. The civil rights movement, which demanded the inclusion of African Americans in the same community of benefits and obligations open to other Americans, seemed to many to signify the completion of the national community, but for others it threatened the very definition of "American." However, the overarching acceptance of the new image of the nation, the state, and sovereignty was palpable, so much so that the very term "sovereignty" was marginalized in popular, political, and intellectual discourse.[35] The search for sovereignty would only reemerge when this national image came to seem disconnected from the actual practices and developments of social, economic, and political life. By examining globalization, we can begin to get a grip on what has—and has not—created a renewed concern for sovereignty in American politics and policymaking.

3

Globalization in the Contemporary World: The End of Sovereignty?

By the 1990s, it became clear to most students of politics and society that the institutions, policies, and shared beliefs of the post-World War II era were facing severe challenges. Within the advanced capitalist countries, the long-established arrangements concerning the relationships of government, the economy, and citizens were undergoing significant changes. From Scandinavia through North America, the various forms of the welfare state were declared obsolete, and market institutions were coming to dominate the structure of society. Governments were reducing the scope of their responsibilities, and many economists and politicians were claiming that states had lost their ability to determine the shape of economic and social development within their societies. In the meantime, economies were undergoing rapid changes in technology and business practices, which were accompanied by the rapid decline of many industries and regions, the emergence of new ones, and a growing inequality of wealth and income, reversing the trends of the previous five decades. Business leaders and economic commentators were also claiming that these developments were being propelled by the necessities of global economic and technological change.

The central issue facing students of these trends concerned interpretation: What was going on, and what were its causes? During the 1980s and 1990s, scholars in political science, sociology, and economics offered two competing approaches for making sense of these developments. The first focuses on the clear political sources of and connections between these developments: state and society were being transformed because of fundamental shifts in the distribution of political power in capitalist democracies. The end of the welfare state, after all, was a key component of the free-market politics associated with the Thatcher and Reagan governments of the 1980s and their successors or imitators.[1] These governments were at the center of a movement to reverse the trend of political economic change from an increasing role for government to a withdrawal of the state in favor of more freedom for markets and individuals. Behind these governments stood many important sectors of the business community. Though this community was not unanimous in its support for every part of the free-market agenda, there was substantial and widespread agreement on the need to reduce the burdens of the taxes and regulations on which the existing social compact was built.[2] In addition, the new power of free-market political economy among political elites and a widespread voter resistance to the further growth of government combined to create a powerful political coalition in favor of market-oriented social and economic change.

Many celebrated observers, however, saw a very different set of causes at work. Rather than political vision, these writers emphasized what they perceived to be a newly dominant set of economic and technological forces transforming politics and society. Instead of reflecting political choice, these forces made politics—and the institution of the modern sovereign state—less and less relevant to the destiny of modern societies. From this perspective, reflected in the writing of Friedman and Ohmae, transformations in the nature of modern economic life, especially those propelled by new communication and production technologies, were making obsolete the kinds of government regulatory activity that had been so prominent for decades, and they turned these policies from necessary checks on the market to obstacles to economic growth and efficiency. Moreover, these transformations were linking the world into one global economic system, over which individual countries had little control. States were reshaping their roles in the economy, and the structure of society was being transformed, because they had little option in the face of powerful new economic pressures. By the later 1990s, these forces came to be widely identified with globalization, and became the central theme in the most widely discussed analyses of contemporary social and economic change.

In this chapter, I will examine more closely the various dimensions and meanings of globalization with the aim of developing a framework to help explain its impact on the politics of American public policymaking. After developing this framework, the chapter will focus on the emergence of the economic aspects of globalization and their impact on American society over the past three decades. In the process, I will review the scholarly debates concerning the relationship between global change and the future of the sovereign state, drawing heavily on the discussion of sovereignty presented in the chapter 2. The ultimate argument of this chapter is that the relationship among globalization, the sovereignty of the state, and the collapse of the post-1945 social consensus is more complex than most observers suggest. Globalization, I contend, is the result of a set of political choices put in motion by states pursuing the free-market project, choices that aim to use a more integrated and open global market economy as a tool to transform the role of the state in society. Though it is often seen as an independent process of change, globalization is better characterized as a new context in which political and economic actors pursue their goals and interests. As its impact in the United States and other states has deepened, globalization has in turn become the object and context of a new set of political struggles that are going to determine the role of the state in the society and polity, and ultimately the structure of power and identity in American society over the coming decades.

Defining and Exploring Globalization

What is globalization? This seems to be a relatively clear and straightforward question, to which an answer should be readily available. However, anyone who begins reading about contemporary global change soon realizes that there are endless definitions of globalization, of which no two are exactly the same.[3] Moreover, there is a wide spectrum of approaches to the phenomenon, ranging from narrow economic analyses to reflections on the future of human civilization, among which there is little common territory. And the problem is only multiplied when one considers the task of explaining and evaluating global change. Thus it is easy and understandable to conclude that the term is simply a catchall for whatever a particular writer wants to praise or condemn, and to dismiss its significance and utility. Because "globalization" has become an important term in political debate and conflict, it is imperative that we come to some clear and useful sense of what it means.

The broadest approaches to globalization see it as a transformation in the relationship of space and time in contemporary world society. In the work of David Harvey, Anthony Giddens, and Malcolm Waters, globalization is an economic, cultural, and technological process that works to override the importance of spatial distance and territorial divisions among human beings.[4] It creates a global system in which individuals around the world are in instantaneous communication with one another and can act together in response to the same developments. In such a system, individuals are part of a globally unified economic system and a globally defined cultural environment, in which territorial divisions mean little, spatial distance can be easily overcome, and individual governments have little power to set the terms on which this system operates. Scholars taking this approach differ over the degree to which the world today is globalized: some see the global system dominated by corporate capitalist institutions, and others think it is beyond anyone's control. They all share the conviction, however, that the world is rapidly moving toward a situation in which territorial divisions and spatial distances among people will matter little in determining the shape of human societies.[5]

A second approach to globalization shares this basic understanding but presents a more complex reading of its implications for world politics. According to Roland Robertson, globalization is not simply about the structural evolution of human relations around the globe but depends also upon a growing awareness of the deepening connections among the fates of human beings. In this view, an essential element of a globalized world is one in which human beings begin to think in global terms about their values, beliefs, and purposes. But, Robertson argues, this does not mean that globalization necessarily brings about a more unified world society. As a more globally oriented society brings different groups into deeper contact with one another, it is just as likely to create a backlash against growing global interdependence, which many perceive as a danger to deeply held values.[6] Thus, deepening globalization can in fact produce an enhanced commitment to territorial borders and divisions as a way of protecting certain groups or societies against perceived dangers generated by the global economic and cultural systems. For Robertson, however, this remains an aspect of globalization; by identifying the global system as a threat to their values, even those who act against it are thinking in global terms about their situation. In a globalized world, a central political dynamic is the tension between forces pushing for deeper integration and those pushing for more separation.[7]

Of course, most discussions of globalization ultimately focus on patterns of economic activity and organization, which most observers would agree are the most important and highly developed aspects of this phenomenon. A third approach, probably the most common, focuses on the increased intertwining of the production, investment, and consumption activities among the economies of the world—a process driven by new technologies of communication, production, and transportation—as the essential element of globalization. In the words of Wolfgang H. Reinicke,

> Globalization finds its origin in the changing pattern of ". . . transborder operations of firms undertaken to organize their development, production, sourcing, marketing, and financing activities." Heightened competition at home and abroad has led not only to new developments in corporate and industrial organization, such as flexible manufacturing, but also to the cross-border movement of increasingly intangible capital, such as finance, technology, knowledge, information, and the ownership or control of assets.[8]

From this perspective, globalization is essentially the story of how economic processes are becoming increasingly global in scope, as firms and capital markets are connected in dense networks of activity and interdependence. As a result, the choices and opportunities available to individuals and organizations are now deeply embedded in a global system of activity that shapes the daily lives of more and more persons.

In this book, I will draw on all three of these approaches and define globalization as a set of economic, cultural, and technological processes that are working to reduce the significance of territorial boundaries in shaping the conditions of life for persons and societies. To put it another way, globalization works to submit the fates of individuals and groups around the world to the operation of the same basic forces of change. This approach closely follows that of Barrie Axford, who presents the following analysis of globalization:

> The core of the idea is that the world is undergoing a process of ever-intensifying interconnectedness and interdependence, so that it is becoming less relevant to speak of separate national economies, or separate national jurisdictions founded upon principles like the sovereignty of the territorial nation-state. The idea of a global system suggests that this interconnectedness and interdependence is making it increasingly difficult for social units like nation-states, localities, and even individuals to sustain identity without reference to more encompassing structures and flows.[9]

In a fully globalized world, the specific place in which one lives—state, region, city, etc.—would make no difference for the opportunities and obstacles that one faced in life; here, all persons would face the same set of constraints irrespective of territorial location.

Do we live in such a world today? It seems pretty clear that we do not. Although there is much evidence that many areas of life are moving in this direction, as we will see shortly, few scholars or observers would claim that the various borders and boundaries that separate human communities are irrelevant at this point. Indeed, if Robertson's argument is correct, we will never see such a fully globalized world; globalization will always lead some groups and leaders to attempt to reinforce the boundaries between societies. Some scholars, impressed by the limits of globalization today, argue that we should distinguish between globalization as presented by Axford and the "internationalization" of relations between states and societies. According to Hirst and Thompson, the latter situation is one in which there is more social, economic, and political interaction between states and societies, but in which political and territorial boundaries remain decisive in shaping the evolution of societies. In their view, this is a much more accurate characterization of the contemporary world than the idea of globalization.[10]

Though we can accept the claim that the idea of globalization does not fully characterize our current world, it remains an extremely useful model to help us understand many of the changes that are shaping our lives. In this sense, I will be using the concept as an "ideal-type": it highlights some crucial dimensions of development and enables us to evaluate the impact of these dimensions on our world.[11] In particular, the concept of globalization helps us think about our increasing dependence on forces and institutions whose activity is not limited by the territorial borders of our society. It helps us, then, to focus on the impact of these forces on the sovereignty of the modern state, which will be the ultimate aim of our inquiry.

The Impacts of Globalization: Cultural, Economic, and Political

Where can we look to see the impact of globalization on our lives today? The scholarly and popular literature on this issue is full of examples, from anecdotes to in-depth investigations of specific areas of life. In this section, I want to present a more overarching picture of the impact of globalization, the details of which will be partially filled in by the chapters in part three of the book. This account is not meant to be comprehensive but to provide the readers with a sense of the significance of globalization and to perhaps provoke them to think about how this impact is felt in daily life.

A good place to begin is with the rapidly changing technological foundations of our society. Over the past decade, changes in the way we travel, communicate, access information, and organize collective action have reshaped lives throughout the globe in tremendous and often simultaneous ways. The most well-known and discussed example of this is the Internet. Increasingly, people around the world are linked by the Internet in all sorts of ways, from consumption and production to access to knowledge and information, and through the various kinds of personal networks established through this medium. Despite the efforts of states to control these linkages, the Internet allows those with access to it to make choices and pursue opportunities irrespective of the particular country in which they happen to reside. Moreover, computer, telecommunications, and transportation technologies have been major factors in the restructuring of production and investment practices in the global economy and major facilitators of the globalization of economic activity. As any follower of business news today will know, this process is now being further intensified through the use of the Internet itself as a major vehicle of global economic activity. It is clear, then, that computers and related technologies, and especially the Internet, provide a key example of the ways globalization is linking the futures of peoples across territorial boundaries.

Just as striking has been the growing cultural intermixing around the world. Cultural life throughout the globe, from forms of music and entertainment to religious community to new forms of environmental awareness, is increasingly moving in directions determined simultaneously on a level larger than that of any state. As a result, the whole notion of a "national culture"—defined primarily by the traditions of the citizens of a given state and developed by those citizens— seems increasingly anachronistic.[12] Diverse cultural traditions still exist, of course, but they are more and more intertwined in a process of mutual fertilization, to the point that all national cultures are becoming hybrid cultures. For anthropologically oriented writers, such as Roland Robertson, cultural change has indeed become the basis for understanding globalization as a whole. In Robertson's view, the essence of globalization is the spread around the world of an awareness of the interdependence of peoples and individuals, a conscious sense that the choices they make are shaped by forces and processes operating on a global level. The spread of cultural influences beyond their sources of origin and the increasing mixture of influences in every country's daily cultural life is central in shaping this awareness.

It remains the case, however, that the discussion of globalization at all levels is dominated by the fact of increasing economic interdependence among states. Economic globalization in this sense has a number of dimensions. The most impressive is the increasing intertwining of global capital markets, a story that dominates Thomas Friedman's book. This linking of markets for stocks, bonds, and currencies has created a world where the value of money and the access to credit are increasingly determined by investors working in continuously active and globally linked markets, especially those in London, New York, and Tokyo. Though governments aim to shape currency values, interest rates, and the money supply, they are only one set of players, and their resources and organization are often dwarfed by those of private institutions. In addition to the emergence of global financial markets, though, the processes of production and consumption are increasingly conducted on a worldwide basis, as corporations and individuals disperse their assets around the globe looking for the most profitable sources of investment. As Reinicke emphasizes, this is one of the most crucial elements of today's global economy, as firms organize their activities in ways that often ignore national boundaries in the search for the most competitive and efficient ways of operation. Indeed, as we will see, an increasing percentage of global trade is now carried out within multinational firms. One result, much discussed by Greider, Reich, and Friedman, is the growing disjunction between a corporation's country of origin and the actual way in which it identifies its interests and conducts its business. As a result, it is increasingly difficult to define the boundaries that distinguish the global economy from any particular national economy.[13]

Globalization, however, is more than a growing interdependence between domestic and global contexts, to which states must react. It is also a central part of the political arena and context in which politics is conducted and states must act in the contemporary world. As societies become more closely linked, and key sources of social change operate on global levels, political conflicts come to involve issues and actors not confined by the territorial boundaries of the state. A classic example of this process is what is often called the globalization of environmental policy and politics. In the past two decades, it has become clear that most of the crucial challenges to the health of the natural environment—from rainforest destruction to global warming to air pollution—are the products of technological and economic forces that are global in scope and operation. As a result of this recognition, states have developed international patterns of negotiation and compromise to promote their goals in the area of environmental protection. The resulting agreements and institutions have injected an essentially global dimension into a sphere of policymaking where it had not existed before.

The globalization of environmental policy, though, goes beyond the level of governmental action. It means that anyone who wants to be a significant player in the politics of the environment must also act globally. This understanding has been especially important in reshaping the strategies of interest groups dedicated to protecting the environment, both those that are primarily national and those that are international in scope. As Friedman effectively presents it, in the Amazon region threats to the rainforest are the product of a set of forces that are both global and local at the same time, and activists attempting to protect the rainforest have had to make global linkages to successfully resist further environmental destruction. Similarly, corporations involved in production activities that potentially harm the environment must now face challenges to their activities from many different parts of the globe, not just those that are based around the site of production. In practice, all this means that environmental policymaking in any particular state will involve the activities of interests and organizations based in other parts of the globe. These players may have a significant impact on any one state's choices but be based in distant political and social contexts.[14]

A similar phenomenon, connected more directly to the evolution of cultural norms and ideals around the globe, has been the emergence of a global politics of human rights. Today, organizations such as Amnesty International and Human Rights Watch work throughout the world to protect the rights of prisoners and more generally to spread high standards of human rights protections to as many states as possible. Moreover, they are backed by major international agreements, key aspects of international law, and many international organizations that share a commitment to promoting uniform standards for the protection of individual dignity around the world. Under the influence of these organizations and institutions, human rights has now been firmly placed on the agenda of both world and domestic politics throughout the globe. States must now be attentive to their own record in this area and must play to or be responsible to a constituency that is at once domestic and international in its makeup, one that is often equipped with substantial sanctions against behavior of which it disapproves.

There is no better example of this process in recent years than the series of events leading to the arrest of General Augusto Pinochet, the former military leader of Chile, in Britain in 1998. After the military coup in Chile in 1973, many left-wing political activists were arrested and tortured by the regime, and many of these persons "disappeared." Among these activists were a number of citizens of foreign countries, including Spain and the United States. In 1996, a Spanish judge, relying on provisions of the United Nations' Declaration of Human Rights, issued a warrant for Pinochet's arrest for violating the human rights of Spanish citizens. Traveling to Britain for medical treatment in October 1998, Pinochet was arrested by British authorities, acting under provisions of the European Treaty on Human Rights, which required the enforcement of the warrant in all European Union (EU) member states. Though the arrest generated much controversy, its legitimacy was upheld by a committee of Britain's House of Lords, operating as the highest judicial authority in the country. Although Pinochet was eventually declared medically unfit to stand trial and was allowed to return to Chile, this process marked a milestone in international law. For the first time, a former head of state was arrested for actions committed while in power, and his arrest in another country was upheld as a logical consequence of the evolving rules of international law to which all states are bound. A more stunning example of the impact of globalization in transforming the boundaries among states cannot be found.[15]

A final example of the way globalization shapes the politics of policymaking, one that returns us to the economic arena, can be seen in the area of capital markets. As Greider and Friedman emphasize, the intertwining of capital and money markets not only links economies but also creates new political actors and constraints on the making of economic policy in even the most powerful states. The most obvious way in which these markets exert political influence is through the decisions they make about the value of investment in a country's currency or productive assets. When market players believe that a state's decisions are misguided, they will withdraw their investment in that state's assets, a phenomenon we have seen clearly in recent years, from Britain to Mexico, Russia to Brazil, and Thailand to South Korea. But this influence is also exerted in more typically political ways. Key market players are often consulted by states concerning economic policy choices. International representatives of the market, from credit rating agencies to the International Monetary Fund, play a central role in providing advice to states on how to maintain the confidence of the markets as they attempt to pursue their economic goals.[16] Once again, we see a process in which globalization transforms the realm of political conflict and policy choice itself, introducing both global and private players and concerns into arenas that were previously considered the exclusive domain of sovereign states.

It is important to emphasize the common features of globalization in these various areas. The emerging patterns of political and economic life that we have seen go beyond the kind of impact of foreign institutions and processes on the actions of states and societies that is a regular part of life in the modern system of sovereign states. Rather, these patterns break down the very distinction between "domestic" and "foreign" that is the basis of so much of our thinking about political life. In a globalized (or globalizing) world, most of the key actors and institutions within the territorial boundaries of any state or society are simultaneously global actors, operating in many countries and making calculations on the basis of a global network of interests, opportunities, and commitments. This is the case whether we are talking about investors, corporations, interest groups, or producers of culture. The activities undertaken by these actors, even though they might be occurring in a particular territory, are just the specific aspects of processes that are global in scope and impact. Thus, it is crucial to remember that we are no longer dealing here with the impact of "outside" forces or institutions; in a globalized world, territorial borders no longer clearly define the boundaries of economic, cultural, or political activity.

Globalization and the Politics of Policymaking in the United States

If this is what globalization is about, what are the implications of these developments and trends for politics and sovereignty in the contemporary state? There is little doubt that such developments are having a profound effect on the ability of states to determine what will happen within their borders. This is especially true of the large group of states—mostly in formerly colonized areas of the world—that are relatively weak to begin with. During the Cold War, these states were subject to the shifting winds of the competitive power politics of the United States and the Soviet Union, often having to bend to the will and influence of one or the other. Today these same states are faced with an onslaught of global forces on every level, from political to economic to cultural to environmental arenas. If it was difficult to preserve some independence and control in the face of the geopolitical game of the Cold War, it becomes even more challenging in a world where the state's control of its borders is subject to simultaneous attacks on a number of levels. Though these states have not been rendered totally helpless, there is little wonder that some of the most vocal opposition to globalization has come from Latin America, Asia, and Africa.

But how do these kinds of trends apply to the United States? To grasp the impact of globalization in the United States, we need to shift our focus away from the simpler question of the control of borders. In chapter 2, I argued that the best way to think about sovereignty is in terms of the boundaries of the state, and that territorial borders are only one aspect of these boundaries. What globalization has done in the United States is to change the boundaries of the polity, of the political process, and of the responsibilities of the states. And it has done so in a way that undermines the assumptions necessary to support the kind of social compact that emerged in the post-World War II era. The reader will recall that this compact was based on a close identification between the borders of the state and those of its constituency, the body of citizens residing in its territory. The aim of the state was to promote the security and opportunities of its citizenry—understood as a nation with a shared set of interests—in return for the loyalty of those citizens. Thus the nation was assumed to have a shared fate as an economic and social community, and the state's purpose was to embody and promote the priorities of this community.

Globalization as we know it has helped to shatter this set of assumptions and expectations. As a result of its impact on American life, it has become more difficult to articulate a clear sense of what holds the community of citizens together, to use the territorial borders of the state as constraints that help to explain the interests of citizens, and to limit the state's obligations and priorities. In the place of these assumptions, a new set of relationships and constraints has come to define the role of the state and the nature of society. Instead of ensuring a common economic fate, globalization has helped divide Americans between those well placed to prosper from an expanding global economy and those likely to experience more insecurity and declining prospects in such a context. For those in the former group, moreover, the territorial borders of the state no longer clearly define the boundary of their interests and identifications. In the meantime, to an increasing degree the economic, social, and cultural developments within the borders of the United States are linked to larger global patterns of activity. Politics and public policy, therefore, are no longer limited to a set of players, interests, and issues defined by the territorial borders of the state. Rather, the state is now involved in exercising power and engaging responsibilities in regard to a global range of actors and interests. The unique link between the priorities of the state and those of the domestic society it is supposed to represent has been severely strained, if not yet totally broken.[17]

We can understand these changes more concretely if we look again at the examples of globalization discussed above. The globalization of American economic life, for instance, has strained the sense in which there exists an "American" economy distinct and independent from the global economy. Whether we consider the capital markets, patterns of corporate ownership, investment, and production, or the labor force, the American economy is now deeply linked to networks of economic activity that stretch across the globe. In this context, the interests of the economy and its participants become much more vague and hard to pinpoint. They certainly are no longer confined by the territorial borders of the state; there are few Americans whose economic fortunes are not deeply tied to economic developments in different parts of the globe. All of this makes it more difficult for government to identify and protect the common economic interests of Americans and renders policies that rely solely on shaping the domestic economy anachronistic at best.

But the situation is even more complex. As Reich has forcefully emphasized, globalization has helped to deepen the divide between Americans positioned to prosper from greater economic integration and those threatened with economic and social disruption. This division has been widely noticed and discussed by economists, sociologists, and political scientists. After reviewing the data, Ethan Kapstein presents the following picture:

> These numbers suggest the "have/have not" nature of contemporary American society. Those who possess education, skill, and investment capital have witnessed a tremendous increase in income growth over

the past two decades, while the unskilled are being left far behind. This development has led Harvard labor economist to assert that the United States is "moving toward an apartheid economy."[18]

It is widely accepted by observers that the causes of this divergence are many and that they are not all linked directly to the impact of globalization. (See the more in-depth discussion of this question in chapter 4.) But to the extent that economic globalization increases the pressures on those with the lowest wages, there is good reason to think that it has worked to deepen this trend. And in the view of one influential scholar, there is evidence that globalization has done exactly that:

> [R]educed barriers to trade and investment accentuate the asymmetries between groups that can cross international borders . . . and those that cannot. In the first category are owners of capital, highly skilled workers, and many professionals, who are free to take their resources where they are most in demand. Unskilled and semiskilled workers and most middle managers belong in the second category. Putting the same point in more technical terms, globalization makes the demand for the services of the individuals in the second category *more elastic*—that is, the services of large segments of the working population can be more easily substituted by the services of other people across national boundaries.[19]

Thus, while those with the financial resources and technological and intellectual skills in demand in the global economy perceive a new world of opportunity, those with fewer resources and marketable skills are faced with a new set of threats and dangers. In this context, policies that are beneficial to one segment of the community can work to the detriment of others. Without a common economic community of fate, there is little left of the notion that the state is the vehicle for promoting the economic well-being of the community as a whole. As a result, the whole social compact based upon this assumption is undermined, leaving the state's priorities up for grabs among those with very different visions of the country's place in the global context. To this point, the resulting struggle has been a very unequal one and has emerged as a central focus of the politics of globalization.

The globalization of culture has had many of the same effects. In one sense, the cultural globalization means the spread of American culture around the world, providing new opportunities for those who create or understand this culture to benefit from increasing interdependence. But these same developments can also work to threaten many Americans' sense of political and cultural identity and security. The same changes in economic activity, communications technology, and popular culture that spread American cultural practices to other parts of the world also work to bring into American life cultural influences from the larger world. Whether one looks at the area of religion, music, cuisine, or language, the daily lives of many Americans over the past three decades have been transformed by an influx of ideas, practices, and values previously absent from the general cultural life of the country. The new waves of immigration from Asia and Latin America, which began in the 1970s, have been central to this process. With the resulting establishment of large communities of persons from linguistic and cultural backgrounds not greatly represented in earlier eras of immigration, Americans have been forced to confront the global variety of cultures in a direct and immediate way at home. Whatever the future of these communities, their impact on American society has been direct and palpable. No longer can the notion of a unified cultural order within the nation's borders—another element of the post-1945 social compact—be sustained. In this much more diverse society, a larger variety of norms and values compete for supremacy, which reinforces the already deep divisions over the relationship of the state to the global economy. Cultural globalization, like economic globalization, becomes a source of conflict over the purposes of the community. Instead of neatly articulating the aims of a cohesive community, the state's priorities become a focus for deep political division.

What has been the effect of these aspects of globalization on the processes of political conflict and policymaking in the United States? As the boundaries of the political world and the territorial borders of the state have begun to diverge, the political arena increasingly includes players and institutions that are global in their interests, outlook, and activities. To take the example of economic policy, the promotion of growth and stability within the United States now requires that policymakers attempt to manipulate economic activity on a global scale. This in turn requires that policymakers engage with a variety of interests and institutions not tied to the polity as a territorially bounded community. These include American individuals and firms that act globally but also foreign-based individuals and firms—many of which play major roles in the American economy—the world of capital and financial markets, the various institutions that shape the evolution of the world economy (such as the International Monetary Fund [IMF] and the World Trade Organization [WTO]), and the other major states and organizations of states (such as the European Union [EU]) that are also major players in that economy. By attempting to shape the actions of this variety of players, American policymakers not only integrate them into the "domestic" policymaking process but also begin incorporating their views and interests into the making of policy choices. As a result, the American state has gradually entered into relationships of obligation and responsibility with agents not based primarily within the territorial boundaries of the state. Many of these relationships are informal, but some have been incorporated into treaties and agreements that carry specific obligations for the United States, such as the North American Free Trade Agreement (NAFTA) and General Agreement on Tariffs and Trade (GATT) treaties. Consequently, distinctly national actors and interests now compete with a variety of multinational and global interests in the economic policymaking process in the United States.

We can observe many of the same developments in the area of environmental policy and politics.[20] United States environmental policy emerged in a systematic way in the late 1960s and early 1970s out of a distinctly domestic set of concerns and pressures. The initial institutions established to promote environmental protections and regulation, at the state and national levels, were also animated by a clearly domestic focus. As in the rest of the world, though, developments over the past two decades have made American environmental policy and policymaking more global in focus. There is now a global environmental policy regime, as embodied in the Montreal Treaty on ozone-producing products and the Rio and Kyoto agreements, in which American policy is constrained and which U.S. policy played an important role in developing. In addition, the network of participants involved in shaping U.S. environmental policy is now global in nature, involving the multinational firms whose activities the policy attempts to regulate, internationally active interest groups such as Greenpeace and increasingly internationally oriented domestic environmental lobbies, the communities of researchers and regulators active in these issues, and the more loosely tied networks of citizens and activists, often linked through the Internet. In the United States this kind of process characterizes the state as well as the national level, as many states have undertaken their own initiatives in environmental protection, often through alliances with other regional authorities, corporations, and interest groups. It is in these senses that environmental policy, like economic policy, has become globalized.

Similar patterns can be seen in a number of other areas of policy, including immigration (see chapter 5), law enforcement,[21] telecommunications, etc. The politics of policymaking in the United States are no longer bounded by a set of players, interests, and priorities defined by a political community contained within the state's territorial borders. Rather, the boundaries within which the state acts and defines its purposes and responsibilities now range far and wide over a global arena of engagement. Most important, the resulting pattern of political conflict shaping policy choice is not defined by a domestic versus global axis. Globalization links all Americans to worldwide processes of change, and global forces, interests, and conflict enter politics and policymaking through their embodiment in the differing directions and outlooks into which the American polity is dividing. The essential political conflicts generated by globalization are not between global and domestic priorities but between different political alliances—each composed of both global and domestic forces—with different visions of the proper relationship between American and international society.

Interlude: Globalization in Modern History

Before exploring the impact of globalization in more detail, we must deal with one of the major weaknesses of most of the popular—and some of the scholarly—literature and discussion of the topic. In reviewing these discussions, our attention has focused on the past two or three decades. This is a reflection of the focus and interest of most writers on globalization, for whom it represents the new system of world politics and economics emerging after the end of the Cold War. But any careful student of modern history will recognize that similar developments have taken place at many different points in the development of the modern system of states. Over the past two centuries, periods of economic closure and nationalism have alternated with periods of great increases in the degree of international economic and cultural interdependence. Though the latter have not been talked about in terms of globalization, they have shared many features with current patterns of global change. The current nature and degree of globalization may seem unprecedented in light of the trends of most of the twentieth century, but it is hardly a new phenomenon.

This is a point made forcefully by a number of scholars of global change, and they are particularly interested in the parallels between contemporary global interdependence and the kinds of relationships that emerged from 1870 through the beginning of the First World War in 1914. During this earlier period, many of the developments often cited today as indicators of globalization were well developed, some to a degree still not reached today. First, the late nineteenth and early twentieth century was a period of great international flows of capital and investment. Under the rubric of the British government's preservation of a gold standard and London's domination of the financial industry, tremendous amounts of money flowed without much regulation between and among the developed and developing countries of the time. English banks and financiers dominated this process, but it also included participants from around the world, especially in the financing of government debts and the construction of modern infrastructure. As a percentage of overall economic activity, it is only in the past decade that the flow of capital around the globe has reached the levels of 1914, when it was cut off by decades of warfare and depression.[22]

Second, the same pattern can be found in the relations of trade among the major and emerging countries of the era. Simply put, the global economy of the turn of the century was one in which all major countries engaged in a great degree of importing and exporting. This was, after all, the era in which the multinational corporation first emerged in something like its contemporary form, as the new industrial giants in Europe and North America both invested abroad and developed complex international networks of suppliers and markets. It was also the era in which countries like the United States, Canada, Argentina, and Australia emerged as major exporters of agricultural products. As indicated in table 3-1, during this period we find that the percentage of overall Gross Domestic Product (GDP) accounted for by trade was higher for all the world's economies than it would be five decades later, reaching levels only recently surpassed in most of the industrialized world. On the level of finance and trade, then, the world of the early

Table 3-1. Merchandise Exports as a Percentage of GDP, 1870–1992. (Three year annual average, except for 1950.)

	Western developed countries	United States	Western Europe	Japan
1870	—	5.4	13.6	—
1890	11.7	6.7	14.9	5.1
1913	12.9	6.4	18.3	12.5
1929	9.8	5.0	14.5	13.6
1938	6.2	3.7	7.1	13.0
1950	7.8	3.8	13.4	6.8
1970	10.2	4.0	17.4	9.7
1992	14.3	7.5	21.7	8.8

Source: Bairoch and Kozul-Wright, *Globalization Myths*, p. 9.

twentieth century was at least as interdependent and globalized as that of the last decade of the century.

There was one resource, however, that was extremely mobile at the turn of the century, and whose level of movement has not been matched since: labor. The mass migration of people searching for work across the Atlantic (and to some degree the Pacific) from 1870 through 1914 was a defining element of the age, without which neither the exporting nor the importing states would have been able to reach the levels of economic development that they did.[23] It is true that the past three decades have seen a new wave of human migration around the world, one that is rapidly changing the face of society and politics in many of the economically advanced countries. But current patterns of migration are controlled and channeled in ways that simply did not exist at the turn of the century. The whole complex web of passports and borders, the network of immigration laws and border controls that we are used to today, existed only in rudimentary form during this period. Instead, the countries that exported labor were generally happy to let what was perceived as a surplus population leave, and the importing countries actively encouraged migrants and competed for them.[24] As a whole, the only significant organization over this process was private, in the hands of corporations that recruited workers, individuals and groups that specialized in organizing emigration, and ethnic organizations that tried to create networks and support for migrants from their own area of origin. For persons, the world was a much easier place to move around in, and borders much easier to cross, than they have ever been since.

To be sure, the similarities between this era and the current period can be overemphasized, especially in the areas of finance and trade. The flow of capital around the world in the 1870–1914 period, for example, was focused on investment in various public forums, such as government debt to support public budgets or to finance massive public works projects. Today, as we have seen, the overwhelming focus is on private investment, especially by multinational corporations. In the earlier era, most of the trade between major states was in the form of finished commodities, a major portion was in the form of agricultural trade, and a good deal of trade took place between what we would now call countries of the "North" and "South." In the current wave of globalization, most trade takes place within corporations themselves, as various inputs are moved around the world to support a global structure of production of finished goods. Moreover, the proportion of trade accounted for by agriculture has fallen sharply, as advanced economies tend to trade mostly with other advanced economies and trade in services has come to take an increasingly prominent role in global economic activity.[25]

But the overall lesson is clear. Globalization is not a phenomenon unique to the late twentieth century; similar patterns have been seen before in the history of the state system. Indeed, some scholars argue that something like globalization occurs in waves throughout modern history, often followed by periods of economic closure.[26] The current process seems so stunning only when it is viewed in comparison with the era that spanned the beginning of World War I through the early 1970s, a period of much closure and reinforcement of borders throughout the world. But seen from the perspective of the previous century or so, this period of closure is what is so unusual, and we can easily conclude that globalization has only put the world economy back on the track on which it was already moving. If we are going to develop a good understanding of contemporary global change, then, we are going to have to look closely at what happened to bring about the opening of political and territorial borders in the last three decades, and compare these developments with the kinds of political, economic, and social arrangements that had dominated life for most of this century.

The Origin and Sources of Contemporary Globalization

What, then, were the origins and sources of globalization and the new political environment that has emerged along with it? Why has the post-1945 set of political, economic, and social arrangements in the United States, the product of much struggle and the source of much of the country's success, been placed under so much stress so quickly? Why did the politics of social consensus give way to the politics of globalization? As we have seen, most influential public discussion of globalization—from Ohmae to Friedman to Greider—presents it as a force of its own, able to transform domestic and international institutions in ways consonant with the needs of a new kind of global economy, technology, and society. In this view, states have had little choice in how to respond to this force; for good or ill, the imperatives of contemporary economics and technology have imposed themselves on our society. The only option facing states, including the United States, has been to adapt or to suffer economic backwardness, and politics is relevant only to the extent that it helps determine which choice will be made. From this perspective, globalization is a reality beyond the control of political or economic authority.

There are good reasons to doubt this account. To be sure, revolutions in technology and economic organization have been a central part of the process of globalization and are likely to continue to shape many of the directions it takes in the future, but we have historical and theoretical reasons to believe that these kinds of factors are not adequate in themselves to account for the emergence of contemporary globalization. First, we have now seen that at the beginning of the twentieth century the world was undergoing a very similar process of globalization, and it is not difficult to locate writers from that period claiming that new inventions in technology and economics had made the interdependence of nations permanent and unstoppable.[27] But the subsequent history of the twentieth century showed that political action and conflict could in fact overcome the pressures of economics and technology. The general closure of national borders to the flow of goods, finance, and persons for much of this century indicates that political factors and the choices of governments are crucial to determining the pace, direction, and impact of economic, technological, and cultural change. All of this suggests that we need to look for political factors to explain the recent reemergence of globalization.

This conclusion is reinforced by the work of earlier students of public policy and political economy such as Adam Smith, Max Weber, and Karl Polanyi, who argued that capitalist economies do not spring to life and function on their own.[28] Rather, capitalist and market economic systems require a framework of law and regulation that sustains the basic rules of the game, providing the confidence and security needed for economic agents to invest capital and produce goods over the long term. Moreover, the kind of legal and regulatory framework adopted at any particular time will shape the direction and pace of economic activity and change; market economies will develop along different paths depending on the political framework in which they operate. From this perspective, the shift from a world of welfare state capitalism to a world of globalization could not have been so quick or successful without substantial change in the political and legal frameworks that governed economic life.

This combination of historical and theoretical interpretations suggests that we look for a political explanation of the globalization of American life and politics. In this section, I will present a framework for doing so, and the next three chapters of the book will fill in the details that provide support for a political approach to globalization. The place to begin is the mid-1970s. This was the period in which the post-World War II social compact came under severe strain around the advanced capitalist world and especially in the United States. The sources of the strain are clear in hindsight. Economic "stagflation" destroyed the confidence in the kind of Keynesian economic management that aimed at providing steady growth and low inflation.[29] Stagnation created demands for greater public spending while reducing growth in revenues; the tax increases that helped to pay for this spending, in turn, helped to spark a tax revolt, leaving the state in a situation of permanent budget deficits eventually referred to as a "fiscal crisis." Meanwhile, it was becoming clear that the growth of productivity was slowing steadily and with it the long-term prospects for increased standards of living.

All these challenges posed a severe dilemma for policymakers in the United States. As we have seen, American leadership, or hegemony, since 1945 had been based on the promotion of world order where a gradual expansion of trade and investment across state boundaries was combined with domestic policies that ensured some amount of equitable sharing of the wealth generated by steady economic expansion, a good part of which resulted from the increase in trade. This international commitment was widely supported in the United States, as long as it seemed to redound to the benefit of America as well as its allies. By the mid-1970s, however, it had become increasingly difficult to sustain this formula of governance, as Americans worried about their own economic security and began to question the policy choices necessary to sustain American leadership in a liberal international economy. An ominous sign of the danger of this situation was the growing impact of imports in the American economy along with the renunciation by organized labor of its commitment to free trade. The accompanying demands for protection seemed to many to further reinforce the dysfunctions of a regulatory system that was increasingly burdensome for business, promoted the corruption of the policy process, and hindered productivity growth. With a future that promised lower living standards, more strain on the middle classes, and more conflict over the direction of economic policy, it was no wonder that observers and policymakers began looking for alternative ways to organize the domestic and international economies.

Not only was the consensus of the postwar years faltering at its economic foundations, but the role of government in the society as a whole was coming under direct fire for reasons linked to a wider set of changes in the United States. Beginning in the 1960s, the national government began to systematically promote a more racially and ethnically inclusive vision of American society. From the Civil Rights Act of 1964 through the emergence of affirmative action programs and the expansion of the domestic welfare state, the national government attempted to use law and policy to break down long-established privileges held by white Americans. In the process, the long-held vision of the meaning and image of American citizenship was challenged by policies that insisted—directly or indirectly—that this narrative pay more attention to the role and suffering of nonwhites.[30] This development was paralleled by the changing role of women and with it the changing structure of the family in American life, which challenged long-held norms concerning gender roles. Along with a changing pattern of racial and gender relations, a new wave of immigration began bringing large numbers of foreign-born persons to American shores, the majority of whom originated from Asia and Latin America. Also facilitated by government action, and deeply linked to America's leading role in global politics and economics, this new wave generated further controversy over the meaning and character of the national community in whose name the government acted.

These may seem to be very different kinds of developments, but together they yield a revealing pattern. During the 1970s, the American state seemed to be losing control over the economic structure of society while at the same time moving to transform the society's view of itself. On both levels, it was contributing by its actions and inactions to a collapse of the kind of guarantees of security and identity that had upheld the post-1945 policy consensus. While the economic and fiscal crises promised to undermine the state's ability to provide the growth and opportunity promised in this consensus, the promotion of a cultural transformation of society worked to alienate many who had previously accepted the bargain implicit in the consensus. This alienation, in turn, further weakened the state's ability to effectively resolve the challenges posed by the new economic climate. By the later 1970s, all signs pointed to the need for a new kind of bargain concerning the role of the state in American society, and the role of the United States in the global political economy.

In hindsight, it is surprising that the most widely discussed alternative at the time involved moving American politics and society in a more "corporatist" direction.[31] For many, the only way to provide for effective government under the circumstances of the time was to strike a bargain between organized representatives of the major social groups and the state. In this view, the state would take a much larger role in overseeing the allocation of economic resources and the distribution of income, in return for a reduction in the degree of social and political division in society. This approach was based on the assumption that the country was facing a long period of stagnating or declining wealth, and that this would mean a dangerous level of social conflict if the resolution of disputes over wealth were left to the marketplace. Pointing to the greater stability of the corporatist states of Western Europe, many observers on the right and left concluded that only a new social bargain that strengthened the authority of the state to resolve such disputes could avoid social and political chaos in the United States.[32]

Of course, these assumptions and predictions proved wrong, and the United States has moved in a very different direction over the past twenty years. Rather than producing a larger government with more detailed control over economic change in a more closed society, American politics is now dominated by a free-market vision closely linked to an immersion of domestic society in a more open international order. What the popular discussion of globalization ignores, however, is that the latter political and economic direction was also developed during the late 1970s, and was put into place well before the "takeoff" of the current wave of globalization. In fact, globalization as we know it in the United States is primarily the result of a political economic program and set of policy choices designed to expand the role of market institutions in American life. The greater immersion of American society into the global economy is one part of this larger strategy of reform, a strategy originating in a set of domestic calculations of interest and power and developed in the realms of politics and policy choice. This market-opening approach to the role of the state in American society was the dominant response to the crisis of the social compact in the 1970s, and it is to this political program that globalization owes its origins.

We can see this new political economy emerge gradually in the 1970s. Its rise was based on the growing acceptance among policymakers and politicians that the opening up of market competition provided the best way out of the conundrum of slow growth and distributional conflict. By 1977, Congress and the Carter administration had embarked on a program of deregulating many of the central sectors of the American economy, such as transportation, telecommunications, and banking. As Derthick and Quirk have shown, this new approach to policymaking and the role of the state was imposed upon often unwilling industries by a coalition of policymakers and policy intellectuals convinced that the traditional tools of government regulation were no longer working.[33] In 1979, a similar recognition led the Federal Reserve Board to abandon the policy of managing interest rates, replacing this with a system of floating rates that would shift responsibility for rates onto the financial markets themselves. Meanwhile, the newly elected Thatcher government was attempting a radical overhaul of the British political, economic, and social systems in a more market-oriented direction, symbolized early on by the decision to remove all remaining controls on the movement of capital across its borders. As in the United States, this policy reversal would have to be imposed upon a variety of social groups, including some elements of the business community. Together, U.S. and U.K. governments would be in the vanguard of a new approach to political economic policy, one that would spread around the world in the following decade and would be central to the creation of a more open and competitive global economic system, transforming the role of the state in society throughout the advanced capitalist world.

These policy changes set the basis and framework for the much more sweeping innovations of the 1980s, which continue today. Despite a good deal of renewed protectionism in response to the deep recession of the early 1980s, the decade as a whole was dominated by the steady advance of the free-market approach to politics and economic policy around the world. Everywhere in the industrialized world, governments were attempting to reduce their responsibilities for managing economic and social change, hoping to devolve these tasks onto newly vibrant and competitive market institutions. Though the movement in this direction was more halting in other states, and generated much more resistance, by the 1990s even the most solidly corporatist and social democratic states in

Europe were attempting to find ways to build more flexible and market-oriented practices into their economic and social structures.

In the United States, the Reagan years saw a spread of the deregulation movement into new areas of the economy, as Congress, the courts, and the states seemed all to be working to displace responsibility for social and economic outcomes onto the operation of markets. Central to these years was the attempt to transform the structure of social security and protection that had been the hallmark of the post-1945 social consensus and embodied the responsibilities of the state assumed in that consensus. Though only partially successful at reducing real spending levels, this movement did seem to make substantial progress in changing the understanding of the appropriate relationship of the state, the market, and individuals in contemporary society. In the place of a social compact in which the state played a central role in providing security and opportunity in a cohesive society, these policy choices were based on a compact in which the state focused on providing the conditions for successfully functioning markets while the task of providing security and taking advantage of opportunities was to be left to individuals.

Despite the Bush administration's more "compassionate" conservatism and the Clinton administration's "new liberalism," the overall direction of social and economic policy remained essentially the same through the 1990s. Slowly but surely new areas of the economy have been opened to competition, more and more government services have been privatized, and a good deal of the social welfare infrastructure established during the 1960s has been dismantled. The only major attempt to move in a different policy direction—Clinton's Health Care Reform Plan—failed abysmally and only reinforced the movement away from the post-1945 understanding of responsibilities of government in society.[34] Especially important, the connections between these domestic changes and the reform of the global economy became more apparent during the 1990s. From the United States–Canada and then North American free-trade agreements through the increasing liberalization of immigration policy to the emergence of a World Trade Organization, policymakers worked to complement domestic policy change with the deeper immersion of American society in a more open, market-oriented global economy. Together, these initiatives amounted to a linked program of domestic change and international opening that has transformed the relationship between the United States and its global environment.

In the process, one central characteristic of American policymaking remained unchanged: the United States continued to play the role of hegemonic power in a liberal or open international order. Indeed, the policy choices that generated the wave of globalization over the past three decades emerged primarily as a means of preserving this global order and America's role in that order by transforming the shape of the global economy and the structure of American politics and society together. The tensions and conflicts of the 1970s had seemed to force a choice between the long-standing goal of promoting the economic interdependence of the major economies of the capitalist world and the maintenance of the structure of social guarantees that had long been understood as necessary to secure liberal democracy. American policymakers found a way out of this dilemma, at least in the short run. By promoting market institutions and introducing more market competition domestically and internationally, they found a means to transform the global economy in a way that played to the strengths of the American economy in the areas of innovation, technological invention, and the provision of highly professionalized services. As a result, the United States has experienced two decades of economic growth in the context of a supportive international environment, which has produced unprecedented prosperity for many. This prosperity, in turn, seemed to cushion the impact of the steady reduction in the guarantees of security and opportunity on the part of the state. All told, this combination of policy choices and some good luck (such as the collapse of the Soviet Union) enabled the United States to enter the twenty-first century with the most competitive economy in a global system organized around the virtues of market competition and efficiency. For the moment, globalization seems to be the solution to the problem of American power and legitimacy.

The Significance of Contemporary Globalization

How does this outline help us understand globalization and its impact on American society and politics? First, it shows that globalization as we know it developed in a way that depended upon political choices and action, on the transformation of the priorities and process of public policymaking. To be sure, technological and cultural changes were important elements in this process, but it seems clear that the degree and speed through which they spread around the world depended upon prior fundamental changes in the legal and policy environment. This conclusion implies that many of the policy changes often attributed to the demands or necessities of globalization—changes in regulatory and welfare state policies, for instance—in fact predated any awareness of the impact of globalization as an independent constraint on the actions of governments. Long before foreign trade, capital markets, or immigration began fundamentally changing American life, policymakers were working to transform the role of the state in the United States to promote a more competitive, market-dominated, and globally integrated economy and society. The historical and policy records suggest that globalization is a phenomenon that emerged and operates through political choice; if global change does often constrain the state, it is also impossible without the positive support of public policy.

Second, this account makes it clear that globalization was to a significant extent an intended outcome of many of the reforms begun in the 1970s. To be sure, few policymakers knew precisely what all the effects would be, and we will discuss instances where the forces unleashed by globalization constrain policymakers in unwanted ways. But, as Philip Cerny has emphasized, it is clear in retrospect that a new form of relationship between state and society emerged in the late 1970s, particularly in the United States and the United Kingdom.[35] Cerny calls this relationship the "competition state," because it emphasized the state's role in subjecting all social actors to the pressures of market competition to improve their economic efficiency and flexibility. His argument, which fits the pattern I have laid out, is that the movement toward a competition state was consciously chosen by policymakers and political elites to pull state and society out of the crises and stagnation of the 1970s. While focusing on domestic change, the building of the competition state also required a transformation of the way the global economy was organized and the relationship between individual states and that economy. Policymakers decided on their own to reduce many of the barriers protecting domestic economy and society from larger global influences, viewing this as a crucial part of the promotion of competition domestically. Globalization, then, emerged as one part of a larger program to rearrange the relationship between state and society in the United States.

Finally, globalization has generated a new pattern and structure of politics and political debate in the United States. Gone are the days when debates and conflicts over economic and social policy can assume a closed and bounded society in which the major issues concern only the distribution of power and wealth within that society's borders. With the spread of globalization, these policy debates must return to and involve the question of the relationship between national and international society. The ultimate questions of the distribution of power and definition of public purposes remain central to this debate, but the pursuit of these ends requires consideration of the relationship of the state to the larger global environment. The struggle over the place of any particular group within the state is now intimately tied to the place of the state in the global environment. Nowhere was this better illustrated than in the November 1999 WTO protests in Seattle. Though some groups involved in these events were clearly protectionist in orientation, one labor official denied that this was the case for the majority of the American and foreign unions represented in the protests. In Jay Mazur's words,

> A broad ideological offensive by corporations has portrayed unions as outmoded relics of a bygone age. But as big business has gone global and waged an increasingly aggressive assault on unions, the labor movement has become more, not less, internationalist. Virtually every major industrial dispute in the United States now has an international dimension. . . . As corporate mergers and alliances accelerate the global integration of capital, more unions find themselves in a similar situation.[36]

In our increasingly globalized context, political success within the state requires a clear and persuasive program for dealing with the boundaries and borders of the state in the larger world. Instead of being the accepted framework within which political conflict takes place, the boundaries are now a central element in political conflict.

Globalization and Sovereignty

We can now return to the question with which we started this chapter: Has globalization, as many popular accounts have it, undermined the sovereignty and relevance of the modern state, especially in the United States? As we have seen, most of the popular accounts assume an image of sovereignty based on the role of government and the state constructed after the Second World War—in the United States, one based on the social compact that emerged from the New Deal and the war experience. Globalization has certainly worked to shatter much of this model of the proper role and responsibilities of the state. Rather than protecting a cohesive national community from threats originating beyond its territory, the borders of the state are now much more porous filters through which global economic and cultural influences flow much more easily. Moreover, successive administrations have been hesitant to develop a set of systematic policies to protect Americans from the disruptions that often come with these flows. Instead, the dominant approach in most areas of policymaking is to expose individuals and institutions to the competition and insecurity of such an environment to create a more competitive and flexible domestic society. No longer is the state actively intervening to protect a cohesive domestic economy from outside disruptions, nor is it committed to preserving the once dominant ethnic-cultural character of the society or ensuring the sacrifices and compromises necessary to hold together something approaching a universal welfare state.[37] It is certainly reasonable to argue that globalization has progressed far enough that these kinds of policies are perhaps impossible and certainly would impose major costs on any state that attempted to pursue them. In this sense, globalization has indeed worked to undermine one version of the sovereign state.

This conclusion is not confined to more popular commentaries. The late distinguished scholar of international relations Susan Strange presented a similar thesis in her book *The Retreat of the State*.[38] Strange begins by describing the basic assumption of her book as the proposition that "the territorial boundaries of states no longer coincide with the extent or limits of political authority over economy and society."[39] I have already indicated that this is a fundamental element of the contemporary context of political life. But she goes further to argue that these developments herald a fundamental diffusion of power in world politics away from states:

Where states were once the masters of markets, now it is the markets which, on many crucial issues, are the masters over the governments of states. And the declining authority of states is reflected in a growing diffusion of authority to other institutions and associations, and to local and regional bodies, and in a growing asymmetry between the larger states with structural power and the weaker ones without it.[40]

In Strange's view, the transformation of the structure of power and wealth in the world economy is threatening to make states as we have known them obsolete. She does not argue that this has happened yet, but she emphasizes that the changes of the past two decades have drained power and sovereignty from the modern state and threaten to continue to do so.[41]

It is misleading, however, to suggest that any of this means that the sovereignty and relevance of the state are things of the past. One way of organizing the sovereign state—involving a specific understanding of the priorities and necessary capacities of the state—may be in decline, but the role of the authority of the state in shaping the boundaries and purposes of the political community remains central to contemporary political life, even in a globalized world. Indeed, my initial account of the sources and impact of globalization in the United States makes it clear that understanding the evolution of the sovereign state is essential to understanding globalization. As we have known it, globalization over the past decades has been the *product* of the actions of the state and the use of its sovereign authority, not the cause of its demise. Despite the real pressures of economic change and technological innovation, global change would not have taken the course and pace that it did without the actions of policymakers, actions that both broke down the obstacles to change and created a framework for a new kind of global economy and society. In the United States, this included a steady transformation of the laws and regulations governing the domestic economic climate, as well as the regulations governing the movement of capital and goods across the nation's borders. Furthermore, the spread of similar policy changes depended upon the active engagement of the power and authority of the United States, which used a combination of constraints, incentives, and force to ensure the foundation for the deepening of globalization over the 1980s and 1990s. Globalization has resulted from the construction of a new kind of liberal capitalist democratic state, and its future is likely to depend on the success or failure of the political project behind this new kind of state.

In the process, globalization has contributed to the transformation of the structure and practice of political life in the United States. Instead of the dominance of purely domestic political actors, interests, and issues, American politics today involves actors and issues that are global as well as local. Whether the question involves the direction of macroeconomic policy, trade agreements, the regulation of corporate activity, the level and nature of immigration, or the cultural values promoted by policy choices, global interests, perspectives, and organizations are now central to political conflict. Indeed, in many cases it is difficult to draw a line between global and domestic actors. The corporations, organized interests, ethnic groups, and even labor unions central to national and local politics are now themselves active on a global level, as they recognize that the state's power itself acts in ways that blur the role of its territorial boundaries. Political conflict itself has been globalized, but the struggle for the control of the state's power and authority remains central to political life.

It will be the burden of the rest of the book to support this argument in more detail and depth. This will also lead us to consider the following problem: If sovereignty remains central to contemporary politics and policymaking, why has there been so much clamor about the end of the state and the irrelevance of sovereignty? The key to answering this question lies in the disparate impact of globalization on different sectors of American society. Many crucial actors and groups in the United States are well positioned to benefit from globalization and have been at the forefront of political support for the policy choices that have been responsible for the emergence of the competition state and its emphasis on immersing American society in a global market economy. But for those groups less able to compete in the global environment, the competition state means insecurity at the least and stagnant or declining opportunities at the worst. In many cases, these are the same groups that benefited from a welfare state and Keynesian political economy in which the priority was to protect vulnerable groups from global changes. More generally, a large segment of the American public still accepts the understanding of the responsibilities and priorities of government that emerged from this period.[42] Faced with the impact of global change and shaped by such expectations, many citizens view globalization as a failure on the part of the state to act as it should, and it is easily blamed for the resulting problems faced by many Americans. The clamor for sovereignty, then, is a call for the reassertion of the social compact that has been uprooted by the new form of state.[43] Is this call the potential basis of an effective challenge to globalization? This is the question to which we will return in the conclusion.

Globalization and Policymaking: A Preface and a Transition

Part three of the book, chapters 4 through 6, will examine in more detail the ways in which globalization has changed the politics of American public policymaking and moved the question of sovereignty to the center of American politics. The analysis of each area of public policy—trade, immigration, and language policy—will emphasize the ways in which policy choices since the late 1960s and early 1970s have worked to immerse aspects of American life in a global context, and how this has resulted in the collapse of the assumptions and practice of state-society relationships put in place during the 1940s. I also trace the development of political conflict in each area of policymaking, focusing on the ways in which this conflict is fueled by competing conceptions of the role and responsibility of the state and its relationship to the new global context of political choice. By examining these policy areas in some detail, we will get a sense of the deeply political origins, nature, and impact of the trends and processes known as globalization.

Before turning to these chapters, it is worthwhile to offer a couple of notes concerning the method and approach I use in presenting the story of globalization in each policy area. First, it remains the predominant approach in policy analysis to explain policy choices and outcomes in terms of the power and play of social groups that attempt to influence government and the political world more generally. Policymakers are forced to respond to the weight of the interests involved, and policy is understood as the result of the balance of power among these interests. In this book I use a different approach, one that treats policy as the result of choices made by political leaders who have a significant degree of autonomy from the play of interests and who can and do act to initiate policy directions unwanted by many of the important interests involved. At the same time, I try to avoid the "statist" extreme of locating all power and initiative with policymakers.[44] The emphasis of my approach is on the interaction of policymakers, policy choices, social groups, and policy outcomes. To highlight the key role of political choice and power in shaping what we now call globalization, however, I do tend to emphasize the relatively independent role of the policy choices made by political elites and government officials. It seems to me a necessary counterweight to the prevalent image of a world where global change and its impact are beyond political control.

Second, my approach to public policy attempts to integrate the "material" and "symbolic" dimensions of policy and political life. Too often, analysts seem satisfied to break these dimensions apart and treat them separately, and among political scientists this usually means the slighting of the importance of the symbolic dimension. In real politics, however, political and policy choices both allocate resources and embody conceptions of the purposes and priorities of the political community, and any satisfactory account of the origins or impact of these decisions must be sensitive to both dimensions of the politics of policymaking.[45] Even some of the most obviously material policy choices—those concerning trade and tariff policy, for instance—are a medium for carrying messages concerning the worth and status of different segments of the polity and thus of the role of the state in society. In the following chapters, I will try to make it clear by example why we need to be aware of the connections between these dimensions of policy choice in order to figure out the impact of globalization on American political life. As the analysis moves from trade policy through immigration and language policy, I hope that the reader will more clearly see that we have entered a period in which even the most basic questions of the allocation of resources through policymaking embody conflict over the purposes of the state, its role in society, and its relationship to a new global context. I have chosen this combination of policy areas to show that globalization requires us to look again at the largest purposes and identity of the American political community.[46]

PART III ☙

Globalization and the Politics of American Public Policy

4 ∾

The Politics of Trade and the Clamor for Sovereignty

The emergence of globalization as a central theme in American politics is intimately tied to the controversies over trade policy. More than any other issue or event, the political debate and mobilization surrounding the ratification of the North American Free Trade Agreement (NAFTA) in 1992–93 marked the maturation of the politics of globalization in the United States. Crafted as an extension of the earlier and less controversial U.S.–Canada Free Trade Agreement, NAFTA was negotiated and signed by the Bush administration with the support of a wide-ranging coalition of major forces in American business and industry. Representing firms and organizations from all regions and sectors of the economy, including many previous bastions of protectionist sentiment, this coalition included the leadership of both major political parties and most influential newspapers and commentators, and even found unusual allies in the environmental and human rights interest group networks. For most observers, and especially for its supporters, quick passage of the treaty seemed an inevitable consequence of such an impressive supporting coalition.

As it turned out, however, the NAFTA ratification process generated the most divisive conflict over trade policy since the 1940s. The treaty was passed only after a tremendous lobbying campaign by its supporters, and it cost the Clinton administration much of its initial political capital. In the time between its negotiation and ratification, NAFTA proved the focal point for the emergence of a powerful opposition movement, which used it to offer a powerful critique of the impact of globalization on American life. The opposition movement spawned the presidential candidacies of Ross Perot and Pat Buchanan, created a mass coalition uniting these figures with Jesse Jackson, Ralph Nader, organized labor, and more critical environmental groups, and deeply divided the congressional Democratic party. Despite their ultimate loss in this conflict, the coalition thus formed and the critique it offered survived to mount a challenge to the Uruguay Round of the

General Agreement on Tariffs and Trade (GATT) treaty that established the World Trade Organization (WTO), and by the late 1990s the coalition had succeeded in preventing the renewal of the president's fast-track authority to negotiate further free-trade agreements.

The controversy over NAFTA put the questions of globalization and sovereignty firmly on the agenda of American politics and policymaking and marked a major transformation of the politics of trade policy. Instead of a relatively obscure and technical arena dominated by experts and business lobbying, the negotiation of trade agreements became a very public process dominated by deeply passionate divisions over the basic values guiding American policy and the nation's place in the world. In the weeks before the WTO meetings in Seattle in November 1999, *The Economist* summarized the current situation in the following manner:

> The result is sobering. With both parties split and Congress divided on partisan lines, the old certainties of American trade policy have gone. The strength of the economy, while it lasts, militates against outright protectionism, of course. But when a new trade round is just starting, America's lack of commitment to greater liberalisation may be almost as bad.[1]

As we now know, the success of protesters in disrupting these meetings, and the divisions among the major states involved in the planning of a new trade round, would make even clearer the depth of the change in the politics of American trade policy over the past decade.[2]

My aim in this chapter is to explain and evaluate the emerging politics of trade policy. I begin by reviewing standard accounts of the politics of U.S. trade policy and show why they fail to provide a full understanding of the role of globalization in shaping current policy conflicts. My account then turns to the history of U.S. trade policy and politics since the 1970s, and I link this history to the larger directions of change in American economic policy over the same era. I then analyze the patterns of political argument and conflict that emerged during the struggle over NAFTA and continue to define American trade policy and politics. The central thread through this analysis is the issue of sovereignty. I argue that the politics of trade have been reshaped by the processes of globalization and the reaction of policymakers and citizens to its impact on American society. The clamor for sovereignty, I conclude, reflects a deepening division over the relationship of state and society in an increasingly globalized world.

Explaining Trade Policy

Controversies over trade policy have played an important role in shaping the relationship of government and the economy in the United States, and the analysis of trade policy and politics has been central to the development of the study of American public policy. During the decades of rapid industrialization that followed the Civil War, the United States erected high tariffs to protect its emerging manufacturing economy from foreign competition. Protection became a tradition that prevailed even during times of relatively open world trade and economic growth, such as the 1920s. When prosperity was followed by economic collapse, Congress reacted by intensifying protective tariffs to secure domestic well-being, passing the Smoot-Hawley tariff hikes in 1933. It was only with the end of the Second World War and the emergence of the United States as the dominant economic power in the world that American policy shifted decisively in the direction of promoting freer trade and that "protectionism" became a term of political opprobrium.

In addition to being a defining moment in American trade policy, Smoot-Hawley also provided the occasion for the seminal study of trade policy in American political science, E. E. Schattschneider's *Politics, Pressure, and the Tariff.*[3] The story told by Schattschneider focused on a society of well-organized protectionist interests with easy access to Congress and a dominant influence on the legislative process. It also highlighted the emerging reaction against this situation in Congress, and the beginning of an attempt to shift power and responsibility over tariffs to the president in an attempt to provide more cohesion to American trade policy. Schattschneider's work also established the key tools with which subsequent political scientists could go about analyzing trade policy. In this account, trade policy is essentially interest politics, mediated by institutional processes and to some extent by perceptions of the national interest. Understanding the formulation of trade policy entailed analyzing the evolving balance between socioeconomic interests, exploring the processes of coalition formation and political leadership around key policy choices, and evaluating the ways in which the operation of Congress, the presidency, and the bureaucracy constrained political mobilization and policy choice.

The specific outline of U.S. trade policy after 1945 took some time to emerge.[4] Under the leadership of Secretary of State Cordell Hull, the Roosevelt administration had begun to try to build a new, protrade orientation into American foreign economic policy in the mid-1930s. During the Second World War, supporters of a more open, "liberal" world trading system used the government's postwar planning process to develop proposals to avoid the competitive protectionism that, they argued, had caused the depression of the 1930s to spread into fascism, communism, and then world war. In the immediate aftermath of the war, American policymakers were successful in securing widespread agreement for the creation of an International Trade Organization (ITO) to parallel the newly created International Monetary Fund (IMF). But the ITO treaty, which would have established a multilateral body that created and enforced a set of rules designed to reduce tariff barriers between states, was defeated in the United States Senate, and supporters of free trade looked for alternative means to promote the same ends.[5]

By the mid-1950s, U.S. and European policymakers had agreed on the approach of using periodic negotiations over the new GATT to gradually reduce tariffs on the movement of goods across borders. The GATT approach, which was based on the principle of each country's extending its "most-favored nation" (MFN) treatment to all other participants, proved a great success, as it allowed gradual tariff reductions in some areas of trade while exempting especially sensitive areas, such as agriculture and textiles.[6] It thus fit well with the larger American goal of promoting a gradual opening of the global economic system to more interdependence, while protecting the ability of states to pursue ambitious programs of economic management and social provisions, the combination John Ruggie terms "embedded liberalism."[7] The United States took the lead in this process, moving the farthest and fastest in reducing its tariffs on manufacturing imports, thus acting as a market for the reemerging industrial economies of Western Europe and Japan. Meanwhile, U.S. policy tolerated much higher levels of tariffs and protection in the latter countries as necessary temporary measures to support economic recovery. In these policy choices, we can see how the United States used its role as hegemonic power in the post-1945 era to begin the process of creating a more interdependent global system, in which the flow of goods and capital across borders was reestablished after a period of severe closure.

Perhaps the most important element of this new direction in U.S. policy was the successful transformation of the domestic politics of trade policymaking. This accomplishment was detailed and analyzed in the next major work in the study of American trade policy, Raymond A. Bauer, Ithiel de Sola Pool, and Louis A. Dexter's *American Business and Public Policy*.[8] Following Schattschneider's model, this work focused on the changing alignments among business and between business and labor that provided a base of support for free trade. But Bauer, Pool, and Dexter also took a significant new direction in emphasizing the central role of the executive branch and the president in helping to create and guide this coalition to sustain the new U.S. commitment to a more open international economy. In their account, the success of the post-1945 reversal of trade policy was based on the emergence and activism of three major political elements—a cohesive internationally oriented set of policymakers, a growing sector of large American corporations who saw their long-term interests tied to a growing and open international trading system, and the decision of the American union movement to put aside its long-standing protectionist orientation and join in support of liberal trading policies. With effective presidential leadership, this coalition was able to provide the political weight necessary to pursue this radical departure from the long-standing American emphasis on high tariffs as a tool for economic development.

This work was one of only a few studies of trade policy until the 1970s. With the emergence of strains in the post-1945 trade regime and the growth of strong protectionist forces in the 1970s, however, political scientists began to reassess the patterns of political conflict over trade policy. The resulting literature has been voluminous and is impossible to survey completely. One body of scholarship on trade policy and politics, central to the development of "international political economy," contributed a new emphasis to a previously neglected factor in the explanation of trade policy, the *international context* in which that policy is formulated and pursued. Whereas earlier scholars had emphasized the role of domestic factors in explaining trade policy, more recent work stressed the global political and economic context as the key explanation for explaining developments in trade policy and politics.

The earliest and most influential approach in this area is the theory of "hegemonic stability," which explained the United States' turn toward free trade in the 1940s as an attempt to take on the responsibilities of hegemonic power to promote the larger interests of the capitalist system.[9] From this perspective, the growth of protectionist pressures in the 1970s followed from the decline of American hegemony and the resulting greater costs that free trade posed to American society. At the same time, other scholars developed the notion that it was the institutions and rules set up to govern the post-1945 global economy—the "regime"—that was crucial to understanding the evolution of trade policy and politics.[10] The elements of this regime—the IMF, the GATT treaties and negotiations, the World Bank, the EU, etc.—developed a life and legitimacy of their own, which could both constrain and empower states as they developed their trade policies. For scholars of the regime school, international institutions and rules could provide a bulwark and mechanism through which policymakers could resist protectionist pressures at home and work out adjustments that smoothed the costs and impact of free trade on key domestic constituencies. Though this approach was more optimistic in its predictions concerning the future of the liberal trade regime, it shared with the hegemonic-stability approach an emphasis on the role of the international context in shaping American trade policy and politics.

In response to the perceived overemphasis on the power of international forces that many scholars found in these accounts, a second school of analysis emerged, which tried to examine the ways in which trade policy is shaped by the *interaction* between international forces and the structure of the economic, social, and political systems in particular states. Using what is referred to as the "second image reversed" approach, these scholars began to investigate the various factors that shaped the political reactions to international economic change in different times and places. An especially dominant example of this approach, represented by the work of writers such as Peter Gourevitch and Ronald Rogowski, argued that international economic changes shift around the political alliances of key elements of the business community and labor organizations in a country.[11] The ultimate policy choices made by the state depend upon the process of coalition formation that results as groups respond to economic changes. Applied to the tensions in American trade policy in the 1970s and 1980s, these approaches mark an attempt to combine the more traditional policymaking emphasis on political interests, coalitions, and institutions with the insights of international political economy. In the American case, both suggest that the power of a dominant free trade oriented coalition based in the business community was likely to preserve the general direction of U.S. policy from any significant challenge.

The third major innovation emerging from recent work in trade policy is the introduction of *ideology* as a factor central to the explanation of U.S. policy choices. The most important contribution in this area has been made by Judith Goldstein, who argues that the analysis of interests, power structures, and institutions is not enough to explain the patterns of change and continuity in American trade policy and politics.[12] The turn toward global free trade in the 1940s, she contends, can be fully grasped only in light of the consolidation of an ideological commitment to the benefits of a liberal trading order, as well as an intellectual critique of the dangers of protectionism. More directly relevant to our concerns, this approach holds that the study of ideology is crucial to understanding the persistence of the elite commitment to open markets since the 1970s in the face of a powerful resurgence of protectionism. The continuing power of free-trade politics in the United States, in Goldstein's argument, stems from the consolidation of a widespread aversion to the protectionist policies that had been central to American political economy before the 1940s.

Meanwhile, the revival of conflict over trade policy led to a renewed attention to the politics of trade by scholars working from the more traditional approaches of Schattschneider and Bauer, Pool, and Dexter. The most outstanding work in this category is I. M. Destler's *American Trade Politics*,[13] which first appeared in 1986. Destler's account of trade policy and politics also focused on the evolution of the political coalitions active in shaping trade policy and highlighted the fragmentation of the post-1945 protrade coalition under the pressures of economic change in the 1970s. But Destler placed special emphasis on the political institutions and processes in which trade policy was determined. In his view, it was the increased deference of Congress to the executive branch in trade policymaking, the isolation of this branch from organized group pressures, and the relative cohesiveness of the main executive actors that were crucial to the success of the pro-free-trade policy emphasis during the 1950s and 1960s. These patterns, however, came under severe strain in the 1970s as a result of broader changes in the American political system, strains responsible for the growing controversy over trade policymaking in the 1980s. As a result, Destler was less optimistic than scholars using other approaches about the future of free trade as the dominant policy direction in the United States.

For the most part, though, the analysis of trade policy and politics in political science relies on a widely shared set of concepts and expectations. In the view of most scholars, the politics of trade policy is dominated by interests, outlooks, and strategies directly related to the impact of trade patterns on American society and to the evolution of the trading system as a whole. Domestic and international groups mobilize to support or oppose policy choices according to the likely impact of these choices on their interests, politicians make calculations of the immediate and long-term costs and benefits of different policy positions, and institutions intervene to shape and constrain the options open to policymakers and political actors. To some degree, the discussion of ideology modifies this picture of the process, since ideological commitments work to limit or redirect the perceptions that political actors have of their interests and priorities. In the form of the influence of experts in international economics, especially, it can be a powerful constraint on the choices considered reasonable by policymakers. In the end, however, most accounts of the politics of trade policy place such factors in a subordinate place, finding them rarely able to overcome the pull of political interests, political power, and the structure of institutions in shaping policy choice.

It is striking that the picture of the contemporary politics of trade policy in the United States presented in most of this work suggests that the NAFTA ratification battle should have been an easy victory for the Bush/Clinton administrations and their supporters. The coalition supporting NAFTA clearly commanded an overwhelming advantage in resources over its opponents, and its domestic power was reinforced by an international system of institutions and interests generally supportive of this kind of agreement. Moreover, the structure of political institutions in the United States—the combination of fast-track negotiating authority and the role of the Office of the U.S. Trade Representative—put the opponents of such a treaty on the political defensive. Finally, decades of criticism of protectionism, combined with the resurgent influence of free-market economic theory in the 1980s and 1990s, meant that the whole network of "established" opinion and expertise supported the treaty. In fact, however, this model of trade politics failed to predict the overwhelming power of the political opposition and the resurgence of a concern over the sovereignty of the United States. In the summer of 1993 the opponents of NAFTA had the upper hand, and only a massive lobbying campaign by its supporters saved the treaty. What had been generally dismissed as a minority and reactionary perspective almost defeated one of the most powerful protrade coalitions in American political history. What had happened that generated such a massive and powerful opposition to a trade agreement? Why did the dominant wisdom in the study of trade politics fail to provide any inkling of the controversy that would emerge over NAFTA?

The Politics of U.S. Trade Policy since the 1970s

To find the answer to these questions, we must explore the ways in which the post-1945 formula for trade politics collapsed and a new formula was constructed during the 1970s. As the previous discussions have shown, beginning in the late

1940s, U.S. policy emphasized the use of GATT and other multilateral negotiations to slowly but steadily promote the reduction of tariffs on trade in manufacturing goods around the world. This approach was widely supported among political and economic elites within the United States, but its success was also based on the ability to deflect potential opposition, which was accomplished in three crucial ways. First, key sectors likely to be threatened by free trade—such as agriculture and textiles—were excluded from the GATT process. Second, traditionally protectionist organized labor was cajoled and bribed to support free trade, largely by the promise that they would share its benefits combined with the reality that imports posed little real threat to U.S. manufacturing industries in the two decades after the Second World War. Third, the long-established power of protectionist pressures in Congress was deflected by the delegation by Congress to the president of almost all the initiative in setting the direction of American trade policy and negotiating tariff reduction treaties. Together, this combination of strategies and interests worked well to allow the smooth reduction of American tariffs to unprecedentedly low levels.

This policy direction, however, depended upon the United States' continued will and ability to live with a steadily increased immersion in the global economy. For the first twenty-five years, the sheer power and dominance of the American economy made this relatively easy. Although the U.S. market was more open than those of its trading partners, the impact of trade on domestic industry and workers remained minimal until the late 1960s. Moreover, during this period American multinational companies dominated the world economy, and the United States remained the leading exporter of goods and services. As a result, the costs of participating more deeply in the global economy were small for the major constituencies in American politics, and the benefits for American leadership in the world remained great. Active support of a more open international economy posed little threat to the social compact upon which post-1945 American politics was built and indeed helped to generate the wealth and stability on which that compact was based.

This formula began to falter in the 1970s. As pressures for increased protection for key industries such as textiles, steel, and shipping grew, President Nixon's 1971 imposition of tariffs on certain Japanese imports marked a fundamentally new situation in trade politics and policy. These actions ushered in a decade of deepening conflict over trade policy, one in which the steady growth of U.S. trade with the larger world met new obstacles, and during which many observers predicted the end of the GATT system and the emergence of a "new protectionism." Indeed, by the end of the 1970s the clamor for protection had come to include such industries as automobiles, electronics, and semiconductors, and trade disputes around the world were growing. Moreover, organized labor had renounced its commitment to a liberal trading system, and Congress was pushing the president to be more aggressive in promoting U.S. trading interests. What explains this reemergence of antiliberal trade pressures, and why did the U.S. commitment to free trade eventually deepen, rather than collapse, in the 1980s and 1990s?

The first part of this question is easier to address and has been the subject of a large body of work by political scientists in recent years. Essentially, it was the revival of the European and Japanese economies and the decline of U.S. dominance in manufacturing that was responsible for the pressure put on the free-trade consensus. With new advantages in cost and technology, manufacturing imports began placing real pressure on American industries, threatening jobs and livelihoods in areas of the economy that were strongholds of organized labor. Americans had paid little in direct costs for keeping markets open in the previous decade, and many began to reconsider the virtues of trade when it meant real competition for domestic industries. Moreover, the global recession and the collapse of the Bretton Woods system of economic management at the international level meant there was no guarantee that the costs of trade would be compensated by overall economic growth. Whether one employs a traditional interest-based approach or complements it with the hegemonic-stability framework, the emergence of protectionist pressures under such conditions is no mystery.

But these pressure were also facilitated by changes in the institutional balance of power at the national level. As I. M. Destler has pointed out, the congressional reforms of the 1973–74 era—the reduction in the power of party leaders, the proliferation of committees, the increased openness of the legislative process, and a general increase in legislative policymaking initiative—served to open up the previously well-guarded process of trade policymaking. With new access points and more activist legislators, protectionist industries and unions could find new paths to influence in a system that had previously been executive-dominated. Most important, Congress in 1974 created the Office of the Trade Representative (OTR) in the executive branch. Though it was often seen as a force for open markets or for deflecting protectionist pressure, Destler and others have shown that the office was initially created to counter the previous dominance of the State and Treasury Departments in trade policymaking. By institutionalizing a congressional voice in trade policy and creating a consultative network of organized interests, the OTR worked to provide protectionist interests easier access to the executive branch policymaking process. Though the OTR would not prove to be a tool of these interests, and indeed has often functioned to deflect them while protecting liberal trading institutions, the immediate effect was to help destabilize the institutional framework that had helped to preserve the liberal trading orientation of American trade policymaking.

Indeed, by the mid-1970s there were many influential voices suggesting that the global capitalist economy, and with it the American economy, could no longer prosper under existing rules and institutions. In this view, the post-1945 approach to governing the domestic and international market systems was one that emphasized management of the economy at the margins; reliance was placed on the basic

efficiencies of the market system while government intervened to tame its instabilities and extremes. But, such critics argued, the market system had shown itself
much more flawed than had been previously assumed. Whether the issue was
equality, environmental protection, the supply of resources, or the control of
macro-economic fluctuations, new conditions required a more organized society
if we were to achieve our basic goals of economic and social security and prosperity. In the area of trade, this meant that the global economic order would need to
be more closely managed by states, with governmentally negotiated agreements
superseding the exchanges that had previously been left to market adjustments.
Only in this way could the growing disruptions caused by competition in key
industries be moderated, and the social and political stability of society be preserved from the ravages of increasingly chaotic market arrangements.

The most impressive fact about these arguments is how little they corre-
spond to the actual direction of U.S. trade policy from the late 1970s to the present
time. To be sure, the United States did develop and use new strategies to protect
key industries from competition in the 1980s, and protectionist forces retained a
presence in Congress during that decade. A variety of "voluntary restraint agreements" (VRAs) were negotiated during this period, especially with Japan, to
protect American products ranging from semiconductors to automobiles to mo-
torcycles. In addition, American industries and unions—most notably in the steel
industry—became much more adept and successful at using the "antidumping"
provisions of American law to protect themselves from lower-priced foreign imports. Nonetheless, as scholars as diverse as I. M. Destler, Graham Wilson, and
Judith Goldstein have argued, the most impressive aspect of U.S. policy during the
past twenty years has been the reassertion of a commitment to a global free trading
system, and in fact the creation of a system much more open and integrated than
the one that prevailed from the 1950s through the 1970s.[14] American policy has
been at the forefront of efforts to further reduce tariffs, minimize "nontariff
barriers," and liberalize trade in many hitherto protected areas. As figure 4-1
indicates, this policy has been extremely successful, as the expansion of world trade
since the late 1970s has outpaced, and has indeed been a major source of, the
growth of economic output around the world. We have already discussed the
persistent protest against the effects of this growth of trade in the United States,
but this movement has had little success in reversing the increasing importance of
trade in the American economy. Why was the system of trade politics and policymaking able to generally withstand the pressures of increased protectionism?

U.S. Trade Policy in the 1980s and 1990s

The key to understanding the impact of globalization and the controversy over
sovereignty in current U.S. politics lies in the forces and choices that sustained this

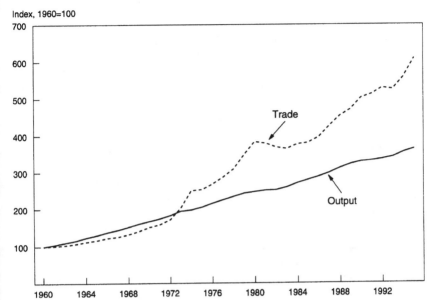

Index, 1960=100

Figure 4-1. Growth of World Trade and Economic Output, 1960–95. *Source: 1997 Economic Report of the President,* February, 1997, Washington, D.C.: U.S. Government Printing Office, p. 248.

project of a revived free-trade and free-market society. As we saw in chapter 3, the shift of U.S. economic policy toward a more militantly market-opening stance began in the late 1970s and was the product of a confluence of trends in the distribution of political power, newly emerging ideas about economic policy, and shifting perceptions of economic interest. In the area of trade policy, the successful conclusion of the Tokyo Round of GATT negotiations in 1979 marked another major element of this new direction in American policy. For the first time, American policymakers had secured an agreement to begin to address the variety of nontariff barriers to trade (NTBs), ranging from social policy regulations and protections to domestic structures of production and retail organization, that were now the major obstacles to increases in the integration of the major capitalist economies around the world. In this agreement, American policymakers were able to push the project of the market-based reconstruction of political economic institutions to the global agenda. The Tokyo Round agreements marked a key step in creating the kind of global context necessary for the building of the "competition state."

At the same time, it became clear to many observers that most of the congressionally initiated changes in the structure of trade policymaking put in place in the mid-1970s were much less threatening to the free-trade direction of American policy than had earlier been believed. Destler's careful work made it clear that the new Office of the Trade Representative in the White House could and did function as a crucial means of deflecting protectionist pressures. By focusing on market-opening initiatives in other countries, successive trade representatives effectively constrained proposals for out-and-out protection, while using the threat of such proposals to great success in negotiations with other governments. Moreover, Congress had come up with a new means of protecting executive dominance of trade policy. This was the creation in 1974 of fast-track authority for the negotiation and ratification of trade agreements. Under this procedure, presidents could apply for the authority to negotiate specific agreements with the promise that, once they were submitted to Congress for approval, there would be no opportunity for representatives to attach any amendments to these treaties. Such an arrangement would provide presidents with greater ability to secure agreements with other states while preventing protectionist forces from modifying them in ways that would undermine their overall aims. Fast-track authority would become a crucial means of extending the free-trade, promarket agenda over the 1980s and 1990s.

Meanwhile, in the controversy over these agreements and in the larger arena of conflict over the new demands for protection, trade politics had begun to take on a general pattern, which it continues to follow, of a give-and-take between those advocating more and those calling for less protection of American firms, jobs, industries, and markets. On the one side is the coalition based in organized labor and older sectors of manufacturing industry. A persistent presence in trade politics, this coalition now has increased support in the Democratic Party, greater access to Congress, and significant local or regional influence where declining sectors of manufacturing are concentrated. This coalition has consistently demanded greater government protection for threatened industries as well as more aggressive moves against states perceived to be violating the rules of fair trade. Given the organization, resources, and public sympathy these forces have been able to command, trade policy has had to respond to their concerns.

On the other side is a growing if more diffuse movement to liberalize trade rules and practices at home and around the globe. Based in the same business and policy groups supporting the larger promarket agenda, this coalition also includes most of the leaders of both the Republican and Democratic parties, much of the mainstream media, and important elements in the environmental and humanitarian interest group circles. Most important, as Helen Milner has pointed out, the growing global immersion and technological innovation of the American economy has worked to strengthen this coalition.[15] As American firms have become more dependent on foreign markets and foreign suppliers—and this is especially true in the more "high-tech" areas of the economy—they have become more active and vocal in opposing any policy choices that might harm the larger global trading system. To their voices have been added those of the increasing number of foreign-based firms who now constitute a significant element in the American economy. Though this coalition has dominated the overall direction of trade policy, it has never been able to fully control the field and has been forced to make some compromises with the more protectionist elements in the polity. The dynamic between these coalitions has been central to the politics of globalization over the past two decades.

In the first years of the Reagan administration, a generally assertive defense and promotion of the interests of American industry seemed to partially satisfy most players in trade policy.[16] During this period, the U.S. government aggressively criticized the trading practices of Europe and Japan, demanding that markets in both areas be made more open to American exports. While this program addressed tariff barriers, it was especially focused on the various kinds of government procurement programs and institutional practices in the economies of these states that worked to favor domestic suppliers over foreign producers. At the same time, as we have seen, the United States negotiated a number of voluntary restraint agreements, especially with Japan, to protect domestic producers under severe pressure from imports. The most well-known involved the auto industry and set specific limits on the number of Japanese-produced cars that could be sold in the United States in any given year. Most observers agree that this combination of policies was designed to avoid any major legislative action on trade while signaling the longer-term U.S. goal of reforming the global trading system. Given the deep worldwide recession of the early 1980s, it seemed a wise and effective approach.

By the second Reagan administration, the recession had lifted in the United States and trade policy became a less volatile issue. This opened up room for the United States to worry less about deflecting domestic protectionist forces and to focus on the longer-term goal of opening up the global trading system. These efforts came to fruition in 1985 with the initiation of a new Uruguay Round of GATT negotiations. Besides attempting to further reduce tariff rates and engage controversies in North-South trade, the Uruguay round aimed to reduce nontariff barriers to trade and—for the first time—to find ways to extend GATT rules to areas such as trade in services and intellectual property. In 1987, the United States and Canada negotiated a free-trade agreement involving bilateral reforms that anticipated the kinds of rules American policymakers aimed to achieve in the GATT arena. To be sure, protectionist pressures remained present, along with attempts to deflect them through market-opening initiatives. Congressional frustrations with these efforts led to the 1988 Omnibus Trade and Competitiveness Act, the first congressionally originated trade bill since 1945. But even here supporters of liberal trade were able to shift the focus away from protection to reducing foreign barriers to U.S. exports, and the Reagan and Bush administrations used these provisions as a negotiating tool, warning other countries of the danger of domestic protectionist forces if they did not reform their own economies.

At this point, a clear pattern was emerging. The overall initiative in U.S. trade policy was with the liberal/market-opening coalition, firmly supported by the executive branch. To more deeply involve the U.S. economy in the global arena and promote American wealth and power, policymakers focused their energy on opening markets abroad and resisting domestic pressures to reduce the penetration of imports at home. The latter pressures were accommodated nonlegislatively where possible and were redirected toward opening foreign markets. In the process, as scholars have pointed out, the United States began developing international agreements and institutions that could be used in the longer run to deflect pressures for trade restriction. Created first in the U.S.–Canada Agreement and then put on the agenda for the North American and GATT negotiations, these multilateral bodies would be given final authority over decisions involving trade disputes previously in the hands of the executive or legislative branches. By institutionalizing the market-opening agenda in supranational bodies, it was hoped, U.S. policy could prevent domestic protectionist forces from undermining America's own immersion in a competitive global economy.

What is most striking for our investigation is how little U.S. trade policy in the 1980s corresponds to the notion of the loss of sovereignty in the face of overwhelming global forces. Indeed, it is more accurate to describe policy during this period as an attempt to mobilize the power of the American state—domestically and internationally—to promote exactly the kinds of economic transformations lamented by critics of globalization. Domestically, a coalition of political elites supported by key segments of the business and policy communities worked systematically to dismantle many of the institutions and practices that insulated the U.S. economy from global pressures. Internationally, U.S. policy during the 1980s seemed determined to apply the same formula to trade policies around the globe, with the aim of reducing barriers to the spread of a globally integrated system of production and trade. To be sure, much of the impetus for this program was the promotion of the power and wealth of American economic interests, but this required a mobilization of the sovereignty of the state to break down restrictive arrangements and create new legal and political structures in which a globally integrated economy could flourish.

The most innovative element of this project was the attempt to shift responsibility for the resolution of many trade disputes to newly active multilateral agencies as a way of securing and protecting the framework of the global market economy. From the various boards established to resolve trade disputes under the U.S.–Canada and NAFTA treaties to the successful creation of a World Trade Organization that would more deeply institutionalize dispute resolution under the GATT rules, American policymakers were effective in promoting the use of these agencies as key elements of a more market-oriented and competitive global economic environment. For some commentators, this marks a significant step toward the "unbundling" of the sovereign power of the state, as parts of it are given up by states who now commit themselves to recognizing the authority of and adhering to the decisions made by multilateral bodies beyond their direct control.[17] There is no doubt that multilateral institutions are exercising more authority in trade policymaking, and this is an important example of the ways in which political authority and territorial boundaries are becoming less directly tied in an age of globalization. But it is also the case that these kind of arrangements are entered into to promote the domestic and international aims of states. As both the growing literature on "two-level" bargaining games and empirical studies of U.S. policymaking show, the delegation of trade policy authority to multilateral agencies is a powerful tool for reducing the ability of protectionist forces to secure their ends by influencing domestic political institutions. By pointing to their obligations under international treaties, policymakers can and do use the existence of these agencies to promote their shared aims of deepening the emerging globalization of the world economy.[18]

Of course, this kind of policy project did not develop as smoothly as my account seems to suggest, and it remains incomplete, but the project has had major successes and has transformed the position of American society in the global setting—and that global setting itself—in fundamental ways. The major problem facing this trade policy direction, however, was a quiet but growing opposition around the country. While the overall growth of trade pulled along a sustained economic recovery, many Americans saw the collapse of jobs and industries that could not compete in a more globalized world and faced little prospect of a smooth transition to more promising alternatives. In addition, the persistence of expectations about the responsibilities of the state to its citizens' economic security made it difficult for many citizens to accept this new direction as anything other than an abdication of government's proper powers. In the early 1990s, two developments would bring this opposition out in the open with surprising vigor. First, the U.S. completed a major agreement extending free-trade principles into the creation of a hemispheric free-trade zone including the clearly less developed Mexican economy. Second, the global economy entered a period of recession, dampening the optimism of the 1980s. When the NAFTA treaty was brought to Congress in the midst of this recession, "all hell broke loose" in the politics of trade policy.

NAFTA and the Contemporary Politics of Globalization

The impetus for NAFTA came from the Mexican government itself in 1990.[19] The Bush administration quickly agreed to the proposal although the Canadians balked for a few months, having endured a deeply divisive struggle over the original U.S.–Canada deal. On both sides, the political and economic calculus seemed clear. For the Mexican government, eager to overcome decades of tension with the United States and looking for new opportunities for rapid economic growth, a hemispheric trade union seemed full of promise and offered the potential to deflect increasing domestic discontent. For the United States, including

Mexico in such a pact promised a number of advantages. First, it would begin a long-desired process of peaceful cooperation over the many issues that involved the two states. Second, the prospect of rapid economic improvement in Mexico promised to reduce the pressures leading to mass illegal immigration into the United States. Third, the completion of a continental trade zone would be a useful negotiating threat and alternative in light of the rapidly deepening European unification process. Finally, opening up the highly protected Mexican economy promised major opportunities for U.S. business while furthering the larger goal of deepening the immersion of the U.S. market into the global economy.

The prospect of a continental free trade zone was well received by the political, intellectual, and economic elites that had dominated trade policy during the 1980s. In addition, the general foreign policy benefits of such an agreement worked to bring many otherwise skeptical individuals and groups into the coalition supporting the agreement. But signs of opposition soon emerged, especially when the Bush administration went to Congress in 1991 to request extension of fast-track authority to negotiate the treaty. Here, the administration faced unexpected opposition from a coalition of labor and environmental groups who believed that including Mexico in a free-trade deal would lead to severe costs for American workers and the environment. Especially influential in the House Democratic Party, this coalition prevented the usual noncontroversial extension of fast-track authority. When this authority was granted in the late spring of 1991, it was done only after the administration had agreed to pursue an agenda of issues surrounding labor rights in Mexico, job loss compensation in the United States, and environmental protection in Mexico as part of the treaty negotiations. Though the protrade coalition had won the fast-track battle, the opposition coalition had shown an unexpected strength that would only embolden its later efforts.

After almost a year of difficult negotiations, NAFTA was concluded in August 1992, committing the three states to the creation of a continental free-trade zone within ten years. By then the negotiations and the treaty itself had already become a major issue in the presidential campaign. In the Republican primaries, George Bush had been forced to fend off a strong challenge from Pat Buchanan, for whom NAFTA symbolized the loss of American sovereignty. The initial success of Buchanan's campaign illustrated the deep dissatisfaction of a substantial segment of Republicans with the globalizing agenda of the party's leadership. At the same time, the surprising emergence of the Ross Perot candidacy had galvanized many voters around a candidate who proved to be one of the most persistent and effective critics of NAFTA. Perot's speeches, television appearances, and books effectively combined an appeal to the protection of American jobs with an ability to tap a widespread sense of lost control over the direction of politics and policy. For Perot, NAFTA's likely outcome of lost jobs and lower wages threatened the destruction of the rights of American workers and citizens.

It was in the Democratic Party's primary contests, however, that the tensions over NAFTA were especially potent. A number of the party's key constituencies, especially the union movement, key environmental groups, and the forces represented by Jesse Jackson's campaign, had made opposition to further globalization a litmus issue for candidates. In addition, a good segment of the party's House leadership was now firmly against the treaty. Though Bill Clinton eventually won the nomination, he did so by carefully avoiding any firm decision on NAFTA. Clinton's strategy had been to combine a generalized commitment to free trade with concerns that trade agreements should specifically incorporate labor and environmental concerns. By the height of the fall campaign, Clinton's position crystallized into support for the agreement conditioned on the further negotiation of specific "side agreements" to address the concerns over dislocated American and low-wage Mexican workers, and to ensure more effective environmental protection in Mexico. While not satisfying NAFTA's most ardent opponents, this position proved palatable to enough constituencies for Clinton to win the election.

After the inauguration, the Clinton administration convened negotiations on the side agreements but turned its major attention to the fight over a budget agreement and the ambitious health-care reform plan. At the same time, however, the emerging coalition opposed to NAFTA jelled and organized an unexpectedly powerful critique and challenge to the treaty. From grassroots union organizing to the constant campaigning of Jackson and Buchanan, to the mobilization of environmental and consumer groups, and culminating in the television appearances by Perot, Americans at all levels of society were exposed to a sustained challenge to the direction of trade policy. This movement was able to combine appeals to constituencies fearful of the loss of jobs, growing illegal immigration, and threats to the environment. In all these appeals, the element that stood out most clearly, and surprised so many observers of trade politics, was the argument that Americans risked losing their sovereignty if NAFTA and similar agreements were allowed to succeed. By the spring of 1993, the opponents of the agreement had managed to define the issues at stake as involving the very independence of the polity, not simply the economic damage NAFTA might pose to specific constituencies.

The side agreements on labor and the environment were concluded in mid-August 1993, and with these at hand NAFTA was submitted to Congress for ratification. But by this point its supporters were clearly on the defensive. Studies of American public opinion showed that a clear majority of citizens opposed the agreement and that citizens had been receptive to the arguments about the loss of sovereignty as well as those focusing on the potential loss of jobs and increase in immigration. Moreover, at this point it was clear that the treaty did not have enough votes in Congress and especially in the House. To secure the ratification of NAFTA, the Clinton administration would have to rely upon a solid majority of Republicans and then work feverishly to draw individual Democrats away from the pull of key constituencies and their own leadership. It was not uncommon at that point for commentators to declare the treaty dead.

As we know, NAFTA was eventually ratified by Congress in November 1993. The effort required to transform public opinion and especially to turn around votes in Congress produced the most massive mobilization of pro-free-trade forces since the 1940s. In the public arena, this included continuous speeches by the president, advertising campaigns by the corporate community, a press conference that brought all the living ex-presidents to the White House to endorse the agreement, and the famous Ross Perot–Al Gore debate on the *Larry King Show*. Behind the scenes, the Administration helped to organize a pro-NAFTA coalition of business groups, centrist environmental groups, and key elements in the foreign policy establishment to support the public relations and legislative efforts. Most important, the administration itself engaged in a sustained lobbying campaign in the House, which resulted in an unprecedented amount of deal making and policy promises targeted at specific legislators. The effort succeeded, though it exhausted the administration's ability to move quickly on other policy fronts.[20]

The Clinton administration's success at turning the tide on the NAFTA agreement was indeed a major accomplishment. It had proved able to mobilize a wide-ranging protrade coalition throughout American society and had withstood the most powerful challenge to free trade since the Second World War. Moreover, the supporters of NAFTA would soon find themselves riding the wave of what would become the longest peacetime economic boom in American history. As in the 1980s, prosperity worked to take the energy out of the protectionist coalition. In this context, it proved much easier for the Administration to secure Congressional approval in 1995 for the treaty that concluded the Uruguay Round of GATT negotiations. This treaty marked some significant reforms in the world trading system—extending GATT rules to incorporate some areas of trade in agricultural goods and the service industries, providing worldwide protection for intellectual property rights, and establishing the WTO as a multilateral body to authoritatively resolve trade disputes under GATT rules. In many ways, this treaty was potentially more radical than NAFTA, and the antiglobalization coalition rallied furiously to oppose its ratification. Without a high level of palpable economic distress, and with a very obscure subject matter, opponents were most effective in emphasizing the WTO's potential threat to American sovereignty. Once again, American politics was flooded with claims and counterclaims about globalization and sovereignty, and once again the conflict was over the terms on which the polity and society would deal with the larger global environment. This time, though, the treaty's supporters were better prepared and the larger economic climate worked to their favor.

By 1996, then, there seemed to be good reason to believe that the proglobalization agenda had been firmly established in U.S. politics and policy. Indeed, the public arena was full of triumphant arguments claiming the inevitability of globalization and the benefits it was bringing Americans, arguments emanating from the administration, the corporate world, leading opinion makers, and policy experts. But things were not really so clear. The political mobilization against NAFTA and the GATT treaty had seen the consolidation of the most effective anti-free-trade coalition in U.S. politics in six decades. In the Republican presidential primaries of 1996, the startling early success of Pat Buchanan again illustrated the depth of this coalition's appeal. In addition, a variety of commentators from across the political spectrum, including some well-respected policy intellectuals, continued to publish a steady stream of warnings concerning the social and political dangers of unhindered globalization. From Buchanan and Perot, to George Soros and William Greider, to the Brookings Institution and the protests in Seattle, came a clear message that serious divisions remained in American politics about deeper involvement of the country in a largely unregulated global marketplace.

As it turned out, these commentators were onto something. Despite a successful reelection bid, the Clinton administration proved unable to persuade Congress to reauthorize fast-track negotiating authority in 1997, and that authority is absent to this day. The global financial chaos beginning in 1998 only boosted the concerns of the critics of globalization. But a serious quandary remained unanswered. Despite the claims of many of the critics, it seemed clear to most scholars that the worst predictions made concerning the impact of NAFTA and the WTO had not materialized. The massive job losses and dislocations these treaties were supposed to generate did not materialize, nor was there a massive upsurge in illegal immigration. Moreover, the United States still seemed quite able to effectively insulate itself from the worst effect of the Asian and Russian financial crises. With so little evidence of any widespread loss of political and economic sovereignty, why did the problem of globalization still appear to be such a potent generator of fear in American politics?

Interlude: The Impact of Globalization on Income Inequality in the United States

As anyone who observed the debates over NAFTA will remember, a central issue dividing supporters and opponents of the treaty was the impact of increased trade on the incomes of American workers. From the late 1970s onward, the degree of income inequality in the United States had been steadily rising. As figure 4-2 indicates, the share of American income distribution of all but the top fifth of American workers dropped from 1979 to 1995, a pattern at odds with that of the post-1945 era. Figure 4-3 shows the particular concentration of this trend among middle-class male workers, precisely the group whose prosperity was at the center of the political bargain of the period after World War II. In addition, the 1980s

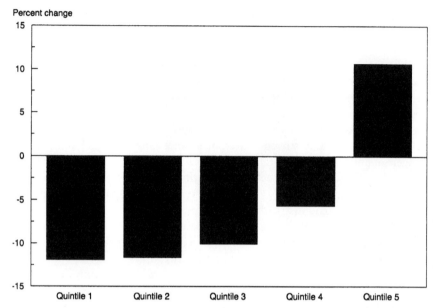

Figure 4-2. Change in Share of Income Received by Each Quintile from 1979 to 1995.
Source: 1997 Economic Report of the President, February, 1997, Washington, D.C.: U.S.
Government Printing Office, p. 178.

and early 1990s saw a great deal of job loss and insecurity as a part of the wave of
corporate "restructuring" or "downsizing" that was undertaken to improve the
competitiveness of American firms. For critics of globalization and NAFTA in
particular, this pattern of increasing inequality and the declining real income of
many lower-skilled workers were directly tied to the increasing role of trade in the
U.S. economy. As lower-priced imports pushed domestically produced goods out
of the market and firms took advantage of the new environment to locate production in lower-wage countries, American workers were faced with the choice of
watching the value of their incomes fall or losing their jobs altogether. From this
perspective, the creation of a continental free-trade zone including Mexico would
only further seal the fate of American workers, condemning them to a future of
fewer and less well-paid jobs. In Ross Perot's memorable phrase, any careful
student of NAFTA could already hear the "giant sucking sound" of jobs moving
south to Mexico, draining the promise of American life out of the future of
American workers.

One result of this combination of real economic trends and loud public
argument was the emergence of a large scholarly literature on the relationship
between greater trade and the incomes of American workers.[21] Although this work
has been conducted primarily by economists, it has had two particularly important

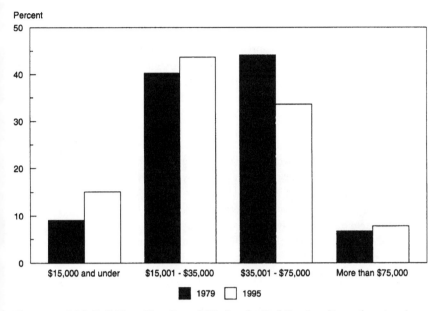

Figure 4-3. Male Full-Time, Year-Round Workers by Real Earnings Range (earnings in 1995 dollars). *Source: 1997 Economic Report of the President,* February, 1997, Washington, D.C.: U.S. Government Printing Office, p. 168.

implications for our understanding of the political dimensions of the question of globalization. First, scholars exploring this issue have had to come to some general assessment of the impact of global economic forces in shaping the social and economic changes of the past two or three decades. In effect, this literature has helped clarify, more precisely than other discussions, the nature and limits of globalization. Second, all the contributors to this scholarly debate have expressed a real concern to find some effective policy response to counteract the trend toward stagnant wages and increasing income inequality. In the process, they have helped to explore the implications of global change for the power, authority, and role of the state in the contemporary world.

What are the general approaches and conclusions that have emerged so far from this literature? For the most part, analysts have attempted to disentangle the effects of three kinds of causes offered for the growing inequality of income in the United States—globalization (including increasing imports and immigration), technological change and its impact on the labor market and the structure of corporations, and various institutional changes in American society (particularly the declining power of labor unions and the changing role of government). The widely accepted conclusion from this analysis is, as Susan Collins writes, that "the weight of evidence supports the view that other factors have been significantly more important than globalization in explaining the rise of the skill premium."[22] For most analysts, the growth of imports and immigration has had a real effect in increasing the amount of inequality among workers but accounts for no more than 20 percent of this increase. Despite the significantly increased role of imports and exports in the American economy, global forces are still clearly secondary to domestic sources of change in shaping the evolution of the American economy, and it is to those domestic changes that we must look to explain the overall direction of that evolution.

Which changes seem the most central to the growth of income inequality? For most economists, the central role has been played by the changing technological environment of the contemporary economy, in particular the spread of computer technology and the growing awareness of technological processes and of the dynamics of quickly changing markets. These developments have worked to increase the demand for highly skilled workers and professionals, often beyond the ability of American society to meet, thus leading to increased wages and benefits for such specialists. At the same time, the declining relevance of low- and semi-skilled workers in an increasingly technological and knowledge-based economy means that there is less demand for these workers and less pressure to raise their wages. Together, these trends have been a central driving force in the growth of income inequality, and their effects can be observed working as early as the late 1970s, well before the recent intensification of globalization.

Analysts also agree, however, that the impact of the changing labor market has been intensified because of important institutional changes in the United States over the same period. First, it is clear that the power of unions to shape the overall distribution of incomes has declined since the 1970s.[23] This decline is the result both of the steady reduction in the percentage of workers who are members of unions and of a legal and political environment much more hostile to unions and more accepting of attempts by corporations to either decertify existing unions or prevent their formation in the first place. Once again, we can see both trends taking shape in the later 1970s. During the Carter administration, unions witnessed a serious hemorrhaging of membership and lost a number of crucial battles in Congress to secure their ability to organize new members and protect themselves against more aggressive management strategies. As the labor movement found itself less and less able to resist the decisions of corporations on wages and benefits, it also lost a good deal of its ability to limit the effect of new labor market trends on the distribution of incomes among workers. When President Reagan successfully destroyed the Air Traffic Controllers union during the strike of 1981, he underscored the decline in union power that had already become a fact of American economic life.

Second, the spread and impact of new technologies and forms of business organization were greatly facilitated and encouraged by the wave of economic deregulation that began in the mid-1970s.[24] We have already explored the sources and general outline of this process, which aimed at forcing key sectors of the American economy to become more responsive to market competition. In the view of most analysts of increasing wage and income inequality, this step was central in allowing firms to employ new technologies and strategies in ways that would change the labor market. Drawing on the work of business organization scholars, students of the labor market note that how fast new technologies were introduced depended on the ability of and need for firms to reshape the ways in which work was organized, and thus the ways in which they themselves worked as organizations. The more competitive and deregulated environment of the last decade or so has provided both the opportunity and the necessity for firms to take full advantage of the power of new technologies. In the process, this environment facilitated the growing premium for highly skilled workers and the surplus of lower-skilled workers. Along with the weakening of unions, then, the policy changes that brought a more dynamic and competitive market economy functioned as crucial intermediate factors in the process whereby new technologies contributed to increasing income inequality.[25]

This does not complete the story. Though scholars widely agree that globalization accounts for a real but secondary share of the growth in income inequality, many of them also warn that the data and models for assessing this issue are quite undeveloped and may be underestimating the impact of trade.[26] Moreover, when the issue is the impact of the immigration of low-skilled workers on the wages of lower-skilled workers generally, scholars seem ready to accept that this aspect of globalization is indeed an important factor in explaining what has been happening at the lower end of the income-distribution scale. Nonetheless, most academics working in this area eventually come to the conclusion expressed most clearly by the authors of *Globaphobia*: the increasing integration of the U.S. economy into the world economy has brought more wealth and higher living standards for Americans as a whole. Certainly, some groups of workers may have suffered from the costs of reshaping individual firms and the economy as a whole to become more competitive in the global economy. But on the whole there is little reason to think that globalization has been the central cause of growing inequality in income distribution.

This understanding of the sources of wage and income inequality helps to clarify and support the analysis of globalization presented throughout the book. As in the case of the changing role of government and shifting social patterns often linked to the impact of globalization, the increase in inequality and stagnation of wages and living standards for many were the result of institutional and political changes that preceded the greater impact of global changes on American society. Though critics of globalization lay the blame for income inequality on the impact of global forces, it turns out that the initial growth of inequality was part and parcel of the transformation in American life brought about by the same policy choices that were responsible for opening the United States to a more globalized world.

Furthermore, the trend toward increased inequality, while partially implicit in new kinds of technological change, required political and institutional reforms that emerged from political action, not any irresistible pressures originating in the global economy itself. As in the larger area of trade policy itself, we need to look to the arena of political action to begin to explain globalization.

A finding that the roots of income inequality go deeper than the impact of globalization, however, does not mean that globalization has not or will not contribute to deepening this trend. If I am correct that globalization emerged as part of the policy choices involved in the creation of the competition state, we should expect that it would work to solidify the institutional and social changes that are part of this new way of looking at the role of government. Indeed, I have already noted that most mainstream analysts do find that some elements of globalization, especially increased imports from lower-wage countries and the immigration of lower-skilled workers, have played a role in reinforcing the trends towards greater income inequality. The most systematic attempt to explore this relationship to date has been presented in the work of Dani Rodrik, who suggests that globalization may indeed be becoming a more important force in its own right in shaping American society.[27] Rodrik begins by asking us to reject the assumption that the factors cited as explaining a growth in inequality—trade, technology, institutional change—should be seen as separate and competing factors. Rather, he suggests that we explore the ways in which they are complementary parts of a more dynamic and competitive economy, reinforcing each other's impact. For instance, Rodrik points out that a more open global economy, with the opportunities it provides for manufacturers to shift their facilities across national borders, functions as a latent or structural element of the situation in which workers and employers negotiate over wages. The simple fact that a particular firm or industry is not heavily involved in globalized production does not mean that the potential to become involved cannot play an important part in shaping the role of unions or the level of wages.

To take another example, Rodrik suggests that the increasing interconnections between the most powerful and dynamic economies around the world may be playing a major role in accelerating the pace of technological change in production activities, thereby enhancing the latter's impact on wages and income distribution. The consequence of these linkages, he argues, is that globalization helps to increase the elasticity of demand for lower-skilled workers, thereby contributing to a drop in their relative share of wages and incomes. Rodrik concludes this discussion the following way:

> There are reasons, then, to think that the main impact of globalization on labor markets may well be the increase in the (actual or perceived) elasticity of demand for unskilled workers and not in the reduction in this demand per se. That is, workers now find them-

selves in an environment in which they can be more easily "ex-changed" for workers in other countries. For those who lack the skills to make themselves hard to replace, the result is greater insecurity and a more precarious existence.[28]

Rodrik's argument remains suggestive and incomplete. Like the other schol-ars in this debate, he is careful to emphasize the preliminary nature of all research into these questions, and like them he remains unwilling to blame globalization for all the trends in income distribution in the United States or to conclude that its overall effects have been negative. But, together with the real if more limited impacts acknowledged by the majority of investigators, his work provides us with good reason to think that in American and other advanced industrial societies globalization is indeed playing an important role in dividing persons who are positioned to take advantage of a more competitive economic context from those who are less so. It is in this sense that there is some real force to the arguments of the critics of globalization. American incomes have not become more unequal because of the impact of uncontrollable global forces, but globalization is indeed an important element of a new context for politics and political choice, one in which it has become more difficult to sustain the kind of social compact that had become widely expected among American workers. In pursuing a new vision of the role of the state and the boundaries of the nation, American policymakers have helped create a world in which the connections between the economic fates of all sections of American society are less clear.

What about the policy conclusions drawn by scholars involved in this de-bate? Here there is much less disagreement or hesitation. The dominant position among analysts rejects increased protectionism for domestic jobs, firms, or indus-tries as counterproductive, promising at best temporary benefits for certain work-ers at the cost of overall reductions in the living standards of the majority of workers. Moreover, from this perspective protection is a response to the wrong problem. Since technological change is usually identified as the primary cause of the problems of greater inequality and lower wages, the common response among scholars is to suggest various forms of adjustment assistance, retraining, and edu-cation to provide opportunities to all workers to develop the kinds of skills that will be well rewarded in a more competitive environment.[29] The only dissenting note comes from scholars such as Rodrik and Ethan Kapstein, who wonder whether governments should slow down the pace of further global immersion of their societies in order to enable the development of effective measures to ensure that the benefits of globalization are not cornered by one already privileged sector of soci-ety. But even supporters of this perspective reject the efficacy of any major rework-ing of the relationship of the United States to the evolving global market economy.

What can we learn from this debate, then, concerning the overall impact of globalization on American society and politics over the past two decades? First, it helps remind us that global change does not operate according to a uniform logic and direction but that its impact on any particular society depends upon the interaction between global forces and domestic institutions and policy choices already in place. In the case of wage and income inequality, these studies show that though globalization has reinforced pressures for increased inequality in all developed economies, it did not create these pressures, and the level and pace of their impact vary significantly depending upon the domestic policy responses.

Second, these studies remind us that it is easy to overestimate the degree to which the American society and economy are integrated into a global system. Although we have seen different ways of thinking about the linkages, all the major works in the area come back to the conclusion that much of the social and economic transformation of the past decades has decidedly domestic origins and operates in ways that depend upon domestic institutions and choices. Indeed, most of these studies are careful to make it clear that much of what has taken place as part of globalization can be traced to policy choices initiated to secure the interests and priorities of domestic political actors. This is, of course, the point of the title of Paul Krugman's essay "We Are Not the World."[30]

Finally, the discussions of policy responses to inequality in this work always stem from the conviction that governments have not lost control of the development of economic processes and institutions to an overwhelming global system. Though globalization pushes social change in certain directions and increases the costs of certain policy choices, states remain active and able to develop a wide variety of responses to the impact of global change. If governments resign themselves to these changes, it is because political alliances and priorities lead them to do so, not because the global economy forces it upon them.

The Globalization of Trade Policy and the Relevance of Sovereignty

Now let's return to the arguments over NAFTA and trade policy in the 1990s. As Frederick Mayer has pointed out, the politics of NAFTA and the related trade issues of the 1990s are not well captured by the usual approaches used by political scientists. This conclusion applies to the organization and activism of both supporters and opponents of the major directions of trade policy. In essence, the immediate and medium-term impacts of NAFTA were expected to be and have been totally out of proportion to the firestorm of controversy the agreement has generated. In the words of one group of commentators, "Despite the preponderance of traditional trade liberalization issues, the debate about NAFTA's passage or defeat was imbued with a level of nearly metaphysical importance seldom seen in foreign trade policy disputes."[31] To be sure, we have already seen the rapid increase in the importance and impact of trade in the U.S. economy over the 1980s and 1990s. But careful analyses have shown that NAFTA's impact on the degree or direction of trade and on the distribution of the costs of trade among Americans has been relatively small.[32] Nor does there appear to have been any significant diminution of American sovereignty as a result of this agreement or the creation of the WTO. Though the U.S. government or particular corporations may lose occasional disputes before multilateral bodies, few question the American state's ultimate ability to promote its own agenda in trade policy.

How, then, can we gain a grasp on the contours of the contemporary politics of trade in the United States? Mayer's important work points us in the direction of "symbolic politics." "The scale of political mobilization is simply incompatible with the likely tiny real effects of NAFTA on the issues ostensibly motivating opponents. The domestic grassroots opposition to NAFTA was based less on what NAFTA *was* and more on what it *symbolized*."[33] To understand the opposition to NAFTA, we must understand that the treaty was a crucial symbol around which were crafted narratives of American economic and social decline, especially the declining fortunes of the working and middle classes. Mayer notes that the narratives of the various elements of the anti-NAFTA coalition—Perot, Buchanan, environmentalists, labor—differed in subtle ways but all returned to this common theme. For him, this conclusion means that analysts of trade policy in political science are going to have to broaden the tools of their discipline and move beyond the focus on interest and institution-based concepts and theories that has dominated the discipline for decades.

Mayer's account fits well with the framework I have been using in this book. NAFTA and its related policy questions tapped into deep uncertainties and hopes throughout the policy, a development that shaped the reactions of many unlikely to be directly affected by the treaty. But we need to go even further with this line of argument and explore the hopes and worries so well manipulated by NAFTA's supporters and opponents. The key step, I have argued, is to look at the politics of trade in the light of the larger direction of economic policy pursued in the United States since the mid-1970s. From this perspective, we can see that the narratives of economic decline and the loss of sovereignty are based in the clash between the expectations of citizens and the changing priorities of government policy. Trade policy and politics came to be a focusing symbol for disagreements concerning the changing place of the state in society over two decades, of which the deepening globalization of the economy was one part. These trends did not amount to a surrender of U.S. sovereignty but they did involve a reworking of its purposes and tools in a way that challenged the consensus about the role of the state that had existed since the 1940s. By the 1990s, the politics of globalization had become the central arena for the struggle over the role of the state in American life and the priorities of the American political community.

Let's look again at the shift in economic policy direction that began in the 1970s. The essential theme in this movement was the reduction in the state's responsibility for securing economic security, opportunities, and outcomes. In the place of regulation and some redistribution, the state would rely on the market mechanism to provide the wealth and dynamism that Americans were used to. With hindsight, it is clear that this project was linked to and was itself a crucial factor setting in motion a more aggressive U.S. trade policy in the 1980s and 1990s. Though this seemed initially to be focused primarily on protecting American interests, it also involved a longer-term project of expanding the American economy's participation in a more competitive global economy. Intended to promote long-term American interests, this larger project meant substantial disruption for many American industries and for the lives and expectations of many workers. The domestic and international dimensions of this new policy direction were clearly linked, as had been the case with the New Deal project. Just as the latter required substantial barriers to protect the domestic economy so that the state could promote the security of its citizens, the former required that the domestic economy be exposed to the pressures of global competition to ensure and support the programs of deregulation and " marketization" of society.

There is and will remain much debate among political scientists concerning the degree to which these policy choices were dictated by a failure of liberal reform programs and the changing realities of the global marketplace. But there is clearly no sense in which the making of these choices and the success of their implementation were inevitable. The political history of U.S. economic and trade policy indicates a major mobilization of the power and authority of the state, in alliance with key elements of the business and policy communities, to break down the commitments, networks, and institutions that had supported the New Deal liberal state. The slow but steady attack on established patterns of policy practice in regulation, macroeconomic management, and social provisions illustrates an attempt to reconfigure the priorities and capacities of the state. It has been a classic case of the mobilization of sovereign power to redirect the relationships between state and society. Whatever the long-term impact of global immersion on the power of the American state, the project itself depended and depends on the active exercise of that power.

So why do we now see the emergence of a coalition of political forces dedicated to the restoration of sovereign power over trade and economic policy? For many Americans, the program of market-based policy directions proved very appealing, as it played well to resentment of and frustration with the social constraints of the reform liberal state. But the impact of these policy changes came to be very disturbing. Rather than making existing patterns of opportunity work better, these choices began causing disruptions of established patterns and expectations in economic life. The transformation of the structure of the corporate world, the destabilization of patterns of employment and compensation, dramatic regional redistributions of economic fate, and a new restraint on the part of the state in the face of these changes brought much insecurity to the lives of many Americans. While some took advantage of many new opportunities, many if not most others grew increasingly confused and indeed resentful of the unanticipated disruptions to established patterns of work and the seeming inability of government to protect citizens from these disruptions.

Much of the rhetoric surrounding NAFTA, both during and after the ratification debates, expresses just this sense of disruption and loss of control. For Pat Buchanan,

> NAFTA is about America's sovereignty, liberty, and destiny. It is about whether we hand down to the next generation the same free and independent country handed down to us; or whether 21st century America becomes but a subsidiary of the New International Economic Order.[34]

As it turns out, the very language and imagery presented in this quote are paralleled by writers far to the left of the mainstream of American politics. For Kim Moody and Michael McGinn of the International Labor Rights Education and Research Fund (ILRER), a key grassroots organization in the anti-NAFTA movement:

> The North American Free Trade Agreement is not about the commerce of nations. This treaty that binds the United States, Canada, and Mexico in economic union is more about corporate profit than trade. It is about letting private businesses reorganize the North American economy without the checks and balances once provided by unions, social movements, or governments. The North American Free Trade Agreement (NAFTA) would roll back a hundred years of controls and restrictions that were placed on private business in the interests of the majority of the people.[35]

We have seen the very same kind of narrative in the general literature about globalization, and there are a multitude of examples of it from all sides of the NAFTA opposition.

Here lies what may be the key to the anti-free-trade, prosovereignty movement: the economic and social insecurity resulting from the new directions of economic change has undermined the expectations about the lifestyles and commitments "due" Americans, expectations set during the 1940s and onward. When government did not respond to protect these expectations in the 1980s and 1990s, many citizens came to feel a loss of control over government policy and the political process. Americans were no longer sovereign in this view because the state no longer enforced the guarantees established in the political culture. As we have seen, the writings and speeches of the leaders of this movement, from Ralph Nader to Pat Buchanan, are replete with exactly this kind of analysis.

In many cases, these kinds of claims overestimate the amount of change that has occurred in the way and degree that government secures its citizens from economic hardship. As Paul Pierson has argued, critics of the Reagan administration and its successors in the United States and the Thatcher governments in Britain have usually overestimated the degree of retrenchment in the scope and resources of the welfare state in the United States.[36] But Pierson's argument is limited in two ways. First, many of the changes that have generated this protest have occurred in the practices of corporations and other private employers, who no longer provide the kind of guarantees of long-term employment and benefits to which many Americans had become accustomed. Although these guarantees were not necessarily the result of public action, the lack of any sustained attempt on the part of the state to counteract these trends has contributed to the sense that the state has failed or broken its promises. Second, the welfare state in the United States has never been very capable of dealing with the problems of retraining and supporting workers who are displaced when their skills become obsolete. But this is exactly the kind of support needed to respond to the impact of the technological changes reinforced by globalization. The lack of sustained and effective policy development in this area, I would suggest, has often been interpreted as a failure to live up to the state's obligation to sustain rising living standards and security among the middle classes. It was this generalized sense of a social compact, I have argued, that fell apart in the face of globalization.

Why did NAFTA and other trade policy choices become the focus of this protest in the face of clear evidence that they were only minimally responsible for the kinds of changes we have discussed? The issue of sovereignty provides a neglected but crucial link here. The most obvious impact of economic change was the growing presence of foreign goods and companies in American life. These have a concrete and palpable presence that issues of market and corporate structure do not. Moreover, global pressures became a recurrent excuse used by many in the corporate and political world to explain or justify the choices they were making. To these must be added the impact of the world of sovereign states itself in shaping the ways we have come to think about threats to our security. Over at least two centuries, international politics has been structured in a way that distinguishes between the security provided by borders and the insecurities threatening any political community from the chaotic world outside its borders. It is understandable that most citizens, influenced by the intensive experience of the Cold War, would tend to look outside the state's borders to explain threats to their security.[37] The language of sovereignty, linked as it has been to issues of globalization, proved an effective narrative pulling all these threads together. While embodying the sense of a loss of control, sovereignty works to focus attention on global forces and links their influence to the issue of security and political independence. In this light, the impending market-opening trade agreements provided a perfect focus to tie the narrative together into a coherent critique of the general direction of American political life.

During the NAFTA and GATT debates, most policymakers and commentators reacted with confusion or disdain to this rhetoric and critique, and many scholars of trade and economic policy continue to do so. In this view, it is clear that the United States is not passively giving away its sovereignty and that globalization is not an overwhelming force responsible for all the ills facing American society today. I have tried to show that this response is essentially correct: sovereignty and the relation of the state to the global economy are changing, but there is no real evidence of the collapse of American independence. However, this response tends to miss a critical dimension of sovereignty that is really behind the critique of trade policy. Sovereignty is not only about the state's resources and capacities but also about the purposes to which these are put and the ends they serve. By renegotiating the deal between state and society—allowing massive shifts in the patterns of economic life and refusing to compensate Americans for the impact these have had on their security—the new competition state has broken the long-established expectations of many Americans. In effect, the state has rejected the purposes these citizens had come to associate with their political membership and identity. Though the American state may still be a very sovereign entity, for many Americans it no longer works to affirm and protect their status as members of the polity. In this sense, the project of globalization has indeed led to a loss of their sovereignty.

As long as American trade policy continues to pursue the immersion of the American economy in a more competitive global market economy, American trade politics will continue to be shaped by the politics of globalization. But concerns about the changing relationship of the United States and the larger world are not limited to trade policy. The opening of American society to global trade and investment also means opening it to new movements of people and the changing patterns of culture linked to these movements. In the next chapter, we will explore the ways that immigration and immigration policy since the 1960s have shaped and become part of the politics of globalization.

5 ∽

Immigration and the Politics of Membership

Over the past two decades, only the issue of immigration has come close to having the kind of impact that trade policy has had on the politics of globalization. Since 1970, the United States has once again become the destination of millions of migrants from around the world, people fleeing civil warfare, ethnic conflict, political repression, and poverty, in numbers not seen (outside wartime) since the turn of the century. As in the earlier era, the promise of prosperity and security has made the United States a central destination for these migrants. The millions who have arrived, most legally and some illegally, have generated much political and social controversy. Predominantly unskilled and of Asian and Latin American origin, these immigrants have in the view of many challenged the economic security and cultural coherence of American life. Though the overall stance of American policy has remained welcoming to immigrants, critics have made important inroads on policy and raised a powerful challenge to the dominant national mythology of immigration.[1]

From the late 1970s to the early 1990s, the movement to restrict immigration was focused primarily on illegal immigrants, especially those coming across the Mexican border. Given the plainly illegal character of this migration, proposals to protect American borders in this area gained widespread support. Even those who supported continued legal immigration found it politically useful and practically important to limit illegal population movements. By the mid-1990s, however, the immigration restriction movement began to attempt to limit all forms of immigration and to clearly distinguish the status and rights of native-born Americans from that of even legal immigrants. Though the generalized attempt to redirect U.S. policy failed, the 1996 Illegal Immigration Reform and Immigrant Responsibility Act and the Personal Responsibility and Work Opportunity Reconciliation Act incorporated numerous provisions reflecting the second part of the restrictionist agenda.[2] In the name of protecting the rights of American citizenship, many legal residents were denied legal protections and access to social benefits they had long enjoyed.

My aim in this chapter is to explore the origins of the recent wave of immigration into the United States and to explain how it has shaped the politics of membership and citizenship in the American polity.[3] In particular, I will focus on the emergence of the immigration restriction movement and the sources of its ability to reshape the dynamics of American immigration and naturalization policy. Changes in U.S. policy beginning in the mid-1960s, I argue, have been linked to and increasingly caught up in the politics of global immersion which we have already explored in the area of trade policy. As immigration policy has been gradually adjusted to facilitate the integration of the American and global economies and societies, it has pushed to the fore key questions about the nature and value of citizenship as an indicator of full standing in the polity. In response, a movement has emerged to revalue the status and benefits of citizenship, usually at the expense of the rights of migrants and legal residents. As the process of globalization continues, immigration and naturalization policy will be a central arena in which the meaning and relevance of citizenship in the American polity will be debated and decided.

"Controlling Our Borders": The Backlash against Immigration

In the 1980s and 1990s, Americans did not have to look very hard to find out that their country was subject to an invasion of foreigners, reducing their living standards and threatening their culture and security. Whether they turned to television, newspapers, the Internet, or public speakers, Americans were being told that their country had "lost control of its borders," that the migrants who crossed those borders were illegally and immorally benefiting from programs funded by the tax dollars of citizens, and that decisive action was necessary to reverse this tide. A wide-ranging group of interests, from organized labor and antitax organizations to anti-immigration groups such as the Federation for American Immigration Reform (FAIR), were steadily promoting this argument. They were supported by politicians from Ross Perot to Pat Buchanan as well as some important representatives of the environmental lobby. Meanwhile, these concerns were increasingly influential in Congress and state legislatures, which moved over these decades from measures directed against illegal immigrants to attempts to develop and enforce policy measures that specifically rewarded citizens and penalized migrants. By the mid-1990s, the Clinton administration was forced to respond to these pressures, pursuing a major revitalization of the budgets and missions of the U.S. Border Patrol.[4]

What generated this kind of movement? In retrospect, it seems clear that the sources of a popular and widespread anti-immigration movement lie in the events of the late 1970s and early 1980s. During this period, activists and policymakers first became aware of the increasing flow of illegal immigrants across the U.S.–Mexico border. Driven by economic collapse and attracted by demands for cheap labor, Mexicans and others were entering the United States—especially California and Texas—in record and continually growing numbers. By the turn of the 1980s, this process was supplemented by the mass migrations from Cuba—the "Mariel boat lift"—and Haiti. Just as these movements tapered off, the deepening of civil wars and revolutions in Central America renewed the push and increased the flow of migrants toward American borders. Despite the system of border checks and controls, it appeared to many Americans that the country had lost the ability to effectively control access to its territory.

In the subsequent campaign to address illegal migration, many of the key coalitions and alignments of immigration politics today were established, as were the key motifs of political argument concerning immigration. Demanding rapid action to limit the flow of migrants was a coalition of cultural nationalists, trade unions fearing competition from low-wage workers, environmentalists concerned with population control, and state governments and taxpayer groups in border regions who paid much of the direct costs of dealing with the migrants. This somewhat crazy-quilt coalition appealed to a combination of economic concerns over the cost of immigration—lost jobs, lower wages, and strains on public budgets—and political-cultural worries over the ethnic makeup and cultural evolution of American society. For example, the preamble of the California ballot initiative Proposition 187, approved in November 1994, contends that the people of America have

> suffered and are suffering economic hardship caused by the presence of illegal aliens in this state. That they have suffered and are suffering personal injury and damage caused by the criminal conduct of illegal aliens in this state. That they have the right to the protection of their government from any person or persons entering this country unlawfully.

In the revived Cold War atmosphere of the early 1980s, the latter concerns were easily combined with fears of the spread of radical politics from Central America. Together, these appeals effectively mobilized many citizens and politicians around a program of reinforcing American borders to stop illegal immigration.

In response, a coalition emerged that aimed to block the more radical moves toward border control. The elements of this grouping proved equally diverse, including businesses that depended on low-wage labor and feared effective employer sanctions against hiring illegal migrants, elements of the foreign policy establishment worried about the impact of immigration policy in Mexico and Central America, human rights activists and civil libertarians who feared the emergence of repressive policies that would penalize an already weak and vulnerable group, and organized interests representing many ethnic groups historically supportive of immigration. This movement responded to the rhetoric of border control with powerful appeals to the mythology of America as a refuge for the downtrodden and a depiction of contemporary migrants as similar to earlier arrivals on America's shores. In the words of Steve Chabot, a Republican congressman from Ohio:

> I deeply value the fundamental character of this Nation as a land of hope and opportunity, and because I cherish our unique American heritage as a country of immigrants, united by shared values, a strong work ethic, and a commitment to freedom. Let us not tarnish that heritage or ignore our greatest strength, which is our people.[5]

In addition, the foreign policy concerns of the restrictionists were countered by the attempt to link the future prosperity of the United States to that of Mexico and the rest of the Americas, arguing that the United States could not afford to adopt restrictions that would alienate potential allies and deepen the sources of conflict in the hemisphere. As the leading state in the world, it was argued, the United States must set an example of openness and accommodation to the globe, even at the expense of some short-term costs to its own society.

The challenge facing these groups and interests, however, was that the migration they seemed to be defending was by definition illegal, and so the debate came to focus on different possible approaches to reducing the flow of illegal migrants. As Congress considered legislation during the early 1980s, this is exactly how the issue was framed. Debates centered around the role and strength of the Border Patrol, the use of employer sanctions to reduce the demand for illegal immigrants, and the possibility of providing amnesty to those who had resided in the United States over a period of years. As we will see, the 1986 Immigration Reform and Control Act (IRCA) represented a compromise between these positions but also signified the emerging strength of the restrictionist coalition. During this entire debate, attention was focused almost exclusively on illegal immigration. Though there were some voices at the peripheries concerned about immigration as a whole, on the level of legislative maneuvering and negotiation, the long-standing pro-immigration mythology still seemed to hold throughout the 1980s.

During the latter part of the decade, immigration seemed to recede from public attention. As in the case of trade policy, a booming economy and the winding down of the conflicts in Central America reduced the urgency of the issue and shifted attention elsewhere. Indeed, the 1990s began with a major revision of policy concerning legal immigration, one that raised the overall limits for migrants and placed more emphasis on attracting highly skilled foreign labor to those areas of the economy facing a shortage of qualified native workers. While policy elites were developing a more accommodating stance, however, support for restrictionist policies was slowly if quietly growing. As Gimpel and Edwards show, public opinion over these years became increasingly skeptical about the benefits of immigration, and the differences in views toward legal and illegal immigration seemed to diminish.[6] Furthermore, the organized groups and advocates demanding more restrictive policies continued to develop resources and strengthen their networks. Most important, key restrictionists began to publicly raise the idea of limiting legal as well as illegal immigration.

The significance of these developments became clear as the U.S. economy settled into the recession of the early 1990s. Another wave of plant closings in manufacturing industries, downsizing in major corporations, and growing insecurity throughout the middle classes transformed political debate and undermined the Bush presidency. In the search for ways to address economic insecurity, immigration once again surfaced as a source of political controversy. The 1992 presidential campaign proved a key forum for this debate, as Pat Buchanan and Ross Perot were able to link the fear of the economic impact of further illegal immigration to the growing public suspicion of NAFTA. Indeed, it seems clear that the fear of competition from low-wage workers, whether in Mexico or through illegal immigration to the United States, provided a major source of opposition to this treaty. Just as important, the link between immigration and NAFTA seemed to broaden and shift perceptions of the immigration issue itself. By linking it to the policy of global economic free trade, the potential was raised for talking seriously about limiting immigration itself, rather than just lamenting its illegal forms.

Nonetheless, the immediate catalyst for political action on immigration remained the continued flow of undocumented workers across the U.S.-Mexican border and the access of such migrants to publicly provided social benefits. This access had been guaranteed by a series of federal court decisions since the 1970s, but came to seem especially controversial as Americans felt increasingly strapped between an uncertain future and rising tax bills. By 1994, the governors of the states (and mayors of cities) that were key destinations for illegal migrants began demanding more national support for paying the costs incurred in extending social, health, and educational benefits to migrants. The most vocal figure, Governor Pete Wilson of California, led a successful campaign in support of California Ballot Proposition 187, which denied all illegal migrants access to any social benefits provided by the state government. This was the most radical attempt to that point to reorient public policy by using citizenship status as a criterion for distributing social benefits. The political year culminated in the Republican capture of majorities in both Houses of Congress, with a leadership whose priorities included legislation that would enact the same kinds of discrimination against noncitizens at the national level.

Of course, the pro-immigration forces were not passive during this period. The controversy over Proposition 187 led to a national mobilization of such forces, which now also included the voices of political leaders from some key immigration-receiving regions, including Governor George Bush, Jr., of Texas and New York City mayor Rudolph Giuliani. Bolstered by a November 1997 federal court decision blocking the implementation of Proposition 187, these groups attempted again to limit the power of restrictionist forces by emphasizing the distinction between legal and illegal immigration. Their strategy was to combine a tougher stance on border control, the crucial element being the Clinton administration's newfound emphasis on tight enforcement and building up the U.S. Border Patrol, with a public relations campaign to extol the benefits immigrants brought to American economic and social life. Increasingly, the debates over the impact of NAFTA merged with those concerning immigration, as all participants came to focus on the benefits and burdens of greater economic integration between the United States and Mexico.

Although most systematic studies concluded that there were no clear grounds for blaming NAFTA and greater immigration for major economic disruption in the United States, the push for immigration restriction continued to grow. When the Republican Congress turned to immigration reform, Americans saw some of the most restrictionist pieces of legislation since the 1960s come to the floor. The central question concerned the readiness of the majority to take seriously Representative Lamar Smith's proposal to reduce overall levels of immigration, turning back a policy direction in place since 1965. Antirestrictionist forces were able to defeat this measure, but Congress moved on to approve major reforms limiting the rights of migrants and legal residents in the areas of social provision and due process procedures. The 1996 Immigration Reform and Welfare Reform acts marked significant victories for those attempting to reorient policy toward the goal of using policy reforms to deepen the distinctions between citizens and noncitizens. Although much of this legislation is now undergoing reconsideration in Congress and the courts, it represents gains for the restrictionist forces that many would have thought unattainable at the beginning of the decade.[7]

What accounts for the successes to date of the restrictionist movement? To this point, political scientists have not come up with a convincing explanation of these developments. For some, this movement is another manifestation of long-standing nativist traditions that have surfaced whenever the United States was subject to a large influx of migrants. Though the definition of a "native" may have changed, the basic dichotomy remains central to the way Americans identify themselves.[8] Moreover, the unprecedented Asian and Hispanic domination of the latest wave has fueled the sense that contemporary migrants are not like earlier immigrants in their ability and willingness to assimilate to American identity. Another strand of analysis emphasizes the generalized economic insecurity facing large sections of American society and the fact that the current stream of migrants is especially threatening because of its generally low level of skills. As Americans worry about potentially declining standards of living, a large influx of unskilled competitors seems a significant challenge to the economic structure undergirding the middle class.[9] A third approach, central to the important study by Gimpel and Edwards, emphasizes that the contemporary politics of immigration is decisively shaped by the controversy over the redistributive state built in the 1960s. As the legitimacy of this state has come under attack and partisan differences have deepened, the strains placed on public services by immigrants have made it easier to link their presence to the larger backlash against the welfare state. Moreover, as DeSipio and de la Garza point out, the fact that the United States has had no specific immigrant policy, but has addressed the problems of migrants through generalized social welfare policies, reinforces the link between the politics of immigration and the politics of redistribution.[10]

Each of these perspectives is crucial to understanding contemporary immigration politics, but what has been missing is a useful framework to pull them together into a coherent and persuasive overall account. In the rest of this chapter, I will try to show how the perspective on globalization that I have developed can provide a step toward this goal. I will focus on the history of immigration policy choices since 1965 and argue that the current politics of immigration is ultimately a product of the policy of global immersion that has guided these choices. In the concluding section, I will use this analysis to link immigration politics and policy to the politics of trade and ultimately the struggle over the way global change will shape the American political community.

Immigration Policy and American Political Identity

In U.S. history, immigration policy has evolved along with changing understandings of the political community. Over time, it has played a crucial but underappreciated role in shaping that community and securing its ends by constituting the boundary between the larger world and American society. Moreover, the mythology surrounding this history has played a central role in the contemporary politics of immigration policy. The general story is familiar. The United States was the haven for the persecuted of the world from its earliest beginnings until the middle part of this century. In the 1920s, in a fit of ethnocentrism and fear, the United States turned its back on this history and closed its doors to most new migration, a policy sustained into the early Cold War era. Beginning in the 1960s, however, we returned to a more enlightened tradition and once again opened the door to the world's oppressed, a change that has brought great cultural, economic, and political benefits. This account contains some truth, but it is also a much too simplified view of the dynamic of American immigration policy.

In fact, there was no national "immigration policy," properly understood, until the 1870s.[11] Before the Civil War, although naturalization was clearly regulated by Congress, decisions on the overall number and destination of migrants were left to the states. Though there was a great deal of similarity among state policies—a preference for Europeans, attempts to limit the migration of the destitute and unhealthy, and a national political movement to oppose Irish and more generally Catholic immigration—Congress and the federal courts took a generally secondary role in these questions. To the extent that budgetary or legal matters drew them into the immigration policy arena, national political institutions deferred to the prevailing practices of the states. On the whole, this arrangement was well adapted to a situation in which national political identity was rudimentary and the issue of slavery and with it citizenship needed to be kept off the national agenda. Immigration policy served to reinforce the dominant Anglo-European and decentralized perception of the American political community.

The emergence of a national immigration policy was possible only after the Fourteenth Amendment created a national definition of citizenship. In the 1870s, Congress passed the first act regulating immigration, and its power to do so was upheld by the Supreme Court in the 1880s and 1890s. But this was more than a question of the structure of federalism. By the 1870s, immigration was already emerging as a national policy issue, and the central problem was its role in changing the ethnic composition of American society. The pressure to close off immigration began on the West Coast in response to an influx of Chinese and Japanese migrants after the Civil War. For its critics, this migration threatened to undermine the cultural and racial coherence of the American polity by introducing peoples believed to be unassimilable to American values and practices. This movement was extremely successful. By the early 1900s, a series of legal regulations and diplomatic agreements had effectively shut off the flow of Asian migration to the United States.

This was only the first step in the growth of the nativist movement, however. By the 1890s, attention turned to the massive inflow of migrants from eastern and southern Europe. For the restrictionists, these populations were equally threatening to the preferred ethnic composition of the United States. As Higham and others have shown, it was widely believed in the American middle and upper classes that these new immigrants could not be assimilated to democratic political and cultural norms and were likely to bring either political radicalism or corruption into the center of American political life. By the early twentieth century, these concerns were bolstered by the growing popularity of racial theories of intelligence and cultural maturity. For many, these provided the historical and scientific confirmation of the existing fear of the new migrants.

For a long period, however, this restrictionist impulse was successfully countered by a powerful pro-immigration coalition. A central element in this coalition consisted of representatives of the new corporate industrial economy, for whom a steady flow of immigration signaled a check on pressures for rising wages and unionization. Alongside this element were the inner-city political machines of the time, primarily Democratic, which drew their support from the immigrant community and saw the continued flow of migrants as a source of increased political power. Finally, an important element of the Progressive cultural and intellectual elite embraced immigration as a means of renewing American power and purpose while promoting an intensive program of assimilation to ensure the immigrants' rapid integration into prevailing political and cultural norms.

The coalition was able to hold off the restrictionists until the 1920s. During this period Congress did gradually tighten restrictions, especially those designed to prevent the entry of political radicals, but immigration rates remained high until World War I. The war and its aftermath, however, changed the balance of power in immigration politics. As the war ended, a widespread "Red scare" led to a rebirth and intensification of nativism while giving further impetus to pseudo-scientific theories of racial hierarchy and a widespread interest in eugenics. By the mid-1920s, Congress responded with a radically new framework for immigration policy. The new system, embodied in the 1921 Quota Law and the 1924 Immigration Act, combined strict limits on the overall numbers of immigrants with a "national origins" quota system heavily biased toward migrants from northern and western Europe. This regime, which remained essentially in place until the 1960s, effectively stemmed the tide of immigration and marked the longest period of closed borders in American history. With the exception of refugees from Communist expansion during the Cold War, immigration was reduced to a trickle during these decades, and the percentage of Americans of foreign birth declined steadily over the middle of the century.

As it turned out, this restrictionist regime fit well with the creation of the new compact between government, corporations, and citizens that emerged during the 1930s and 1940s. Behind the now highly protected borders of the polity, the immigrants of the past six decades could be gradually assimilated into the national community, a process facilitated by their incorporation into the polity during the Roosevelt administrations. This stabilization of the boundaries of the community in turn made it much easier to forge the new set of expectations, responsibilities, and privileges attached to American citizenship in the post-1945 era.[12] Indeed, in retrospect we can see a "bargain" being struck, in which the immigrant communities would accept full immersion into the national community in return for a new set of commitments from its political and economic institutions to provide guarantees of economic security and opportunity.

Nevertheless, this remained a community with a clear ethnic-cultural identity. As Michael Lind has argued, the New Deal redefinition of the polity retained the sense of the United States as a national community with clearly European roots. The earlier emphasis on distinctions among Europeans was dropped as all persons of European origin were incorporated into the emerging category of "white" persons, but this remained the defining character of American identity for most citizens. In the aftermath of the Second World War, however, this understanding became an increasing source of tension, for reasons of both foreign policy and domestic stability. How could a country claiming to protect liberty for all retain laws of immigration and citizenship that defined those of African, Asian, and Hispanic descent as second-class citizens or even ineligible for citizenship? In the 1950s, immigration laws began to change, albeit slowly, under these pressures. The long-standing ban on Chinese naturalization, dating from 1882, was lifted in 1943, and the 1952 McCarren-Walters Act created new exceptions to the ethnic quota system. But the real push for change came in response to the Civil Rights movement and the emerging U.S.–Soviet competition for the loyalty of the newly independent states of the Third World. Under these pressures, policymakers in the early 1960s came to accept the fact the United States could no longer afford to officially designate itself a polity open only to those of European background. Once again, the demands of global leadership pushed policymakers to begin the process of opening the borders of the polity to a changing international environment.

The result was the Immigration Act of 1965, which revolutionized the immigration policy regime in the United States. This legislation eliminated the system of ethnic quotas, replacing them with overall immigration limits for persons from the Eastern and Western Hemispheres, and established a limit for the number of immigrants from any one country. Within these limitations, the new regime was based on a set of preferences or criteria to choose among applicants for legal immigration. These preferences favored the aim of family reunification, and secondarily emphasized the need to attract workers with skills that were in short supply in the United States. Although the law did establish the first specific limitations on immigration from Latin America, the overall emphasis was to raise the level of legal immigration and put an end to preferences for those of particular ethnic or racial backgrounds. By all accounts, the primary motive behind the change was symbolic: it would complete the legal revolution embodied in the 1964 Civil Rights Act and 1965 Voting Rights Acts and end a source of embarrassment for U.S. foreign policy. Few expected that it would have any substantial practical impact on the nature or politics of immigration in the United States.

Immigration Policy and the Politics of Global Immersion

Subsequent history shows how misguided these expectations turned out to be. Immigration policy was transformed just as a new wave of global migration began to reshape the distribution of the world's population. This time, it was not Europeans but persons from the economically backward and/or formerly colonized states who began to look for a refuge and opportunity and who turned to the United States, as their predecessors in the nineteenth and twentieth centuries had done. As American policy became more active in these areas of the world, it helped stimulate the desire of the inhabitants to migrate to the United States and created some of the networks vital to sustaining such a movement. The new shape of U.S.

policy presented a new opportunity and set the basis for a new wave of Asian and Latin American immigration into American society.

By now scholars have come to recognize that the growth of migration around the world has been the result of a number of forces, many mutually reinforcing ones.[13] On the one hand, there are the factors pushing migrants from around the world to leave their homes to resettle in the more developed parts of the world economy. It is clear, for instance, that the process of creating independent states in formerly colonized areas helped to touch off the latest period of human migration. The violence, warfare, instability, and repression characteristic of the creation of new states in Africa and Asia led to the displacements of large groups of persons, many of whom decided that their chances at a better life would be best served by migrating to more prosperous states, usually to the former colonial power in their place of origin. Though these kinds of conflict have continued over the decades, the growing economic chaos, inequality, and lack of opportunity in the Third World since the 1970s have provided added impetus. Even in relatively stable societies, the combination of growing populations and limited economic growth has been a continuous factor leading many to emigrate, and these pressures were deeply compounded by the global recession of the early to mid-1980s. Finally, this migration was further facilitated by the growth of multinational investment in many parts of the underdeveloped world. The linkage between home country and the place of investment created by multinational corporations created natural chains of population movements in the same directions.[14]

On the other hand, from the late 1960s onward these forces were complemented by many factors pulling migrants toward more prosperous states, especially the United States. For one thing, the gradual establishment of economic and political linkages described above led to the emergence of informal family and regional networks joining already settled migrants with potential ones. Migration would become a much easier and more attractive option when there were already established support networks to help with the trip itself and the settlement process once a migrant arrived. Second, by the 1970s prosperity and changing patterns of economic organization had created a growing demand for cheap, unskilled labor in the increasingly affluent states of the West, particularly the United States. As low-skilled jobs proliferated and unions lost much influence over the next two decades, the American economy would be generating great numbers of jobs for which migrants, even illegal ones, were the most attractive labor force. The more employers came to depend on immigrant labor, the more they became involved in actively recruiting such labor, often working in tandem with family or ethnically based networks. Finally, as I will discuss in more detail, various developments in law and social policy in the 1960s and 1970s created an environment much more favorable for migrants to the West than any that had existed since the era before World War I. By the late 1970s, then, the new wave of migration had established a significant presence throughout the advanced capitalist world, including the United States, and the only real issue would be the policy response to this changed context.

It took time before policymakers in the United States realized what was happening, but by the mid-1970s they had recognized that American society was entering a new era as a recipient of immigrants, and these were coming from areas from which immigration had previously been restricted. As figure 5-1 shows, legal immigration has reached absolute levels unparalleled since the 1920s. The most impressive aspect of American policy in this period has been its clear acceptance and indeed encouragement of this new wave of immigration. From the mid-1970s onward, the overall limits placed on non-preference-based legal immigration were steadily increased, reaching the level of 675,000 in the 1990 Immigration Act. Moreover, the provision for unlimited migration of immediate family members has turned into a key vehicle for further migration, and no serious attempt to change this policy has come close to success. Rather, three key pieces of legislation over this era worked to deepen the U.S. commitment to maintaining a steady influx of immigrants.[15]

First, the 1980 Refugee Act replaced a very haphazard system of ad hoc exceptions to the overall immigration totals with a more systematized U.S. policy toward refugees, creating a new and expanded category for further legal entry into the country. This act brought U.S. policy in line with evolving international standards on the treatment of refugees and asylum seekers, which meant among other things the creation of new legal protection for those claiming refugee or asylum status in the United States.

Second, the Immigration Reform and Control Act (IRCA) of 1986 worked in unexpected ways to solidify the commitment to continued immigration. Although the act was directed at curbing illegal immigration, the great emphasis on the legal/illegal division during the debates over the legislation worked to further

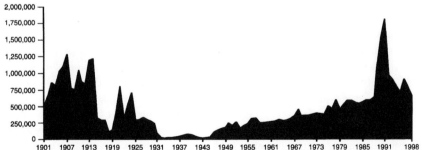

Figure 5-1. Legal Immigration to the United States, Fiscal Years 1901–1998. *Source: Fiscal Year 1998 Annual Report*, Office of Policy and Planning Statistics Branch, Immigration and Naturalization Service, May 1999, p. 1.

protect the status of legal immigrants. Moreover, key provisions of the act, such as the amnesty for illegal migrants who had been residing in the United States for seven years and the creation of a new program for temporary migration of agricultural workers, promised to further increase the presence of immigrants in American society. Finally, the 1990 Immigration Act reorganized and systematized the policy regime for legal immigration and reaffirmed the goal of high and regular levels of legal immigration from all over the globe. Two aspects of this legislation stand out. First, the rearrangement of the immigrant preference system to put more emphasis on the entry of highly skilled workers, at the expense of family reunification, indicated the growing acceptance of the notion that immigration was a fundamental element of the emerging American economic order. Second, the fact that such a major piece of legislation was debated and passed without any significant public controversy indicated how widely this view was accepted by American political elites. As America's economy was being pushed into deeper immersion in the global economy, then, U.S. policymakers created a regime for immigration aimed at making the movement of persons as flexible as possible, helping to accommodate a regime based on the continued movement of capital and goods across national borders.

The impact on American society has been striking. Despite much popular wisdom, the large majority of immigrants to the United States since the late 1960s have come through the legal channels established under this policy regime. Today, the percentage of Americans who are foreign-born is approaching levels not seen since the beginning of the century. The overwhelming majority of the migrants have origins in Asia, Latin America, and the Caribbean. Though there remains a steady flow of migrants from Europe, now sustained by the "diversity" category established in 1990, it is dominated by source countries that had never been central to American immigration.[16] For the first time in our history, the standard claim that immigration has made American society the most diverse in the world is close to truth. This pattern would not have been possible without the transformation of the policy regime brought about by the 1965 Immigration Act and its successors. To be sure, the global rise in human migration is a necessary prerequisite to these changes, but it has only been in combination with the new policy regime that American society itself has been transformed.

I have suggested that this direction in immigration policy is linked to American society's greater immersion in the global environment, a direction sustained for three decades at the national level. What are the main elements of this connection? First, it is clear that the impetus behind the elimination of the national origin quota system was a desire to eliminate a blemish frustrating the increasingly active pursuit of American foreign policy goals in the new states emerging from colonization. This exercise of U.S. power in turn stimulated new flows of migrants, especially from Southeast Asia, Central America, and the Caribbean (see table 5-1). Although shaped by Cold War concerns, American policy was adapted in the

Table 5-1. Percentage of Immigrants Admitted to the United States by Region and Period, Fiscal Years 1955–97.

Region	1955–64	1965–74	1975–84	1985–94	1995–97
All regions	100.0	100.0	100.0	100.0	100.0
Europe	50.2	29.8	13.4	11.0	16.2
Asia	7.7	22.4	43.3	32.2	34.6
Africa	.7	1.5	2.4	2.6	5.9
Oceania	.4	.7	.8	.5	.6
North America	35.9	39.6	33.6	48.0	36.1
Caribbean	7.0	18.0	15.1	11.0	13.1
Central America	2.4	2.5	3.7	6.6	4.9
Other North America	26.4	19.0	14.8	30.5	18.1
South America	5.1	6.0	6.6	5.7	6.6

Source: Immigration and Naturalization Service, *1997 Statistical Yearbook*, p. 20.

1970s and 1980s in light of the evolution of foreign policy aims, especially in its willingness to accept more refugees from political conflicts in Southeast Asia and Central America. In the past decade, as the extension of the global market economy has become more central to U.S. policy, immigration policy has again been adapted to new ends. The shift in the preferences system to place more emphasis on attracting workers with the advanced skills and investors with the capital necessary to a growing economy—a key part of the 1990 Immigration Act—reflects the new emphasis on ensuring American competitiveness in this expanding global economy. In effect, as policy priorities shifted from ideological conflict to economic growth and human rights, immigration policy was adjusted to fit new rationales for the active presence of American power around the globe.

The policy regime governing immigration has also responded to globalization in other ways as well. The most important concerns the legal framework under which migrants and residents are treated. The 1980 Refugee Act, with subsequent amendments, was itself partly an attempt to bring U.S. law into line with emerging norms in international law. But, as David Jacobson has argued, a variety of other developments reflected the slow but steady impact of international norms on the American judicial system. In areas such as the treatment of applicants for asylum, the standards of due process in the consideration of deportation actions, and the legal standing of aliens and residents, American law and practice in the 1970s and 1980s reflected an attempt by those acting in the field to incorporate more liberal global norms into domestic administrative practice. There is no doubt that the United States has proceeded more slowly in this area than some other countries have, but it remains clear that active participation in promoting a more globalized world has reshaped the American policy regime.[17]

Another factor that shaped the impact of this wave of immigration was the expanded framework of social policy provisions dating from the Great Society of the 1960s. Of course, these policies were not designed with immigration in mind, but constitutional precedent and emerging legal doctrines expanded these new social policy benefits to all legal residents of the United States, not just citizens. As a result, immigrants entered into a context in which there existed a whole range of publicly provided guarantees against insecurity that did not exist during earlier waves of immigration. But it was not only legal immigrants that could take advantage of such provisions. In the 1982 *Plyer v. Doe* decision (457 U.S. 202), the Supreme Court ruled that states could not deny children of illegal immigrants access to the public education system. Moreover, undocumented migrants were in fact taking advantage of other kinds of public provisions, especially emergency medical care. In effect, as DeSipio and de la Garza point out, by the 1980s the United States had allowed the established set of social policies to substitute for any clear and specific policy regime directed at migrant settlement and adjustment to the new society.[18] The implications of this would be significant, since it effectively implicated immigration policy in the increasing controversy over redistributive policies during the 1980s and 1990s. From the perspectives of the critics of such policies, the benefits available to migrants were a large part of a perceived unjust transfer of resources from the deserving to the undeserving. Immigration and immigrant policy thus proved a lightning rod for critics of redistributive policy and at the same time worked to weaken the long-standing distinction between legal and illegal migrants in the debate over immigration in American society.

Assessing the Impact of Immigration Policy

Where does this leave us? By the mid-1990s American life had been transformed by a two-decade-long flow of immigration, one that promised to continue indefinitely into the future. The United States was the preferred destination for the millions who were on the move around the world, but the impact of this migration was not inevitable. Crucial policy changes begun in the 1960s determined the specific contours of this impact and shaped the way in which immigration entered the realm of political conflict. What were the main features of immigration policy and politics? First, policy choices ensured that American society would be one of the more open destinations for migrants and that the flow of legal immigrants would continue at a relatively high rate. While other advanced industrial states tightened restrictions on migration, U.S. policy preserved a relatively accommodating stance. The emphasis on family reunification, the growing openness to refugees and asylum seekers, and the relatively generous framework of social provision all worked to ensure that immigration would remain a part of the landscape of American society. Moreover, during this period Congress steadily increased the levels of allowable immigration, moving gradually in the direction of greater preferences for migrants with skills and resources needed in a competitive economy. These choices signaled a commitment to using a relatively open immigration policy to facilitate the immersion of America's economy and society in a larger global marketplace.

Indeed, it can even be argued that this policy was applied to illegal immigration as well.[19] It is true, as we have seen, that the United States began efforts to effectively control the flow of illegal migrants in the mid-1980s. These included much tighter measures of border control, bolstering the Border Patrol, and requiring that all workers certify their legal status to employers. Though these measures did help to curb the growth of illegal migration, their effects were limited by two other developments. First, the American economy over this period came to depend much more on low-wage labor in a variety of sectors, from nonunion manufacturing to agriculture to the personal services industry. In all these areas, employers continued to employ illegal migrants, and sophisticated networks emerged to supply these industries from various areas of the world. Second, a powerful coalition of businesses, civil libertarians, and ethnic group organizations succeeded in preventing the adoption of effective employer sanctions for the use of illegal migrants, a policy most experts agreed would be the only effective way of limiting this practice. Though stated policy goals and political rhetoric aimed for greater control, the actual "on the ground" policy regime worked to ensure that illegal migration would continue to be a steady factor in American labor markets. As Peter Andreas notes, regarding the growth in policing of the U.S.-Mexico border:

> At the same time, the policy focus on the border has drawn attention away from confronting a long-established and deeply-entrenched cross-border labor market that is an integral (even if clandestine) dimension of U.S.-Mexican interdependence. As the United States and Mexico have grown closer together in recent years, there has been an increasingly sharp tension between the push to open the border and liberalize markets and the push to close the border to immigrant labor.[20]

In this situation, Andreas emphasizes, increased efforts at border control reshape the direction of migration but not its overall volume. "Border control" policies satisfy political pressures for a show of efforts to limit illegal crossing without actually striking at the roots of the movement of migrants and thus without significantly affecting the practice.[21]

A second crucial element of the contemporary environment of immigration is the racial and ethnic composition of the migrant population. As we have seen, the overwhelming majority of legal and illegal migrants since the early 1970s have arrived from Latin America, Asia, and the Caribbean. For the first time in American history, large numbers of non-Europeans were voluntarily and legally entering the United States. To be sure, this reflected the overall population moving around the globe during this period. But it was by no means guaranteed that such migrants would be welcomed into the United States. Policy choices established and reinforced since 1965 have been central in shaping the characteristics of immigration into the country. By eliminating ethnic origin quotas, promoting family reunification, and establishing a separate refugee regime, these policies regulated the overall flow but worked with rather than against the composition of the immigrant community. Moreover, this policy direction was supported by a powerful coalition of forces committed to preserving a steady flow of migrants for reasons of interest, principle, or both.

The lesson of this policy record is clear. The increased movement of persons, like that of goods and capital, is a central fact of the process of globalization in the contemporary world. But the ways in which these movements have affected the United States have been mediated by the policy regime and choices of the state. Global processes of change dictated increased pressures to enter the United States, but the outcome of these pressures can be explained only on the basis of choices and constraints created by policy choices. To be sure, the initial policy choices were not made with these ends in mind; however, they were necessary to the outcomes we have seen, and policymakers remained committed to the resulting policy regime even when its impact became clear. Indeed, the policy record of the 1980s and 1990s suggests that U.S. policy embodied a clear commitment to continue this process of domestic transformation. As in the case of trade policy, policy choices over this period seemed to point inevitably toward a commitment to more deeply engage the American economy, society, and polity in the currents reshaping the globe.

Interlude: Globalization, Immigration, and Sovereignty

An emerging scholarly literature on migration, immigration, and globalization helps to clarify the relationship between globalization and immigration. As in the case of trade, much of the work in the area of immigration explores the question of sovereignty and the continuing relevance of the state in the face of the pressures of global migration. For some scholars, the combination of the new waves of migration and changing global norms of human rights has indeed posed a serious challenge to the continued ability of states to control the movement of persons across their borders. This challenge has come in two areas. First, as Saskia Sassen emphasizes, the evolution of the global economy has led to the emergence of new, nonpublic mechanisms for the organization and promotion of labor migration from underdeveloped to advanced societies. In particular, multinational corporations and the networks they have created have come to be dependent on the movement of labor across national boundaries, and corporations have in turn become key agents promoting this movement. Moreover, family, regional, and ethnic-based networks have emerged to facilitate the continued flow of migrants and their settlement in established immigrant communities. Often working together, these two forces have organized labor migration in the global migration outside the control or supervision of sovereign states.[22]

Second, the ability of states to respond effectively to this challenge has been hindered by the emergence of a global regime of human rights protections for migrants, refugees, and asylum seekers.[23] The common aim of this regime, increasingly promoted by a growing network of organized interests, is to limit the ability of states to act unilaterally in their dealings with migrants and to discriminate in favor of citizens in policy choices and legal protections. In some of the more ambitious presentations of this argument, such as those by David Jacobson and Yasemin Soysal, these evolving legal practices threaten to undermine the future relevance of the status of citizenship and to break the link between the borders of states and the boundaries of political communities, rights, and obligations.[24] Sassen is not ready to go as far in describing the existing situation, but her work does contend that these kinds of challenges are indeed posing real difficulties for states as they attempt to preserve their role in determining the nature of their boundaries.

Other scholars have offered important criticisms of these arguments. Their arguments are of two kinds. First, while recognizing many of the legal and practical constraints facing states that are recipients of large-scale migration, such as the United States, they contend that these constraints are essentially domestic in nature, not creatures of the operation of global forces. As Christian Joppke and James Hollifield have argued, the legal constraints on the treatment of migrants in Western Europe and North America are primarily the result of the liberal norms of individual rights and equality of treatment that have become deeply embedded in the legal and policy regimes of these states.[25] International norms and agreements are of a clearly secondary importance in explaining these norms or the force of their constraints on the actions of the state. The same can be said for the difficulties such states face in controlling the labor market activities of corporations; the basic legal and policy framework of a liberal capitalist economy works against the ability and willingness of these states to interfere too deeply with the employment activities of most firms. Finally, the pluralist nature of politics in these states contributes to the other major political constraints on immigration policy, the emerging influence of ethnically based political organizations and human rights interest groups. As Jeannette Money has emphasized, the more entrenched immigrant communities become in particular regions of a country, the more effective they become at playing the game of pluralist politics to defend the interests of immigrants.[26] The combination of such forces certainly constrains a state's freedom in policymaking, but these are the same kinds of political constraints that are found throughout liberal democratic systems.

These arguments take on special significance in United States immigration policy. As even Jacobson admits, much of the transformation of the legal protections for migrants in the United States was a product of the spread of "liberal" norms and practices throughout the polity in the 1960s and 1970s, and these norms are clearly rooted in the U.S. Constitution and its more liberal interpretations. In particular, "alienage" became an increasingly "suspect" legal classification during this era primarily as a result of the attempts to expand the Fourteenth Amendment's guarantee of equality before the law; as long established practices in the areas of race and gender were challenged, activists turned to other kinds of discrimination with an increasingly critical eye. In the same vein, there is no doubt that increasing protections for refugees and the conflicts over their application were driven by controversies closely linked to the dynamics of domestic politics. As I will emphasize in the next section, the same can be said about conflicts in the 1990s over the access of migrants to the variety of social provisions that are a legacy of the redistributive programs of the 1960s. It is especially clear in the case of the United States that the emergence of a more accommodating legal and political environment for migrants cannot be considered primarily or simply a response to a more globalized political context.

Second, scholars also note that, despite such constraints, states have remained quite effective in setting the terms of the movement of persons across their borders. While the United States, for instance, has remained relatively open to further immigration, during the 1990s many European states successfully reduced the flow of migrants across their borders. This was accomplished by a combination of more forceful unilateral actions and the formation of a relatively effective EU-based regime for controlling immigration, which emerged out of the Schengen Accords of 1995.[27] To be sure, these efforts have not been totally effective, and the turn to multi-lateral enforcement mechanisms may indeed reinforce the argument that contemporary migration is forcing fundamental changes in the ways states must operate in order to control the movement of persons across their borders and is thus forcing real changes in the politics of migration.[28] But the overall lesson seems clear: states retain much of their sovereign authority and practical capacities to control the movement of persons across their borders. If they choose not to exercise them, it is primarily because of legal, political, economic, and cultural factors shaped by the domestic evolution of these states, not because of any disappearance of sovereignty.

These criticisms, however, do not exhaust the relevance of the arguments presented by Sassen and others concerning the way immigration policy plays into the politics of globalization. As Sassen points out, even if the growth of immigration in contemporary states has been driven as much by political choice as by economic necessity, this movement does challenge long-held notions about the proper role of the state in maintaining the borders and boundaries of the political community.

> Immigrants and refugees bring to the fore the tension between the protection of human rights and the protection of state sovereignty. This tension is particularly sharp in the case of undocumented immigrants, because their mere existence signifies an erosion of sovereignty. At least in part the tension originates in the state itself, in the conflict between its authority to control ingress and its obligation to protect those in its territory.[29]

The result is that immigration becomes a crucial arena in the political conflict over the changing role of the territorial borders of the state. While advocates of increased globalization attempt to open flows across this border, opponents focus on immigration control as a key mechanism for promoting the "renationalizing" of the state, in Sassen's phrase. And, indeed, this has been exactly the case in recent European and American politics; the entry of large numbers of seemingly "unwanted" migrants becomes a central test case for the longer-term viability of globalization.

Now, as Peter Andreas has noted, immigration also provides a means by which supporters of global integration can promote their goals.[30] By placing great emphasis on a symbolic commitment to control illegal migration, supporters can go a great distance toward deflecting the larger resistance to globalization, and Andreas makes a persuasive case that this explains much of the recent politics of "border control" in the United States. In the next section, we will examine the limitations of this strategy. But the larger point being raised here brings us back to one of the book's central arguments about globalization. In the political struggle over immigration, we can see the way in which globalization makes the boundaries and borders of the state a central question of political conflict within the contemporary state. Global change reshapes the contours of domestic political conflict as it transforms the nature of domestic society, making domestic politics into an arena in which political actors and coalitions struggle over the future of the state's relationship to the global arena and the shape of that arena itself.

The "Worth of Citizenship" and the Backlash against Immigration

As growing numbers of immigrants brought new economic and cultural vitality to the United States, however, their presence seemed to raise new questions about the meaning of American citizenship. In an earlier chapter, I argued that the post-World War II bargain in the United States was based on policies that provided unique benefits and guarantees for American citizens. The restrictive immigration policy regime of the middle of this century played an important role in the success of this bargain and symbolized the state's commitment to the security and prosperity of its citizens. For many Americans, the increasingly open policy regime since the 1960s, combined with the range of new social benefits available to migrants, seemed to embody a change in the state's role and commitments. By the mid-1990s, these perceptions fueled the most powerful challenge to date against post-1965 U.S. immigration policy.

In a series of essays, Peter Schuck has coined the phrase "the declining worth of citizenship" to capture the changes in the role of the state as it relates to immigration policy.[31] The essential idea is that by the 1980s, there was little practical difference between the rights, privileges, and responsibilities of native-born or naturalized citizens and those of legally resident noncitizens. With the exception of the right to vote, legal residents enjoyed the same set of constitutional protections, social benefits, and legal obligations as citizens. In particular, the variety of social benefits available to residents—from education to health care to security against poverty—stood out in public perceptions. Instituted during the Great Society era, these programs seemed to provide a variety of benefits to new arrivals who had not necessarily made any significant contribution to the community and certainly did not have the historically grounded loyalties assumed in the case of citizens. As Schuck put it,

> I contend that the distinctive meaning of American citizenship, as revealed by the distinctive rights and obligations it entails, has been transformed in recent decades by a public philosophy that is steadily expanding the equality and due process principles in pursuit of liberal values. These changes have reduced almost to the vanishing point the marginal value of citizenship as compared to resident alien status. These changes have not only minimized the alien's incentive to naturalize; they have also altered the social significance of citizenship.[32]

The declining worth of citizenship can also be seen in another, more deeply seated and symbolic sense. For Americans who believed that the state was abandoning commitments to economic security, the encouragement and facilitation of high levels of immigration could easily be understood as part of a larger attack on the priority their interests should have in the making of public policy. Initially, these concerns focused on the threat posed by illegal migrants to the wages and tax burdens of American workers. The demand that the United States regain "control of its borders" embodied a call for the state to fulfill its obligations to protect the interests of its citizens. But the evolution of the issue and the continued flow of migrants led many to generalize their protest to the structure of legal immigration as well. From this perspective, government's encouragement of migrants combined with its refusal to protect citizens against the threats posed by freer trade came to appear as part of a larger abandonment of the interests and needs of citizens. Closing American borders to global movements would be the only effective means of retethering the state to the national community and thus reestablishing the national and symbolic distinctiveness of citizenship.[33]

The political environment of the early to mid-1990s proved especially propitious for the restrictionist movement. In the controversy over NAFTA, figures such as Ross Perot and Pat Buchanan effectively linked the deepening of regional economic integration with a continued uncontrolled growth of immigration. At the height of this controversy, Peter Birmelow's *Alien Nation* became an unexpected national best-seller.[34] Brimelow's book presented the most radical and powerful case for an end to immigration in recent decades, claiming that immigration was threatening the economic, cultural, and racial composition of American society. Its popularity indicated the depth of the growing opposition to immigration. In this context, control of Congress shifted to the Republican Party in the 1994 midterm elections. The new Republican majority included a significant number of sympathizers with the restrictionist agenda. While some were willing to reconsider the whole direction of immigration policy, many more aimed their criticism at redistributive policies that produced the programs from which migrants had benefited. In their general desire to further shrink the whole welfare state, these politicians were open to measures aimed at prohibiting the "undeserving" from access to public provisions.

It is thus not coincidental that the new Congress worked simultaneously to reform the welfare system and redesign immigration and naturalization law.[35] In the initial maneuvering over the latter, restrictionists such as Representative Lamar Smith attempted to raise the general issue of legal immigration levels as well as the questions of social provisions, legal procedures for reviewing asylum claims pursuing deportation, and illegal immigration. Though unexpectedly powerful, the attempt to reconsider overall immigration policy failed in the face of the continued strength of the pro-immigration coalition, especially the business community. But the most impressive outcome of these legislative efforts was a set of legal and policy changes that marked the greatest inroads for the restrictionist approach since the 1960s. In the 1996 Immigration and Welfare Reform Acts, Congress took the first major steps to reverse the "devaluation" of citizenship.

The major provisions of these two laws fall into two broad categories.[36] First, a whole variety of social benefits will now be denied to both legally resident aliens and recently naturalized citizens. This includes the new forms of assistance that replace Aid to Families with Dependent Children (AFDC), the Supplemental Security Income program, and the Food Stamp program. From the perspective of immigration policy, the message behind these changes is clear. The fundamental guarantees against economic insecurity provided by the state ought to belong only to native-born citizens, and the operation of these programs ought to work to distinguish and affirm the privileges of citizens. Second, the Immigration Act contains a number of provisions narrowing the grounds upon which migrants can claim asylum or refugee status and granting the Immigration and Naturalization

Service (INS) and the Justice Department greater flexibility and autonomy in moving to deport illegal residents. A central provision, ratified by the Supreme Court in February 1999, significantly reduces the jurisdiction of federal courts over appeals of INS deportation rulings.[37] This is accompanied by provisions to weaken the variety of due process and habeas corpus protections that had been made available to even illegal residents over the past two decades. The message of these reforms seems to parallel those concerning social services: the highest level of constitutional protections should apply only to full citizens of the polity, as they are properly understood as part of the "compact" of American citizenship, and not to all persons coming under the sphere of American power and law.[38]

For the moment, conflict over immigration policy may be muted, as the U.S. economy prospers and the 1996 legislation is reviewed in Congress, implemented in the states, and litigated in the courts. As we have seen, periods of economic well-being tend to diminish the audience for criticisms of immigration, and this seems to be the case in the late 1990s. Moreover, pro-immigration sentiment is deeply embedded in American politics and law, in ways that may in fact produce significant modification to the 1996 reforms. But we cannot forget that the late 1980s, too, was a period of prosperity in which many observers predicted the demise of any widespread anti-immigration movement. As long as American society is placed in more intensive contact with the changing global context, and many Americans come to see their security and their vision of the meaning of citizenship threatened, immigration policy will emerge as a decisive arena in which to battle over the nature and purposes of the American political community.

Conclusions: Immigration, Citizenship, and Globalization

The politics of immigration, like the politics of trade, is essentially the politics of citizenship. Contests over border control and public services are battlefields in which competing conceptions of the proper relationship of the state and society are fought out. On the one side is a program that emphasizes the need to minimize the distinction between American citizens and noncitizens as part of a recognition and promotion of the greater immersion of American society into global society. From this perspective, all residents of the territory of the United States should have the same legal and social opportunities, and borders should remain relatively open to further migration. However the rights of residents are defined, the state should minimize any attempt to distinguish between citizens and noncitizens.[39]

It is precisely this distinction that opponents of current immigration policies want to reassert and that they have had some recent success in promoting in American law and social policy. In this perspective, citizenship creates a relationship between government and the citizen that goes beyond the basics of holding a passport and enjoying protection from foreign military attack. Citizenship creates an obligation on the part of the state to secure the conditions for real economic and social security in the face of economic change, including changes connected to global economic activity. Moreover, this obligation must be clearly limited to those who are full citizens and, for some critics, only native-born citizens; only such persons can be considered to have made the kind of commitment to the polity or nation that can be the basis of such an obligation. In the view of these activists, the trend toward weakening the boundary between citizens and noncitizens is a violation of the state's primary obligations, a violation that parallels the state's unwillingness to counteract the upheavals of global economic integration.

As in the area of trade politics and policy, it is this reconstitution of the relationship of state and citizen that is central to the emergence of a politics of sovereignty. As more immigrants enter the United States and are granted eligibility for a variety of benefits and legal protections, and as native-born citizens see less and less protection from economic insecurity, it becomes easy to suggest that somehow American sovereignty over their lives is being eroded. Too often, critics of this response dismiss it as a misreading of the continuing powers of government over migration (and trade, for that matter). This is true but misses the point. Today, demands for sovereignty and border control reflect a sense that the sovereignty of "the people" is waning as government ignores their interests. The criticism of globalization is a demand for a recommitment of the state to the priority of the needs of its "own" citizens. As global changes have deeper impacts on American life and generate more insecurity, they fuel the demand for sovereignty.

But the concern for citizenship is not only one of rights and obligations. As the conflicts over immigration make clear, citizenship and sovereignty are also matters that evoke powerful symbolic and cultural meanings. Because citizenship is a question of status, meaning, and identity, it is common for citizens in the modern state to expect government to ratify the values and purposes that tie the community together. Usually, this is closely tied to an affirmation of the worth of citizens themselves. Policy choices that distribute wealth and rights in ways that privilege citizens are part of this process; their material consequences carry larger symbolic meanings. Among immigration restrictionists, these connections are clearly perceived and unambiguously interpreted. For these citizens, policies that seem to minimize the distinctive value of citizens—whether the substantive issue is social benefits or legal protections—are understood to embody a disregard for the interests and purposes shared by those citizens. In this view, there is little a state could do that would amount to a more egregious violation of its obligations.

These kinds of considerations emerged in the analysis of anti-free-trade rhetoric but are even more prominent in immigration politics. Here the consequences of policy choices are actual persons and communities rather than foreign goods or abstract statistics. We now come to a potentially sensitive but important element of the restrictionist movement. For the right wing of this movement, ranging from Brimelow to Buchanan, talk about the sovereignty of Americans inevitably leads to a conception of the polity as properly based on persons of European ethnic, racial, and cultural backgrounds. The "people" whose sovereignty they would restore is not equivalent to all the current citizens of the United States. It is rather the citizenry as they perceive it used to be and ought to be—white and of European descent. In a curious parallel to the operation of globalization, even its opposition comes to accept some sort of disengagement between the state and the persons within its territory. Despite their rhetoric, the "nation" whose identity such writers want to promote is no longer equivalent to the community of persons existing within the borders of the state.

The pattern of immigration since 1965 has proved an effective focus for these kinds of restrictionist sentiments. Since the overwhelming majority of immigrants have been from nonwhite and non-European backgrounds, the impact has been to transform many of the ethnocultural assumptions and images that dominated the closed polity built in the 1930s and 1940s. At best, these kinds of concerns lead to a focus on the real problems of adjustment and assimilation posed by the new migrants. At the worst, they produce a revived nativism in which the American polity is defined as including only those of certain ascriptive characteristics. In this formulation, an image of popular sovereignty is mobilized to support a political program of exclusion, one that would use the tools of domestic policy to reproduce the results that earlier immigration policies secured.

The battlefields on which this conflict is fought are those of culture, language, and education, and this brings us to our final dimension of the politics of globalization. As American life becomes more intertwined with global trends, American culture is increasingly shaped by global patterns of culture. These are transmitted by information technology, represented by the goods that flow across borders, and embodied in those migrants who settle in our communities. To get a more encompassing view of how global change is reshaping American politics, the next chapter will examine the emergence of a politics of language in the United States.

6 ∽

E Pluribus Unum? The Politics of Official English and Bilingual Education

Trade and immigration are familiar topics for political scientists and policy analysts. Both have been persistent themes in American political life, and they have been the subject of some important works in the discipline. As a result, political scientists have been generally confident that many of the discipline's key theories and concepts can be used to provide a coherent understanding of the political conflict surrounding these issues. I have suggested, however, that this confidence is misplaced. My alternative accounts of the evolution of the politics of trade and immigration have emphasized the need for analysts to take seriously the process of globalization as a force reshaping the reactions of key segments of the American public to the actions and choices of the state. Not only does the impact of globalization show the limits of standard approaches to the politics of policymaking, but it also requires political scientists to think again about such fundamental concepts as sovereignty, citizenship, the state, and the nation. Attempts to analyze contemporary political conflict in the United States that do not integrate the role of global change remain limited and unsatisfactory.

In the process of developing this account, I have moved from a policy area in which the distribution of material benefits and opportunities is central to political conflict (trade) to one where questions of distribution and redistribution are closely linked to conflicts over the national identity (immigration). I have taken this approach to show in some detail how globalization is challenging the basic elements of modern political identity and membership at their roots. At this point, we have already seen some of the close links between conflicts over the material benefits and costs of policy choices and conflicts over the values and purposes of the political community. It is not accidental, for instance, that the issues of trade and immigration were closely linked in the early 1990s, especially by the opponents of NAFTA. The opening of the borders to more trade and more migrants seemed to threaten both the economic opportunities of many Americans and their right to recognition as citizens and the privileges that should come with citizenship. What we now need is an issue that clearly highlights the nature of conflict over political identity, and allows us to round out the account of globalization's challenge to the polity.

The politics of Official English and bilingual education provide an excellent area for studying the politics of identity. In the 1980s and 1990s, the status of English as the dominant language of American life and politics suddenly emerged as a focus of political conflict. The closely related controversies over the "official" status of English and over bilingual education erupted in many different areas of the country and periodically became the focus of intense national concern. Political scientists on the whole were unprepared for this development and have produced relatively few substantial analyses of its origins or importance. Why has this been the case? First, language had ceased to be a question of national significance in the United States by the 1920s, when political science was first forming its major concepts and approaches. At best, it seemed a question of relevance to linguists and sociologists studying cultural trends among subgroups of American society. Second, as we have seen, political scientists have long been trained to see the essence of politics as "power" and "interests."[1] As a primarily symbolic question, it would be natural for most in the discipline to dismiss language conflict as a secondary issue, a reflection of some more important question about the distribution of material resources. Though analysts could do much with this approach in the areas of trade and immigration, the absence of attention to symbolic issues left little room for a serious consideration of language politics.

My aim in this chapter is twofold. First, I will analyze the issue of language in recent American politics, focusing on the conflicts over the status of English in public life and public education. In this analysis, I will try to show how the debates and conflicts over language policy have been shaped by the impact of globalization on American life, and I will argue that this area of policymaking provides a crucial dimension for understanding the impact of global change on American politics in the largest sense. To make this argument, I will pursue a second aim, which is to explore the way policy and political analysts usually treat the role of cultural and symbolic dimensions of politics. This chapter will offer what I believe is a more useful approach to the role of culture and symbolism in politics, one that takes it more seriously on its own but also links symbolic analysis with the "power" and "interest" dimensions more familiar to political scientists.[2] A complete understanding of the impact of globalization, I argue, requires that we understand the way in which it raises questions concerning the cultural and symbolic dimensions of political community.

This chapter, then, will be the culmination of my attempt to show how globalization has been a major force helping to raise the question of identity to the center of contemporary political conflict. In the modern world of nation-states, the predominant source of political identity for most persons has been their membership in one of these states, understood as a national community of common background, understandings, and fate. Political identity in this sense has in turn played an important role in shaping the personal and social identity and sense of belonging of the citizens of such states. Globalization, as it opens up the boundaries between states and weakens the sense of shared interests and obligation within the national community, works to undermine long-established political identities. In response, globalization seems to help generate a backlash, in which citizens attempt to reassert the cohesion and value of the national identity and culture against these pressures. The emergence of a politics of language in the United States, I argue, is a prime example of this kind of political movement.

Globalization in American Politics and Policy: An Interlude and Review

What have been the main arguments of the book to this point? I began with a review of the prominent debate over the impact of globalization on American society and politics and indicated in chapter 1 why I felt that the most important contributors have misunderstood the issue. Both supporters and opponents of globalization have tended to link its spread with the declining power and sovereignty of the state, an argument that actually misleads Americans about the real importance of global change. In chapters 2 and 3, the book takes a step back from the contemporary landscape to look more closely at the nature of the modern state, the meaning of sovereignty, and the nature and impact of globalization in the contemporary world. There I argued that the modern state's central role is the creation and regulation of the boundaries around the political community. In the twentieth century, these boundaries have been understood to match the territorial borders of the state, within which a national community of shared economic and social destiny exists, protected by a government that defends that community from the disturbances of the larger global scene. Seen in this light, the real significance of globalization is that it works to transform the meaning of the state's borders and boundaries, as states increasingly replace the protection of domestic society with immersion of communities in the movements of a global market economy.

In the subsequent two chapters on American trade and immigration policy, I have tried to bring out and substantiate two central arguments or themes concerning the impact of globalization on the politics of American public policy. The first theme has been the argument that globalization as we know it today is as much a creation of public policy choices as a force impinging upon the freedom of states to pursue their objectives. In the areas of both trade and immigration, the relationship between domestic and global society has been transformed because of conscious decisions of policymakers, supported by key constituencies in the

United States, to more deeply integrate American society into a more dynamic global economy. These choices, in turn, were the outcome of a political process driven by an assessment of the particular national interests and purposes of the United States in the international environment, a process deeply shaped by the evolution of domestic political and economic institutions. The second theme has been that globalization has deeply divided American society between those likely to prosper in this new global economy and those threatened with insecurity in this same context. The result has been the emergence of new kinds of political divisions centered over the policy choices defining the boundaries of the polity. In both trade and immigration politics, we have seen new coalitions emerge around the competing goals of preserving and deepening the opening of American society to global change, on the one hand, and on the other, reversing this direction and providing more protections for Americans against the changes and disruptions brought about by this new global context. Globalization, I have concluded, does not undermine the importance of politics but works to create a new kind of politics centered around the conceptions of the proper position of the political community in relationship to the emerging global society.

Throughout the analysis, I have emphasized how policy choices and the political conflicts that shape them center around the allocation of power, resources, and opportunities. This is the standard focus in political science, and it is extremely important for understanding the politics of globalization. Thus, we have seen how the state's power and responsibility to determine the nature of the boundaries of the community have played a central role in shaping the degree of power and opportunity available to different segments of society. The movement from a relatively closed society to one in which capital, production, and goods from abroad more freely flow across the borders of the United States has worked to redistribute power and opportunities among different groups. Similarly, changing rules as to who may reside in the United States and the benefits available to residents and citizens have had a significant impact on the distribution of the protections and opportunities available to individuals in the United States. It is no wonder, then, that the policy decisions that define the United States' relationship to the rest of the world have become a source of deep controversy and political mobilization.

At the same time the analysis has raised issues about the symbolic and cultural dimensions of these policy choices and political struggles. I noted in chapter 2 that the creation of certain kinds of boundaries around the states amounts to endorsing a certain vision of the meaning and priorities of the polity, and I argued that the post-1945 set of boundaries incorporated a particular, ethnically and ideologically limited vision of American citizenship. The analysis presented in chapters 4 and 5 shows how the policy choices that have led to an increasing immersion of American society in the global economy have also challenged this vision of the polity. Opening the American economy to these forces has involved an attempt by the state to renounce its commitment to provide a secure middle-class status to all working Americans, while also reducing the commitment to ensuring that the most privileged Americans contribute to make this program work. The impact of the transformation of immigration policy on the meaning of citizenship is even clearer. The elimination of the system of national origin quotas marked a decisive move away from the notion that full American citizenship was available to whites only and helped diversify the racial and cultural makeup of the citizenry. At the same time, the subsequent policy decisions extending social welfare benefits to all legal residents worked to devalue the status of citizenship itself. By the 1990s, the policy changes that globalized American life had undermined the expectations of many Americans about the proper role and responsibilities of the state. In the minds of many, government no longer protected the understandings, symbols, and values of American citizenship.

Symbolism, Culture, and Political Identity

There is no uniform or dominant approach in political science to help us understand the role of this symbolic or cultural dimension of political conflict. For many if not most analysts, this whole dimension is barely relevant to the essence of politics, a distraction from the real play of power and interests. Despite this general emphasis, though, over the years we can find a number of suggestions from important political scientists concerning the best ways to incorporate symbolic and cultural themes into political analysis. One of the most interesting and surprising sources was the early work of David Easton. Though known as a key figure in the post-World War II push towards the empirical and behavioral study of politics, Easton was keenly aware of the multidimensional aspect of political conflict and incorporated this into *The Political System*, his blueprint for a new kind of political science.[3] This is evident in his classic definition of politics as the struggle over "the authoritative allocation of values." It has long been standard practice to emphasize that the "values" discussed here refer not only to normative conceptions of politics but also to the material goods and opportunities distributed through the actions of the state. But it is just as important to turn this argument around and to note that Easton's broad use of the term "values" *does* place normative and symbolic themes at the center of politics. Indeed, we can take this definition as an attempt to move beyond the usual division between material and symbolic values and to remind us that normative conceptions of the polity are in fact embodied and realized in the distribution of resources and opportunities.

A different approach to the role of symbolism in politics is offered in the work of Murray Edelman.[4] Perhaps the single most influential student of symbolism in contemporary political science, Edelman has long argued that in modern democratic politics the "real interests" of most participants matter less than the interpretations placed on policy choices and the persuasiveness of the narratives through which they are justified. In his earlier work, Edelman tended to emphasize the ways in which symbols, myths, and narratives were manipulated to justify policies that served political elites at the expense of the majority of citizens. From the regulation of business to social welfare policy, he traced the ways in which policy choices and political rhetoric were used to deceive citizens about the control that they had over government and the responsiveness of political elites to their interests. Edelman's more recent work, while not rejecting this argument, places less emphasis on the conscious manipulation of rhetoric and symbols by elites, and focuses instead on the ways in which political life as a whole is constituted by the myths and narratives constructed and competing within a given culture. In explorations that range from the role of the media in constructing a "political spectacle" to the interaction between art and politics, Edelman offers a vision of political life in which citizens act and react in a world dominated by competing, interacting, and usually "deconstructing" narratives of political reality. Policymaking and policy choice, in his view, gain their meaning and relevance from the way they are integrated into these narratives, or "constructions."

We need not accept all of the emphasis on elite manipulation or deconstruction in Edelman's work to see how it can work along with Easton's argument to help us build a framework for thinking about the role of symbolism and culture in the politics of policymaking.[5] The understanding of politics and policy choice that emerges from these writers is one in which there is always an interaction of symbol and interest, meaning and power, as political choices allocate meanings as well as resources, and symbolic conflicts draw upon real grievances concerning the role of the state in sustaining the identity and values of citizens. We have already seen examples of this in the politics of globalization. For instance, when the priorities of economic policy are changed to promoting free markets instead of regulating them, a new set of opportunities and obstacles is created for citizens, and with them a new relationship between the state and the individual. As the state redefines its boundaries and obligations, it is redefining the purposes of the polity as well as reallocating resources—at the same time. The same kind of relationship can be seen when the nature of immigration policy is transformed. As the debate over immigration policy indicates, these policy choices reshape the meaning of citizenship and challenge the identity of citizens while also involving the practical questions of taxation and social policy. In the politics of globalization, the struggles of interests and meanings seem best understood as different but closely linked dimensions of the same political actions and policy choices. They work together as political alliances develop competing visions of the structure and purposes of the polity.

To fully understand the politics of language, though, we need to link this understanding of politics as an arena that is simultaneously one of interests, power, and symbols to the basic structure of modern political identity. Here the work of Benedict Anderson is central. In his classic book *Imagined Com-*

munities, Anderson explores the ways in which modern nationalism emerged from the social and technological changes that accompanied the emergence of modern states in western Europe and the Americas. He argues that the modern nation attempted to create a new kind of political society, one in which individuals would identify and feel as if they belonged to a community the majority of whose members they would never meet, let alone come to know. Unlike earlier societies, in which the primary source of identity would come from face-to-face contact in a small local community, the creators of the modern nation attempted to link each individual's sense of fate to a large, territorially bounded and abstract community.

Anderson calls this kind of community an "imagined community" because it is based on the ability of each person to imagine himself or herself as part of a larger whole in which persons never met or seen are felt to be sharing the same experiences, interests, obligations, and fate. As Anderson describes the nation,

> It is *imagined* because the members of even the smallest nation will never know most of their fellow-members, meet them, or even hear them, yet in the minds of each lives the image of their communion. . . . [Finally] it is imagined as a *community*, because, regardless of the actual inequality and exploitation that may prevail in each, the nation is always conceived as a deep, horizontal comradeship.[6]

Much of his work explores the ways in which the emergence of the modern state called this kind of community into being, and he pays particular attention to the role of modernizing "bourgeois" elites in forming the bonds that would link different parts of a territory together. Anderson also places much emphasis on the role of new communication technologies—especially the emergence of a mass market for newspapers and periodicals—in mediating between individuals and the larger nation, helping to provide the sense of common experience necessary for a truly national identity. In addition, these forms of communication depended upon the articulation and spread of a common national language as their medium, a task usually reinforced by the state's promotion of public education in that language. For our purposes, Anderson's account is especially important because it indicates that common symbols, mythologies, and narratives are central to the shape of political identity in the modern world. The very size of a modern nation-state makes it impossible for individuals to feel a real belonging to a larger community unless they experience this through the political-cultural practices—and the language in which they experience them—that they share and that differentiate them from members of other states. Even the institutions and policy choices that are central to political life must be placed within such context for citizens to understand them as part of the process through which the nation is defined and maintained.

This is an approach that fits well with the arguments of Easton and Edelman and has two other important implications for the study of the contemporary politics of globalization and language. First, Anderson makes clear how fundamental national and political identity is to the way citizens of modern states understand their personal fate and define the community of which they are a part. For all the talk about the pressures on the state as a result of global change, it is clear that no form of community has emerged to challenge the nation-state as the basic source of common identity in contemporary politics. Changes that do seem to undermine this community or to draw the state away from protecting the community it represents, then, can be expected to generate a powerful response in defense of that community. Second, Anderson's account suggests that challenges to the cohesiveness of the political community will be felt and articulated in terms of the cultural symbols and narratives that are essential to the very existence of that community. Any political response that attempts to defend the community, then, should include if not emphasize a defense of what its supporters understand to be the essential norms and symbols of the polity. Since these symbols and narratives are closely identified with the language in which they are expressed, Anderson's account suggests that in most cases the politics of globalization will generate, as one of its central elements, a politics of language.

We must begin to think in these terms to fully come to grips with the political impact of globalization. In the contemporary world, as many have noted, the primary source of political identity for most persons is drawn from the political community of which they are a part, of which they are citizens if they are lucky. The state's presence as representative and guarantee of this community is central in shaping the terms of this identity. Globalization generates pressures on established patterns of identity because it brings with it new boundaries of the community and new roles for government. Much of the resulting controversy is played out in terms of policy issues that often seem to focus primarily on the distribution of resources in society. But such fundamental challenges to the role of the state also challenge the sense of identity that is fundamental to all citizens' sense of who they are, of the obligations they owe to others and that are owed to them.

The Politics of Language in American History

Although absent from political conflict for most of this century, the issue of language is an important part of American history and national identity.[7] During the founding period and the two succeeding decades, a great deal of attention was paid to the question of whether the new nation should have an official language and what that should be. Though there was no practical competition to English, many argued that "American" English should be promoted as a different, more democratic or republican language, and that efforts should be made to purify it of the feudal and aristocratic influences of British history. The most famous such advocate was Noah Webster, who connected his project of systematizing an American language with the larger Federalist aim of nation and state building. In the end, these efforts had few practical political consequences, and there remained no national language policy in the United States during the nineteenth century.

This did not mean, however, that linguistic diversity and usage were not often the sources of political conflict during this era. One important source of controversy emerged out of the territorial expansion of the United States. While the standard approach toward Native American languages was suppression, much controversy surrounded the question of how to treat native French speakers in Louisiana and especially Spanish speakers in the territories gained from Mexico. Although there was little debate over the necessity for English to become the dominant language in these areas, there was much variety in the degree of tolerance and even protection given to Spanish in the newly conquered areas. Indeed, the relatively indulgent policy practiced in the New Mexico territory contributed to the long delay in accepting that state into the Union.

The other key source of controversy was the continued use of native languages by immigrants, especially the Germans. As in the case of Spanish speakers today, a steady flow of immigrants from Germany kept the German language a vibrant force throughout the nineteenth century, helping it maintain a strong institutional base in the networks of churches, newspapers, and fraternal organizations serving the German immigrant communities. Indeed, German was clearly the leading second language in the United States throughout this period, and responses varied. In many areas, such as Pennsylvania and some Midwestern states, local governments accommodated German to the point of printing legislative proceedings in the language and allowing a good deal of public education to be conducted in German. In many of the same areas, immigrants also were granted the right to vote upon their arrival, without the requirement of naturalization and citizenship, as an incentive for settling particular states.[8] Other groups of Americans found this very disturbing and mobilized to secure the dominance of English in all public spheres. Still, no national response along these lines appeared, as a combination of politicians' interests in the votes of citizens of German descent and a clear dominance of English in the larger culture worked to minimize the perceived need for such an approach.

The political and cultural calculations surrounding language changed in the late nineteenth century, inaugurating three decades of major political activism and conflict concerning language. Not surprisingly, it was the growth of mass immigration from eastern and southern Europe that accounted for this change. We have already seen how this phenomenon generated concern over the political and cultural future of the American polity, and in no area was this more prominent than in that area of language.[9] A concern for the future of the English language as the dominant language of the polity was central to the restrictionist movement that emerged in the early 1900s. Indeed, the creation of a literacy test (in their native language) for all immigrants in 1917 was one of the first victories of this movement, which also brought substantial pressure on state and local governments to eliminate the use of non-English ballots and the publication of public business and records in German and other languages. Meanwhile, a smaller but more progressive wing of the movement focused on the problem of "Americanizing" the new immigrants. Two central aspects of this wide-ranging project were the creation of special classes for teaching English to adults and the elimination of the use of other languages in public education.

Such efforts often met with resistance early on, but the United States' entrance into World War I, and the antiradical politics of the years after the war, effectively secured the victory of the pro-English forces. During these years, the heightened patriotism and xenophobia led to a sustained attack on the use of German in the United States, from which that language has not recovered. In addition, all attempts to accommodate other immigrant languages in the polity and education system fell under the pressure to promote the use of English as rapidly as possible. Assimilation became the official policy of all levels of government and proved remarkably effective in changing the larger cultural attitudes of the migrants themselves. During this period, some states went so far as to try to prohibit the use of all other languages not only in education but in churches and other private institutions. These efforts were rebuffed by the Supreme Court, but the overall dominance of English was nonetheless secured by the mid-1920s, just in time for the enactment of systematic immigration restrictions.

By the late 1920s, then, the establishment English as the dominant American language had been secured. This can be seen as part of the larger movement to create a more cohesive and uniform national polity, in which the state used its control over borders to close the nation to the flow of "outside" influences, thereby facilitating the creation of a community of identity within its borders. To be sure, the dominance of English was not directly enacted into law, and much of the work of assimilation would be accomplished by powerful economic and social pressures. But language was effectively depoliticized during the following decades, as the United States moved toward the establishment of a new sense of national identity and a new compact concerning the role of the state, the purposes of the polity, and the rights and responsibilities of citizens.

The Reemergence of the Politics of Language

Like the controversies over immigration, the roots of the contemporary politics of language are found in a set of legal and policy changes that began in the mid-1960s.[10] The first of these was the Supreme Court decision in *Katzenbach v. Morgan*, 384 U.S. 641 (1966), in which the Court ruled that residents of New York State who were American citizens educated in Puerto Rico—and who had thus been provided public education in Spanish—had a right to be provided with ballots in Spanish when they voted. This decision was partly the product of the unique history of U.S. colonial rule in Puerto Rico and the link between that island and New York City. But the most important context for understanding the Court's position was the impact of the victories of the civil rights movement in the previous three years. In this decision, the Court attempted to extend the new orientation of American law and policy to ensure that all persons had equal effective access to the ballot. It marked the beginning of the use of bi- or multilingual ballots across the United States, under the rubric of the enforcement of the 1965 Voting Rights Act.

The other two major contributions to the emergence of language politics concerned education policy. As part of its growing role in public education during the Great Society, Congress in 1968 passed the Bilingual Education Act. The main purpose of the act was to provide funding for programs aimed at providing a smoother transition to an English-dominated curriculum for students from backgrounds in which English was not the primary language. Children from Spanish-speaking backgrounds, especially in the Southwest and key urban areas, were the main focus of this legislation, and bilingual education soon became an issue of intense local conflict in these areas. The initial challenge to the constitutionality of bilingual education reached the Supreme Court in 1974. In *Lau v. Nichols*, 414 U.S. 563 (1974), the third major step in the emergence of language politics, the Court ruled that "Title VI of the 1964 Civil Rights Act required school districts to take steps to ensure that non-English speaking children can participate meaningfully in the education system."[11] While not providing much detail on what this meant, the Court upheld a California bilingual education program as a reasonable method to achieve this goal, emphasizing the ultimate aim of ensuring that all students have an effective grasp of English.

By the late 1970s, the question of the use of non-English languages (especially Spanish) in public education, voting, and the provision of public services had become closely linked to the growing controversy over immigration. The major increase in immigration from Latin America and Asia, and especially the growth of illegal immigration from Mexico, led to a rapid growth in the use and presence of Spanish in the United States, especially in those regions that attracted the largest concentration of migrants. For a small but growing sector of Americans, this phenomenon and the official public sanction it was receiving seemed to pose a threat to the preservation of their distinct national identity. As in the case of immigration, this movement was divided between those opposed to the influx of non-English speakers generally and those primarily concerned with the success of the assimilationist program of integrating migrants into the larger society. But supporters of both approaches shared the sense that the growing presence of non-English speakers in the United States posed a real or potential threat to the cohesion of the national community.

The connection between language and immigration during this period was only one aspect of a larger development. In essence, beginning in the 1970s Americans were being forced to increasingly engage—often on a day-to-day basis—with the presence of cultural influences from around the world. Whether these took the form of the cultural practices brought by immigrants, the goods brought by trade, or the variety of languages now heard in many parts of the country, the larger global context was now forcing its way into the daily lives of Americans. Rather than blocking these out and protecting the distinctiveness of national traditions, government policy and economic forces were opening American society, forcing it to deal directly with the global environment in which it existed. Americans now had to recognize the relationship between their own traditions and those of the rest of the world, rather than ignoring the latter in a world of fixed borders around the country. Language proved an especially potent symbol and arena of this change. The dominance and almost uniform presence of English had been a crucial if uncodified symbol of the shared community of fate upon which the post-1945 political and social compact had been built. For many, the growing presence of other languages in public and private life signaled a threat that this vision of the national community was coming apart. As Jack Citrin put it, discussing the emerging politics of language:

> Underlying the political confrontation between "language rights" and "English only" is a deeper debate over the meaning of American identity and the means of preserving it. Is speaking English a condition of full membership in American society? Does government support for bilingualism erode the foundations of national unity, or does it enhance ethnic harmony?[12]

Indeed, it was a combination of these larger cultural trends with the specific legal and policy changes in the area of education that led in 1983 to the formation of U.S. English, the central organization behind the movement for the recognition of English as the "official language" of the United States. This movement, the major manifestation of concerns over language in the 1980s, grew out of California Senator S.I. Hayakawa's 1981 proposed constitutional amendment declaring English the country's official language. Though the amendment failed on the national level, U.S. English and its supporters spawned a wide-ranging campaign for the adoption of similar amendments in state constitutions. These amendments, though varying in form, share a number of common provisions: a declaration that English is the "official language" of the particular state, an enforcement clause providing that the legislature has the power to enforce this declaration, an explanation of the rationale for the amendment and thus the importance of maintaining English as the common language, and (in some cases) a declaration that the amendment is not aimed at denying any persons or groups equal protection under the law.[13] Such amendments were adopted in California in 1986 and in Florida,

Arizona, and Colorado in 1988. Though the movement to adopt Official English amendments was only partially successful, its support in areas of heavy Latin American immigration ensured that language politics was back on the agenda in the United States.

Of course, a substantial segment of Americans opposed these amendments and embraced the social and cultural trends that had fostered the growing use of other languages in the United States. In 1987, representatives of twenty-seven groups that shared this view, ranging from the American Civil Liberties Union to the Mexican American Legal Defense and Education Fund and the National Education Association, formed the English Plus Information Clearinghouse (EPIC). For these groups, the spread of multilingualism and multiculturalism was part of the movement for full equality of all ethnic groups, which promised to strengthen America.[14] Rather than defending English, which these groups believed was unnecessary, EPIC tried to promote the notion of "English-plus." The central idea here was that Americans needed more exposure to the diversity of cultures and languages if they were going to be able to function well in an increasingly integrated global society. Focusing especially on education, EPIC accepted the dominance of English in American life but tried to emphasize the need to broaden the exposure of American students to the larger world. In terms of public life, EPIC emphasized the need to help facilitate the acquisition of English while allowing persons whose native language was different to retain the viability of that language and the culture it embodied. Though a number of municipalities have adopted statements of support for EPIC's goals, EPIC has had only small success in combating the more widespread support for English-only amendments.

What would be the practical impact of these amendments? This is not necessarily clear. Some, like Arizona's, prohibit the use of any language other than English by state workers in the fulfillment of any official duty, including any kind of interaction with citizens. This most extreme form of official English legislation was successfully challenged in the federal courts as an unconstitutional violation of the First Amendment's free speech provisions. But most versions of the amendment did not go this far. Rather, they amounted to a general commitment to the primacy of English and called in general for governments to act to promote English fluency and usage. For most analysts, this very vagueness indicates that the issue is a symbolic one, which taps feelings of national identity and pride but has little connection to the more material aspects of political conflict. As Citrin et al. sum up their argument: "The evidence strongly suggests that an important reason for the popularity of 'official English' is the pervasive public desire to reaffirm an attachment to a traditional image of Americanism that now seems vulnerable."[15]

But why does this image now seem vulnerable to so many Americans? Before simply accepting this conclusion, we need to look more closely at the politics of the Official English controversy. As it turns out, the divisions surrounding this issue closely match the cleavages seen in the politics of immigration. Supporters of the English-only amendments tend to be those constituencies closely tied to the image of a cohesive state-society relationship based on a clear sense of national unity, and very skeptical of the deeper immersion of the United States into a global society. They are dispersed among various sectors of the population, though they are somewhat more likely to be found among citizens of lower income and education levels, union members and representatives concerned about the influx of immigrant labor, and policy analysts worried about the preservation of a national culture. Opponents, on the other hand, tend to represent the same supporters of open immigration policies, including most leaders of the two major political parties, key segments of the international and domestic business communities, and the variety of civil libertarian and ethnically based interest groups.[16]

There remains one crucial difference between the politics of immigration and that of language, however. Supporters of more liberal immigration politics could draw on the deeply rooted national mythology of the United States as a haven for persecuted migrants from around the globe, and they include those with very different views of the way migrants should be integrated into the larger society. In the case of language, however, this very same tradition was not necessarily helpful, as it contained a strong dose of assimilationist sentiment and symbolism. Though the national identity may help resist anti-immigration politics, it is clearly biased against attempts to question the necessity and primacy of English as a unifying force in the polity. Thus, to take the example of California, many of the same sectors of the electorate hostile to anti-immigrant themes and propositions were solid supporters of the Official English ballot measures, including a good share of the immigrant communities themselves.[17]

A very similar set of developments can be seen in the closely related question of bilingual education.[18] Indeed, it is hard to separate the politics of language generally from the emergence of the controversy over the spread of bilingual education. As we have seen, this approach to the promotion of English language acquisition among the children of immigrants emerged as a centerpiece of federal and state education policies in the 1970s. Criticism began almost immediately. The attack on bilingual education has played and continues to play a central role in the arguments offered by the Official English movement, and ballot measures attempting to eliminate it appeared even earlier than the English-only measures. If anything, the conflict over bilingual education is the more intense of the two, as it involves the crucial role of schools in socializing future generations of citizens, and the use of large sums of taxpayer money to fund a particular vision of the role of language in the polity.

Of course, there are many different practices that are often grouped under the rubric of "bilingual education," as well as a large volume of studies concerning the impact and effect of the various approaches. As is often the case in public policy, the results of these studies are highly mixed but also seem of little relevance to most public debate on the issue. For its opponents, bilingual education is a direct attack on the national culture and values that hold the community together. In this view, such programs promote the retention of the student's native language over the quick immersion into English, threatening to create self-sustaining ethnic divisions and to break up the common culture based on a common language and values. To have the state promote such a program, it appears, provides one more example of its refusal to uphold the purposes and values of the American polity.

Supporters of bilingual education point out that its purpose is to facilitate the learning of English and that it is more effective at this than are any alternative approaches. But this argument has not proved very compelling to many, for two different reasons. First, some organizations and spokespersons, claiming to represent the non-English-speaking communities, have argued that bilingual education in practice was a means of enabling these communities to resist assimilation into the broader culture. Drawing on some strands of the "multiculturalism" project, these activists have specifically criticized the assimilationist ideal and promoted a much more culturally pluralist conception of the polity. Though not necessarily representing the views of most of the nonnative English speakers, this rhetoric has been effectively used to spur the opposition to bilingual education. Second, it has become clear that effective bilingual programs are very expensive and require a large pool of talented and specially trained teachers. The absence of such funds and talent has in many cases meant that bilingual programs have not worked well at promoting English acquisition, furthering the sense that their real impact is to undermine the role of English in the polity.

The movements for English-only laws and against bilingual education have also grown in tandem. The 1980s saw the first heyday of English-only statutes and amendments at the state level. From 1981 to 1990, fourteen states—including California, Virginia, Arizona, Colorado, and Florida—passed one or the other type of measure. After some quieting of activity in the early 1990s, four more states passed such statutes in 1995 and 1996, meaning that close to one-half of the states now officially support the dominance of English in American life.[19] Moreover, in 1996 the House of Representatives passed a similar bill, though it did not become law.[20] Meanwhile, mobilization against bilingual education continued, although supporters of such measures had to struggle against the entrenched opposition of the education bureaucracies and much of the political elites in most states. Nonetheless, in a striking victory that has shaken the future of bilingual education, California voters in 1998 overwhelmingly endorsed Proposition 217, which limits bilingual education programs in the state to one year for each student, after which students must be put into rapid English immersion programs. In the wake of the widespread disappointment with the success of bilingual programs, educators around the country are now working to fashion alternative strategies for dealing with the large and still growing population of children whose native language is not English.[21]

To be sure, opposition to the pro-English movements remains powerful. In 1998, the Arizona Supreme Court struck down that state's English-only law as an abridgement of the first amendment, and it is unlikely that such laws would fare well in Supreme Court challenges.[22] Meanwhile, the English-plus alternative movement has had a number of successes of its own in the states, and political elites in states and cities with substantial immigrant populations remain skeptical of the nativist tendencies of the pro-English movements and resistant to its demands. But it is fair to conclude that the political movements to officially recognize the unique status of English and its role in the polity remain strong and growing, and their success even with immigrant voters suggests a powerful future. So what is really going on here? How can we explain this powerful movement to defend a language that most analysts believe faces little threat, and what does this movement tell us about the impact of globalization on American society and politics?

Explaining the Politics of Language: Back to Globalization

Though few political scientists have studied the debate over language policy in any depth, those who have come to a very similar set of conclusions. First, it is widely agreed that socioeconomic cleavages help explain only a small amount of the variation among the views of citizens and elites on Official English measures. With the possible exception of levels of education—the less the level of formal education, the more likely voters are to support such measures—the relationship between support for such measures and such indicators as income, wealth, type of occupation, or even the presence of non-English speakers in a given area is relatively minimal. Though the latter is much higher in states that have passed referenda (as opposed to ordinary legislation) on English, support for such measures seems equally high in states and regions with very different levels of immigrant presence. Second, the one variable that does tend to show a significant relationship to the divisions over language policy is partisanship. In most parts of the country, conservatives and Republicans are clearly more likely to support pro-English measures than are liberals and Democrats. Or as Citrin et al. put it, supporters seem much more likely to display high levels of "Americanism," a composite of measures linked to what we tend to call "conservative" positions on the nature of the American polity.

But the overwhelming finding of these studies is that support for pro-English measures is widespread throughout the United States. As Tatalovich emphasizes, there remains a deep-rooted belief that speaking and commanding English is a central part of American identity, and this is a belief that immigrants themselves tend to support. It is reflected in the fact that English-only referenda have never failed to secure a majority of voters in any state. To be sure, the issue of language policy does not seem to rank high among the conscious priorities of most Americans. Moreover, when English-only measures threaten to interfere with private practices of non-English speakers or to significantly disadvantage these groups—as in the case of the Arizona referendum—support drops dramatically. But there remains a real concern in the polity over the status of English, and this concern can be effectively mobilized by those who wish to place it on the public agenda of state and national governments.

The most surprising aspect of language use in the United States, given this widespread concern, is the lack of any evidence suggesting that there is any real threat to the status and dominance of English in the United States.[23] As study after study emphasizes, immigrants to the United States are interested in learning English and do so over time. More important, it seems clear that the pattern found at the turn of the twentieth century—the steady decline in the use of the native language over generations—is again repeating itself as the more recent waves of immigrants settle into American society and succeeding generations mature in this context. To be sure, there is more public use of other languages, especially Spanish, in the United States than what many remember from the three decades following 1945, and there are pockets of American society—in certain urban areas and in the Southwest—where English is not the most commonly used language. But none of this amounts to a threat to the long-term dominance of English. As Portes and Rumbaut argue in their discussion of the issue:

> These conclusions reverse the usual concerns and alarms found in the popular literature, which call attention to the proliferation of foreign languages and to the threat they pose to English dominance. Historical and contemporary evidence indicates that English has never been seriously threatened as the dominant language in the United States and that—with over two hundred million monolingual English speakers—it is certainly not threatened today.[24]

If there is widespread support among Americans for declaring English the official language of the country, it is not because of any real threat posed by other languages.

So why has the question of language emerged in the 1980s and 1990s, and what does the support for Official English really indicate about American politics? Since this phenomenon is clearly linked to both the growth of immigration and concern about the coherence of the American political community, we must return to the issue of globalization to put this movement into perspective. To do this, though, we must refer once more to the basic definition and analysis of globalization. Though it is often discussed solely in terms of deepening connections and interdependence between developments in different parts of the world, I have argued that globalization cannot have a decisive impact on political conflict unless people actually develop an awareness of it. This is the central contribution of Roland Robertson's important analysis, which we have encountered earlier.[25] According to Robertson, globalization "relativizes" our perceptions about our place in the world, and that of the society in which we live. As a result of the increased presence of other societies and cultures in our lives, we come to think differently and less confidently about where we are in the world.

Robertson's approach is especially useful because it helps us understand both the dynamics of increasing interconnectedness between societies and the divergent ways in which this affects political change within societies. It enables us to see that global change is not something that simply happens "out there" but is manifested in the structure of social life within societies and communities. This contention has been central to my argument that the politics of globalization is primarily a struggle between political forces that—though these forces are increasingly global in definition and interests—is largely played out within the realm of particular states. In addition, Robertson argues that the widespread reactions against globalization—the attempts to define and defend borders against the forces of global change—are central to understanding the process of globalization. Only with the vital impact of global forces and their relativizing effect on our self-perceptions can citizens begin to think about the possibility of threats to the existing structure of society and be motivated to act to resist such changes.

In this sense, Robertson's work provides the theoretical basis for the kinds of insights about the interaction of globalism and localism offered by writers such as Benjamin Barber and Thomas Friedman. Though the earlier discussions focused on their analyses of the sources and nature of globalization, this is only one part of the argument in their books, which also focus on the sources and impact of the backlash against globalization that has emerged in different forms around the world.[26] Whether it takes the form of "Jihad" or the "Olive Tree," Barber and Friedman emphasize that the spread of globalism generates a constant reaction that attempts to defend national sovereignty, traditions, and institutions against the homogenizing and overpowering forces of the global economy. Both writers worry about some of the chauvinistic tendencies of this backlash, though they seem to place their bets on the long-term staying power of globalizing forces, but they note that such movements are understandable defenses against a type of social change that threatens to undermine most familiar forms of political community and identity. Whereas Barber and Friedman trace this backlash and examine the connections between these movements and the changes brought about by globalization, Robertson's account provides a crucial conceptual and theoretical foundation for the pattern they observe. When it reaches a certain point, globalization inevitably challenges some of the fundamental values, narratives, and symbols that have held communities together, and some sort of reaction is inevitable. What many of the opponents don't realize, Robertson emphasizes, is the way their own agendas depend on the real power of global change for their meaning and direction.

The implications of this approach for analyzing the rise of language politics in the United States are clear. It is not only coincidence or simply political manipulation that explains the emergence of English-only politics at the same time as we see the conflicts over trade and immigration. The increasing immersion of the U.S. economy into the global economic system, along with the growing presence of immigrants in American society, has brought the globe "home" into the borders of polity and society. Globalization has introduced cultural practices and languages that were at best strange when viewed in the context of the relatively closed American society of the middle of this century. The sudden presence of the globe in American life has forced Americans to come to terms with the new place of their nation in the world and has worked to challenge many of the institutional and cultural foundations of the post-World War II social compact. No aspect of this presence is more tangible or obvious than the increasing use of languages other than English. Globalization has pushed language onto the political agenda as a central symbolic and practical aspect of the struggle over how American society will adapt to its growing engagement with the larger world.

The links between the Official English and bilingual education controversies are very clear in this perspective. As we have seen, the conception of a cohesive national identity and community in the United States since the 1940s was based upon the closing of the society to further immigration, which allowed a sustained period of assimilation of southern and eastern European immigrants into the dominant political and cultural ethos of American life. Out of this real experience came the classic mythology of the immigrant experience, in which the reception given to immigrants was exchanged for their commitment to assimilate quickly, quietly, and definitively into American culture. Though this mythology greatly simplified and even distorted the historical reality, it was based on enough real experience and aspiration to become central to the meaning of American citizenship in the twentieth century. As part of its role in securing the boundaries of the polity, the state was expected to promote this assimilationist vision in its policy choices.

For the most part, there was no major controversy over this question before the 1970s, as the tightly guarded borders of the polity and the demands of the Cold War effectively eliminated the need or possibility of debate on the role of language. But the combination of increased levels of immigration and a new approach to education and public policy helped bring these issues to a head. For many Americans, bilingual ballots, bilingual education, and the larger project of multiculturalism represented a retreat by the state from its obligations to promote the established national ethos and mythology. From this perspective, the very identity and meaning of their membership in the polity was being denied by law and policy, and the fact that the public school system was a part of this could seem especially threatening. Not only was the globe increasingly impinging on the daily life of Americans in the form of new languages, but the government's seeming encouragement of the preservation and protection of these languages amounted to an abdication of its responsibility to value and sanction the long-established national mythology. Whatever the practical threat to the dominance of English in American life, the real threat that the state would no longer secure what many perceived to be the very essence of the national community was enough to generate a backlash in the form of Official English.

Conclusions

The divisions emerging in the politics of language policy, then, show the same conflict over the meaning, purpose, and structure of the American polity that we have seen in other policy areas. Since the 1960s and 1970s, a dominant trend in policy choice at the national and state levels has been to accommodate greater openness to the world by accepting and encouraging a more diverse conception of the cultural life of the nation. Instead of the forceful emphasis on cultural uniformity and assimilation begun in the 1920s, important policy and legal choices have emphasized the need for a more open and loose pattern of cultural expression.[27] The very success of this policy orientation in transforming the daily experiences of American life, however, has helped to generate an alternative movement that seeks to reassert a cohesive national identity emphasizing the distinctiveness and hegemony of the national culture as it was for most of the twentieth century.

In one of the most perceptive treatments of the Official English movement, Geoffrey Nunberg also emphasizes the way in which the rise of language politics is connected to deeper changes in American politics and society.[28] Unlike the historic notion that American national identity is based primarily on a set of ideological commitments—a notion long emphasized in political science[29]—Nunberg argues that recent decades have seen the emergence of a specifically cultural definition of American identity. In his view, this is the crucial significance of the Official English movement.

> To make the English language "official," however, is not merely to acknowledge it as the language commonly used in commerce, mass communications, and public affairs. Rather, it is to invest English with a symbolic role in national life and to endorse a cultural conception of American identity as the basis for political unity. And while the general communicative role of English in America has not changed over the past two hundred years, the cultural importance that people attach to the language has evolved considerably.[30]

He explores many potential explanations for this development, including the changing nature of community in the United States and the growing recognition of cultural diversity around the world, but is most interested in the implications of this development. Linguistic diversity or change is not a central concern when the community is defined ideologically. But when common cultural experiences become the basis of national identity, Nunberg argues, language becomes a crucial issue, and the pressure for a public guarantee and promotion of the dominant language becomes much clearer. The emergence of an American politics of language, then, is linked to an increasing sense that American identity is embodied in cultural practices and that these practices are increasingly under threat.

Nunberg's approach fits well with the patterns of argument and politics we have seen surrounding the language and education controversies, but it leaves us with another kind of question. To the extent that an increasing contact with global patterns of change has led Americans to question the stability of their national identity, how does this relate to the controversies over trade and immigration? Of course, immigration has been a central cause of the rise of the language question, but is there anything more to this story? It seems to me that there is, and that in this area lies the ultimate key to the politics of globalization in the United States and to the limits of Nunberg's argument and the political science arguments on which it draws. If my analysis and argument are correct, the sharp division between an ideological or political and a cultural definition of American identity that Nunberg assumes is a mistake. Since the 1930s and 1940s, Americans have looked to the state to promote and protect a vision of a cohesive nation based on mutual sacrifice to promote the benefit of all. The particular content of this vision was based on a political-economic bargain but also included an often underestimated cultural dimension. Central to this vision of a cohesive nation was the assumption that this community was defined by a European-based tradition of values, cultural practices, and ethnic origins. This tradition was understood to be the source of the political values on which the nation was built, and acceptance of it was a central part of the bargain on which mutual sacrifice was built. If these assumptions went unnoticed by most observers, it is primarily because they were too powerful to be challenged effectively. Globalization has not created cultural politics or cultural definitions of the nation. Instead, it has undermined the easy dominance of one kind of cultural vision, and the resulting conflict has brought an already existing cultural dimension of our politics and identity out into the open.

The emerging concern with language and linguistic unity, then, can be understood as part of the larger set of worries and divisions linked to the breakdown of the social compact, and through this to the growing immersion of the United States in the global environment. Since the rise of globalization has matched the dismantling of the post-1945 social compact, it has prompted a defense of this compact and the cultural vision behind it, articulated through attempts to limit or reverse the impact of global forces. The politics of language mirrors the divisions in the politics of trade and immigration, both at the level of elite politics and at the level of public opinion and mobilization. What Nunberg identifies as an increasing focus on cultural uniformity is not just the result of widespread insecurity but is linked closely to a set of structural and policy changes that involve the distribution of political, economic, and social power in the United States. In turn, the politics of language and culture is one of the most important aspects of the reaction to these changes, since it clearly emphasizes the fundamental challenge of globalization—the demand that we rethink the nature and purposes of the nation as a political community.

Of course, the connection between the politics of trade, immigration, and language is not exact and perfect. The relative weight of support for and against the manifestations of globalization varies across these areas in important ways. In the conclusion, I will review the analysis of the three policy areas, compare and evaluate the patterns of politics they illustrate, and consider the largest question that globalization poses for political choice in the United States.

PART IV ☙

Conclusions

7 ∞

Which Future for the American Polity?

What has the study of the politics of public policymaking revealed about globalization and its impact on the United States? My analysis of the history, structure, and impact of globalization is much different from the picture presented in the popular works discussed at the beginning of the book. As we look more closely and carefully at the various phenomena that make up globalization, the image of a vast and unified process that is at once all-encompassing and beyond anyone's control—taking the world in one direction whether we like it or not—seems less and less accurate or useful. In its place emerges a set of developments closely connected to the evolution of political power and ideology, interacting in many different ways with the choices of policymakers, and often contradictory in their impact on American politics and society. This concluding chapter aims to pull together the major elements of globalization presented in the book, present an overall interpretation of the impact of globalization on the American polity, and raise some of the basic questions that it poses for citizens and policymakers as they participate in the choices that will shape the future of American politics.

Globalization: A New Political Context Shaped by Political Choices

In this book, I have argued that we should understand globalization as a new *context* for political life and policy choice, itself the result of political choices made by sovereign states. Over the past three decades, the relationships between states, nations, and individuals have been rearranged as the boundaries of political communities have been transformed from tightly patrolled borders into rules and institutions that facilitate the immersion of domestic societies into a global economic and social structure dominated by loosely regulated market institutions. States still exist and remain central actors in the ongoing relationships that shape political and economic life around the world, but they now operate to set the terms upon which individuals, companies, and institutions interact with the larger global environment. As the major states attempt to reconstruct themselves along the lines of "competition states," rejecting the model of welfare states, they create a new environment in which all citizens are increasingly faced with the challenge of competing in a global terrain in order to prosper and promote their goals. States themselves, of course, are attempting to do the same thing. Globalization, I have suggested, is best understood as this new context in world politics, in which states increasingly focus on managing the movement of capital, goods, and persons across their borders, and in which they and all other social actors are preoccupied with finding the right kinds of rules that will use this movement to the promotion of their ends and interests.[1]

Seen in this light, globalization is best defined as part of a new approach to the exercise of the power, authority, and sovereignty of the state.[2] At the least, this is an essential aspect of the phenomenon, one ignored by most of the popular and a good deal of the scholarly literature on the subject. The growth of economic, technological, and cultural interdependence that has occurred in this context has been dependent upon this new approach to use of political power by states. To be sure, these processes are not simply the products of political choices, and they do indeed have their own internal dynamics, as any observer of financial markets or technological innovation will attest. But time and again our survey has shown that these kinds of processes were set in motion and/or facilitated by changes in the role and policy choices of governments. Whether it concerns the growing global interdependence of production and consumption, the increasing human migration into the United States and other countries, or the emergence of a global capital market, the analysis in this book has always found that key political choices and adjustments were necessary to allow these processes to reach their current level of development.

Of course, this account applies best to the United States, which has been the focus of my argument and analysis. As the politically and economically dominant state in the world, the United States has been at the center of the push for the market-centered global society we now see emerging throughout key regions of the world. Only Britain has played a role that was nearly comparable, but it has been important primarily in the area of the global financial system. How did the United States promote this transformation? First, it did so by transforming the role of the state in American society. The spread of deregulation, the renunciation of full employment as a central goal of economic management, and the build-down of the welfare state were all crucial steps in this process, along with the encouragement of immigration, begun earlier and for different reasons. Together, these policy choices transformed the role of the state and began the process of forcing a more competitive and market-oriented context on domestic society. Second, U.S. policymakers made a concerted effort to push other states into a similar posture. Partly, this was done through the exercise of the United States' hegemonic position in the global political and economic system—i.e., once the U.S. and the U.K. capital markets and financial systems were revolutionized, all other major states had little choice but to follow. At the same time, the United States acted through international organizations to promote these changes, as in the case of the GATT process in areas ranging from tariffs to nontariff barriers to intellectual property issues. Moreover, these efforts reinforced the ability of U.S. policymakers to secure their domestic goals as well.

Why did the United States promote the changes that led to globalization? A central theme running throughout the book has been the domestic origins and context of the choices that promoted global change. These origins are complex and at times surprising. One key element was the search by policymakers and political elites for a new approach to economic policy in the wake of the collapse of standard Keynesian approaches in the 1970s. By the late 1970s, an increasingly powerful current in elite opinion and practice came to embrace the need to expose the American economy to more market competition to revive its efficiency and productivity. Over time, this program gathered the support of key elements in the business community as well, especially those poised to take advantage of a less regulated and structured environment. This combination was crucial to the political mix that led to a new kind of state-society relationship; by withdrawing most of their support for established New Deal-type approaches, the most dynamic elements of the economy helped turn free-market political economics into the new guiding principles of the economy. A third link was the sustained activity of the policy entrepreneurs and intellectuals who successfully spread free-market ideas and policies in the 1970s, just as policymakers and business interests were looking for a new direction for state and society. Together, policymakers' interest in reviving the economy, business interest in greater profit opportunities, and a new set of ideas about politics and economics combined into a powerful force for a new kind of state. Stitched together in the 1970s, by the later 1980s this coalition helped to consolidate a new "policy paradigm" for the United States.

Globalization played an important but derivative role in this paradigm. The central aim was the promotion by government of a more competitive market-based economic context, one that would free business from much direct state intervention while subjecting it to more formidable market forces. As we have seen, though, it was clear by the 1970s that the U.S. economy was already deeply linked to the international economy, and that a domestic market revolution could not survive in a protectionist global environment. It turned out that the mid- to late 1970s was the crucial period for determining the fate of the global financial and trading systems established in the 1940s. Faced with the choice of limiting further economic openness—and initiating larger protectionist policies—or moving toward a much more open global economy, American policymakers successfully pushed for the latter as the only way to secure the larger agenda of transforming the role of the state. Such calculations, and the combination of ideas and interests supporting them, were central to the emergence of globalization as we have come to know it.

But this is not the total story. By the 1980s, more open immigration policies and a greater willingness to accept the diverse cultural influences they brought came to be a central part of the free-market agenda. They also became central to the emerging political conflict over globalization. It is clear, however, that these policies were not only the product of a free-market agenda but emerged also from the politics of equality and the expansion of rights that peaked in power in the United States in the 1960s. Both the reform of immigration policy and the introduction of bilingualism and other multicultural policy initiatives were responses to the spread of the Civil Rights movement and the embrace of its politics by the reform liberalism of the 1960s. In many ways, the success of this movement marked the first major challenge to the boundaries and understandings of the post-1940s state. While they were in one sense an extension of its egalitarian themes, they also marked a clear break from the dominant sense of national identity on which New Deal politics was based. During the 1980s, many supporters of free-market politics began to see clear advantages of open immigration and multiculturalism. But this was a much later development made possible by a different set of political forces and calculations.

Nonetheless, the alliance between the promarket, pro-immigration, and cultural diversity agendas and coalitions played an important role in sustaining the globalization project in the 1980s and 1990s. As we saw in the politics of immigration, each of these groups plays a crucial part in preserving a relatively open posture toward legal immigration in the United States, though developments in the late 1990s may have begun to overwhelm their efforts. Most important, the unusual nature of this alliance indicates some of the definitive aspects of globalization's impact in the United States. Rather than just a set of economic developments, globalization is the product of a broad movement to dismantle the elements of state power and authority that enabled states to insulate political communities from sources of instability in the larger world. This was the essence of the political formula that John Gerald Ruggie terms "embedded liberalism" and that predominated throughout Western Europe and North America after the 1940s. Whether it concerns the movement of capital, goods, persons, or ideas, whether the focus is on the domestic or international level, globalization embodies a political project to replace this model of state-society relationships with one based on open borders, free movement, market competition, and the preference for self-reliance over security.

Policy Creates Politics: The Impact of Globalization on American Politics

In the study of public policy, it is common to see the idea expressed that policies create or shape politics. This notion was advanced to remind us that policy choices are not simply the product of political conflict but that by creating new kinds of social relationships, changing the allocation of power and resources among social and political groups, and creating new institutions and rules, the choices themselves reshape the patterns of political conflict. My study of globalization has provided many examples of this. The policy choices that have rearranged the context of political and social life have had a dramatic effect in reshaping the distribution of power, resources, and opportunities in the United States and as a result have generated new patterns of political conflict. The second major aim of this book has been to show in some detail exactly what the effects of globalization on political life have been.

My central argument has been that globalization divides the polity between those segments likely to prosper from the spread of market competition and openness to global changes and those segments threatened with insecurity, declining opportunities, and a devaluation of their sense of political identity. Following Robert Reich, Ethan Kapstein, and Dani Rodrik, I have argued that globalization has worked to undermine the sense that the national community is one of shared fate, destiny, and identity and has left a profoundly divided society. In the area of trade, we have seen the global immersion of the American economy benefit those groups with skills or resources valued by the fast-changing, technologically revolutionary global economy—many professionals, highly skilled workers, and those with capital to invest. At the same time, this evolution of society often works to the detriment of persons whose position or skills—lower-skilled labor, traditional manufacturing, government-based service providers—face stagnant or declining opportunities.[3] Moreover, all groups and actors accustomed to a sense of economic security have found themselves in an unfamiliar terrain in which few jobs or institutions are protected for long.

The growth of legal and illegal immigration has generated its own set of winners and losers. Here, we can also see a division on economic lines, between lower-skilled workers for whom immigrants pose a threat to wage levels and job security and those who are consumers of lower-skilled labor who now find more opportunities to use this resource at lower cost. Of course, economists are almost unanimous in the contention that freer trade and immigration will increase the overall level of wealth and opportunity in society. And it cannot be denied that in the 1980s and 1990s we have seen such gains in overall levels of efficiency, productivity, and wealth in the American economy. But we also know that these gains have been unequally distributed and that those who are displaced or threatened by displacement must suffer many of the short- and long-term costs that come with these overall gains. As the politics of trade and immigration focuses on the distribution of these costs, globalization has created and sustains deep divisions between these two segments of American society. It has been increasingly difficult to sustain the idea that improving overall conditions for American business and workers will lead to the benefit of all citizens.

Similar divisions have been generated by the state's accommodation to the growing presence of non-English languages in American life, especially in voting, public services, and education policy. As we have seen, the issue here concerns divergent visions of the cultural identity of the national political community, with some segments welcoming a more diverse and inclusive national culture and others wanting to assert the value and distinctiveness of American identity as understood for most of this century. Though this area of division is more focused on symbolic issues, I have argued that politics in all three policy areas is shaped by the very same concern centering on the relationship of state and society: Will the priority of the state be the promotion of an open, liberal, competitive order domestically and globally, or will it be to protect and promote the distinctive interests, values, and security of the national community?

This question brings us to the heart of the growing impact of globalization on American politics. The project of globalization does not simply divide the polity between different coalitions but works to change the boundaries of polity. In a globalized polity, the interests, constituencies, and purposes promoted by the state are not confined within the territorial borders of the state. Policymakers now have a global agenda and are responsive to agents and interests attempting to act globally or positioned to benefit from doing so. This includes many key elements of domestic society but also multinational and international interests, institutions, and organizations; it excludes many domestic interests and institutions that resist the thrust of globalization. As Saskia Sassen notes, in exploring the notion of "economic citizenship" in a globalized context, the former groups become the true "constituents" of the state, which now defines the limits of its responsibilities less and less in terms of its territorial boundaries.

> But this economic citizenship does not belong to citizens. It belongs
> to firms and markets, particularly the global financial markets, and it
> is located not in individuals, not in citizens, but in global economic
> actors. The fact of being global gives these actors power over individ-
> ual governments.[4]

As a result, the very agenda of government becomes dominated by these actors, the interests they articulate, and their impact on the ability of the state to achieve its policy priorities.

It is important to be careful and specific on this point. The U.S. policymak-ing process is not becoming captive to institutions or interests that are international in the simple sense of being located outside American borders. There is no evidence that American policymakers are now the tools of global markets and corporations, or of the WTO. What globalization has done is to create a context where firms, interest groups, and markets that are global in aspiration have deep and specific roots within the borders of the polity itself.[5] The playing field of political conflict and choice remains predominantly domestic, as do the players themselves, but now many of the key players are deeply implicated in a global network of markets, contacts, and activity and attempt to shape policy to promote the interests of this larger network. The politics of policymaking now divides those "domestic" interests linked to and promoting such global networks and institutions from those "domestic" interests whose networks and interests are still primarily defined by the territorial borders of the polity. As politics becomes globalized, the key lines of political division are less and less between states and nations and increasingly within the national community.[6]

How have these developments affected American political life? One thing that is certain is that the new pattern of political conflict is playing out in a way that confounds many established routines in and assumptions about American politics. On the central policy choices of globalization, for instance, the differences between the two major political parties matter less than the divisions within each party. The leadership of both parties has been generally supportive of the globalization project, while resistance has appeared within the ranks of each party, in different ways. For instance, we have seen that labor union discontent is more likely to be expressed in Democratic circles, as are the concerns of environmentalists. Those who object to the cultural aspects of immigration and linguistic diversity, on the other hand, have had more success in the dissident—and more recently the leadership—ranks of the Republican Party. This running battle within both political parties has been a central story of American politics during the 1990s, coming to the surface during battles over trade agreements, immigration policy reform, and every four years during the presidential primary season.

Even more interesting have been the attempts to put together unprecedented political alliances at the edges of or outside the established parties. The opposition to globalization has generated phenomena such as Pat Buchanan's attempt to develop a consistently "nationalist" approach on all issues related to trade, and the coalitions surrounding Ralph Nader's network of consumer and environmental groups, which oppose globalization in the name of equality and reform. Both coalitions, and the alliances they have occasionally made, are consistent in the aim of rebuilding the boundaries that protect American life from the political, economic, and social dangers associated with globalization. The most audacious attempt to move this tendency forward has been Ross Perot's creation of the Reform Party, which identifies more responsive and principled politics with a rejection of much of the openness to the economic and population changes that have occurred over the past two decades. Initially considered little more than a vehicle for Perot's personal political ambitions, in 1999 the party became the focus for debate of the direction of a new "third force" or direction in American politics, as Pat Buchanan formally joined the party and began the process of contending for its presidential nomination. At the time of writing, the wide-open conflict created by this move indicated the diversity of the forces involved in the antiglobalization movement, only some of which are part of the Reform Party, and the future of the party and movement it aims to create remain uncertain. As the Reform Party seemed to decline into chaos, however, the Green Party presidential campaign of Ralph Nader was picking up steam. Nader's campaign is also based on a clear opposition to globalization but not one that stems from the nativism characteristic of the Buchanan campaign. At this point it seems to have a broader appeal. The continuing power of the various challenges to globalization and the real possibility of a significant third-party movement are clear signs of the kind of tension that global change has generated in American politics.

In essence, this discussion brings us back to the beginning of the book, where I linked the politics of globalization to the larger phenomenon of discontent in American politics. A main contention of this book has been that we need to grasp the political impact of global change to understand this discontent and anger. The sense of a loss of influence over political life and policy choice, my analysis suggests, is deeply linked to the way in which the new kind of politics associated with globalization has questioned or rejected many long-dominant assumptions about the purposes and role of government in American life, purposes still widely shared in the political community. The demand for a restoration of sovereignty is best understood as a way of capturing this sense of lost influence or responsiveness by the state to these assumptions and purposes. As government has embraced a vision of the political, economic, and cultural destiny of the polity centered around an acceptance of this new global context, it has generated a deepening cleavage between those willing to accept this vision and those whose interests and/or values seem lost or ignored.[7]

At this point, the future of the political conflict over globalization is uncertain. The policies that have helped construct a globalized polity seem most dominant in the areas of finance and trade. Although the future of trade negotiations is stalled by the inability of the Clinton administration to secure the renewal of fast-track authority, it seemed until recently that protectionist forces remained on the defensive, at least as long as the economy's performance remains strong. But the success of the anti-WTO demonstrators in Seattle in November of 1999, combined with the internal disarray among the negotiators, has signaled a new power and determination among these groups. Most important, many unions, environmentalists, and human rights activists seemed to have coalesced around a program of accepting some globalization while reforming the resulting international order in a way that places the goals of equality, human dignity, and environmental protection at the center of international action. As Destler and Balint have put it,

> the political dynamics of the trade debate have changed in significant ways. The good news for trade advocates is that traditional protectionism remains surprisingly weak, recent steel industry activism notwithstanding. The challenging news is that trade liberalization is threatened from another direction—from politically important constituencies alarmed over the impact of globalization on widely shared social values.[8]

The future of this coalition and approach remains unclear, but the confidence of the protrade community in the inevitability of further international tariff-reducing agreements is lower than at any point since the late 1970s.

In the area of immigration, supporters of relatively open borders have been successful in deflecting major challenges to the general framework of policy, partly by co-opting demands for stronger action against illegal immigration. Moreover, the continued presence of immigrant communities bodes well for their supporters. As migrants have become citizens, their votes are becoming increasingly important in national and local elections, making it more difficult for many politicians to openly court the anti-immigrant constituencies. And the economic boom of the late 1990s, with its accompanying labor shortages, has further weakened the force of criticisms of immigration. But opponents made strong gains in 1996 in their attempts to raise new boundaries between the rights accorded citizens and the treatment provided for resident aliens and potential migrants. More ominously for supporters of more open borders, public opinion in the United States remains highly skeptical of the value of immigration, and opponents of further immigration have been relatively successful in mobilizing public opinion in certain contexts.

Most important, it seems to me, the legacy of the post-New Deal vision of the polity is strongest in the area of cultural and national identity. In the overwhelming majority of cases in which the question of an official English language, bilingual education, or even multiculturalism has been raised, large majorities of Americans have thrown their support behind measures demanding that the state promote a cohesive sense of national identity. Whatever their tolerance for diversity in private relationships, Americans seem to want their government to firmly endorse and promote one vision of the national identity—an assimilation to the dominant national identity—and one national language. And even though evidence suggests that most immigrants rapidly adopt a similar view, continuing high levels of immigration are likely to feed this concern and preference. To be sure, such issues are not generally at the top of the list of political concerns for most citizens. But the evidence suggests a deep reservoir of attachment to a vision of the national community as a uniform community of public values, identity, and fate, a vision with little place in the project of globalization. Whatever inroads the latter may have made in shaping the politics of economic policy, to this point it has not firmly found its place in the national political culture.

The Politics of Globalization and the Future of the American Polity

The future shape of the American polity, then, will be determined by a battle over this political culture and the way Americans understand their relationship to the larger world. On a terrain that was once clearly demarcated by the Cold War, competing visions of the relationship between American society and the global environment are now competing for the allegiance of citizens. One vision, the globalized polity, presents a minimal construction of political community, in which citizens are loosely tied by a common attempt to pursue their own economic fates and personal identity, protected by a state that tries to provide a social order in which individuals have the maximum opportunity to secure their own interests and purposes in a global context of alternatives. The other vision, steeped in the legacy of post-1940s American politics, offers a cohesive and closed community of shared economic and cultural destiny, in which the state works to secure these ends by protecting domestic society from the threatening forces of a competitive global economy and a diverse and changing set of cultural influences. I will end the book by considering the issues at stake in this choice of alternatives.

We can begin with the challenge to globalization. This program asks for a resurrection of the kind of political community assumed to be the norm for most of this century in the United States. This is a state within whose borders there exists a cohesive nation with a common set of purposes and interests. In this model, the role of the institutions of state power is to promote and protect this community or nation against outside threats; its success in doing this becomes the source of the government's legitimacy and authority. In the American context, this means a reassertion of the commitment to the economic security of the middle class and to a cohesive national culture undisturbed by the influx of persons or practices from the rest of the world. It means a reassertion of American identity and the value of American citizenship against the challenges of global interdependence.

The movement for globalization, on the other hand, has taken many powerful steps away from this model of political community. Here the political community has only a minimal purchase on the lives of most persons. The state provides only a framework of legal and social order and leaves individuals and institutions to pursue their own ends for themselves. It neither promises nor provides any larger sense of the purposes or guarantees of membership in a particular political community. Citizenship becomes a formal legal status, and a national political culture or tradition plays little role in holding citizens together or in providing any common meaning that valorizes their membership in the polity. Indeed, in this model the state may even promote a diversity of identities among its citizens as a vehicle for facilitating the greatest possible integration of domestic and international societies and as a tool for economic competitiveness. At a minimum, it insists that questions of identity are privatized, taken off the agenda of the state.

There is no question that the project of accommodating and promoting globalization has some major attractions. To this point, it has been successful enough in promoting economic growth and restructuring the economy that preservation of much of this policy regime seems almost a necessity of rational policymaking, a recognition of reality. Today, any attempt to significantly close the United States to global economic and social change would place many costs on Americans in terms of economic growth and prosperity, costs that would not easily be paid. Such a recognition is clear in the rhetoric and policy of the Clinton administration. While attempting to support and promote smoother adjustment to globalization and trying to minimize its impact on the distribution of income, the administration has accepted the notion that globalization is a reality and necessity in the current structure of the American economy.[9] But the dominant strain of opinion in Republican presidential politics, established media, policy professional, and academic circles, and among the organized business community has differed only in small nuances. There may not be much left of the old establishment in American politics, but globalization is the central issue for whatever passes as the current establishment.

Moreover, the globalization program has the virtue of resisting the potentially dark side of its opponents' position—the spread of ethnic and national chauvinism and repression. Here again, the success of globalization has transformed many of the real conditions of American politics. The critics of globalization often talk of restoring the responsiveness of the state to "the people," or the cohesive national community. But the vision of the nation usually operative in this rhetoric is no longer even a reasonable approximation to the actual makeup of American society. From an economic vantage point, so many Americans are now dependent upon the global economy for their livelihood that it is unrealistic to argue that there is a common economic fate shared by all Americans in opposition to the larger world. In terms of the cultural and ethnic makeup of society, the nation is no longer the clearly European ethnically based community celebrated in the midcentury national mythology of the melting pot. When opponents of globalization call for the defense of national sovereignty, they are, knowingly or not, in fact proposing a defense of only part of the national community against the rest. We know the potential dangers of this kind of program, and the politics behind the globalization project avoids them by minimizing the importance of citizenship and national identity.

But the globalization project also leaves unaddressed a central fact of modern political life. As Helen Thompson has persuasively argued, it is not the growth of global economic interdependence that creates new political problems in the modern state.[10] In the form of global financial markets, in particular, states have been dealing with this kind of problem for centuries; indeed, global capital markets have been around as long as the modern state. Stephen Krasner has made the same point:

> I do not want to claim that globalization has had no impact on state control, but these challenges are not new. Rulers have always operated in a transnational environment; autarky has rarely been an option; regulation and monitoring of transborder flows have always been problematic. The difficulties for states have become more acute in some areas, but less in others.[11]

The middle of the twentieth century, during which states successfully disciplined such markets and radically insulated their economies, is truly the exception in modern political economic history. But we are not *simply* returning to an earlier situation. During these decades, modern democratic states radically redefined their relationships to the market economy and to the economic fortunes of their citizens. The expectations that this history created—that states would act to protect citizens from economic distress, that the economic well-being of all the nation is the primary purpose of the state, and that the state's legitimacy is ultimately based on its ability to accomplish this aim—remain powerfully implanted among the citizens of the capitalist democracies. For good or ill, citizenship is still believed to bring with it the right to have the state pursue these ends in the name of securing the value and prosperity of the nation.

In a globalized polity, however, the state no longer willingly undertakes these ends. Instead, governments attempt to return to an earlier era, in which protection from foreign invasion and internal crime was the main obligation of the state to the citizen. This contrast between what states are trying to do and what citizens continue to expect from them, Thompson argues, is at the heart of the challenge globalization presents to modern politics.

> As the twenty-first century dawns, citizens have what they believe to be the legitimate expectation that states will do far more. If the political elites of the oldest, and previously most capable, nation-states can in present circumstances no longer oblige, they will either systematically destroy those expectations at the same time as finding a new statecraft through which they can govern reasonably competently and win elections, or find a way of collectively reregulating some international capital flows. . . . If they can do neither, they will fact the most profound crisis of legitimacy.[12]

In effect, democratic capitalist states are now constrained by popular expectations in a way that was not the case at the beginning of the century. If they push the program of globalization "too far," as Dani Rodrik has put it, or turn out to be unable to stop it, they risk unleashing major social conflicts the future of which cannot be anticipated.

One way out of this dilemma, explored by Reinicke as well as Destler and Balint, is a program to use the proliferating institutions of the globalized world to help temper the impact of global change. In this approach, a new institutional and legal framework would be created to help govern the increasingly global forces of economic change, a parallel to the international institutions used in the post-1945 era to secure the goals of embedded liberalism. The basis of this framework would be the global promotion of such shared aims as improved living and working standards, environmental protection, and political reform, and the model would be the European Union. But there are good reasons to be cautious here. It is quite unclear how much these goals are shared by all the major participants in the global economy, or how they are interpreted by those who do share them. Moreover, the difficulties of securing common action on a global scale remain enormous, as illustrated by the havoc caused inside the Seattle meetings by U.S. attempts to incorporate elements of these demands in a new trade round. For the immediate future, it seems, states will be left primarily to their own resources to balance the promotion of global integration with the continuing demands for securing the values of equity and security still widely shared by their citizens.

In the American context, this dilemma takes on a special kind of resonance, which links it back to the broadest questions of political culture. As Judith Shklar has argued, American political culture in the twentieth century has defined full membership or citizenship to a great degree in terms of the ability of citizens to participate fully and productively in the economic order.[13] As the globalized polity creates a society in which many citizens can no longer find satisfactory ways of economic participation, it generates a sense that the very meaning and value of citizenship are being lost. This sense of loss will not be confined simply to one aspect of political identity but to the whole bundle of political, economic, and cultural expectations that it has developed over time. I have already argued, in effect, that the movement against globalization represents precisely this kind of development. It stands to reason that the longer this continues, the more likely it is that we will face the problem of legitimacy that Thompson suggests. We have already seen some of the dangers this presents in the spread of political violence and renewed nativisms over the past two decades. It behooves policymakers to find ways to ensure that globalization becomes a force for renewing an inclusive vision of American citizenship and not to allow it to spawn reactions that will threaten the best aspirations of American democracy. America needs a new vision of its place in the world, one that links the promotion of American values to its participation in a new, globalized world.

Notes

Notes to Chapter 1

1. Paul Krugman, "Once and Again," *New York Times*, 2 January 2000, at www. nytimes.com/library/opinion/010200krug.html, January 3, 2000.

2. Kenichi Ohmae, *The End of the Nation State* (New York: The Free Press, 1995).

3. Thomas Friedman, *The Lexus and the Olive Tree* (New York: Farrar, Straus, and Giroux, 1999).

4. Ibid., p. 309.

5. William Greider, *One World, Ready or Not* (New York: Simon & Schuster, 1997).

6. Patrick J. Buchanan, *The Great Betrayal* (Boston: Little, Brown and Co, 1998).

7. Greider, *One World*, 210.

8. Benjamin Barber, *Jihad vs. McWorld* (New York: Ballantine Books, 1996).

9. Robert Kuttner, *Everything for Sale* (New York: Alfred A. Knopf, 1997).

10. Jerry Mander and Edward Goldsmith, eds., *The Case Against the Global Economy* (San Francisco: Sierra Club Books, 1996).

11. James Davison Hunter, *Culture Wars* (New York: Basic Books, 1991).

12. Christopher Lasch, *The Revolt of the Elites and the Betrayal of Democracy* (New York: W.W. Norton & Co., 1995).

13. Susan Tolchin, *The Angry American*, 2d ed. (Boulder, Colo: Westview Press, 1999).

14. Michael Sandel, *Democracy's Discontent* (Cambridge, Mass: Harvard University Press, 1996).

15. Catherine McNicol Stock, *Rural Radicals: Righteous Rage in the American Grain* (Ithaca: Cornell University Press, 1996).

16. "The Politics of Trade: Despite the Boom, Globalization Is One of the Hottest Issues Around. Why?" *The Economist*, 23 October 1999, p. 27.

17. The "Bretton Woods" system refers to the institutions and rules that were approved by the representatives of forty-four allied nations but drawn up by officials of the United States and British governments at a meeting in Bretton Woods, New Hampshire, in July 1944 to plan the post-World War II political and economic order. The main goal of

this system was to establish a system of fixed exchange rates to ensure the steady reemergence of international trade while preserving flexibility for individual governments to pursue their own objectives in economic policy. (Originally, this system was to be one based on the gold standard, in which each government would preserve a fixed value of its currency in terms of gold. As it turned out, the Bretton Woods system came to rely on the U.S. dollar as the main reserve currency and standard by which other currencies were valued.) To manage this system, the plan called for the creation of an International Monetary Fund (IMF) to stabilize currency values, and an International Bank for Reconstruction and Development (IBRD, which came to be known as the World Bank), to support economic reconstruction after the war. By the late 1960s, growing threats to the value of the U.S. dollar led to conflict among the major economies, and the system of fixed exchange rates finally collapsed in 1971 when the Nixon administration ended the policy of attempting to maintain a fixed price for the dollar in terms of gold. The best short account of this system and its evolution can be found in Joan E. Spero and Jeffrey A. Hart, *The Politics of International Economic Relations*, 5th ed. (New York: St. Martin's Press, 1997), chap. 2.

18. An excellent source for this information, providing good overviews of the way the U.S. economy has become increasingly embedded in the global economy, is *The Economic Report of the President*, which is issued annually by the Council of Economic Advisers.

19. My discussion of the evolution of the politics of trade relies on the following two excellent overviews: Stephen D. Cohen, Joel R. Paul, and Robert A. Blecker, *Fundamentals of U.S. Foreign Trade Policy* (Boulder, Colo: Westview Press, 1996), and I. M. Destler, *American Trade Politics*, 3d ed. (Washington, D.C.: Institute for International Economics and New York: Twentieth Century Fund, 1995).

20. *Remarks by the President at Annual Meeting of IMF and World Bank*, White House Press Release, 11 October 1995. This is not the sole theme in President Clinton's treatment of global change, but it is by far the dominant one. Another good example of these arguments, though framed for a different audience, can be found in Robert Wright, "We're All One-Worlders Now," *Slate*, 24 April 1997. See also Wright's more recent essay, "Continental Drift," *New Republic*, 17 January 2000, 18–23.

21. Buchanan, *The Great Betrayal*, 16–17.

22. For a good concise example of Perot's criticism of NAFTA, see H. Ross Perot, "Keep Wealth in the North," *New Perspectives Quarterly* 10 (fall 1993): 30–32.

23. For good overviews of contemporary immigration and immigration policy, see David Heer, *Immigration in America's Future* (Boulder, Colo.: Westview Press, 1996), and Alejandro Portes and Ruben G. Rumbaut, *Immigrant America*, 2d ed. (Berkeley: University of California Press, 1996). My discussion of the politics of immigration policy also relies heavily on Peter H. Schuck, "The Politics of Rapid Legal Change: Immigration Policy in the 1980's," *Studies in American Political Development* 6 (spring 1992): 37-92.

24. These figures are from Bureau of the Census, *Profile of the Foreign Born Population in the United States: 1997.* Current Population Reports, Special Studies P23-195 (August 1999). The figures include Census Bureau estimates of the number of illegal aliens in the United States.

25. An excellent treatment of all sides of the debate on immigration is found in John Isbister, *The Immigration Debate* (West Hartford, Conn.: Kumarian Press, 1996).

26. In this and the following section, my treatment of the debates concerning globalization focuses on economic globalization. My approach is dictated by the nature of the material. To this point, most of the public debate about the general nature of global change, especially as it may relate to political conflict and policy choice, focuses on the significance of economic processes. In the next section of the book, as I look more closely at the scholarly analysis of sovereignty and global change, the importance and relevance of global migration and cultural change will become clearer and more central to the argument.

27. William Greider, *One World*, 11.

28. Friedman, *The Lexus and the Olive Tree*, chapter 5 especially.

29. Wright, "We're All One-Worlders Now," 7.

30. David Rothkopf, "In Praise of Cultural Imperialism?" *Foreign Policy* 107 (summer 1997): 38–53.

31. Greider, *One World*, 334. Similar accounts are presented in Barber, *Jihad vs. McWorld*, and Mander and Goldsmith, *The Case Against the Global Economy*.

32. These distinct programs and directions were clearly present among the protesters during the Seattle WTO meetings, and they remain a source of tension among the opponents of the current direction of globalization.

33. My focus in this discussion is on scholarly work that has crossed over the boundary of academia into the world of current political commentary, as these scholars attempt to influence the larger public debate on globalization. In chapter 3, I present a more in-depth discussion of the wider scholarly debate on the nature, sources, and impact of globalization.

34. For a good sample of this work, see the collection edited by Jeffry A. Frieden and David A. Lake, eds., *International Political Economy*, 4th ed. (New York: St. Martin's Press, 2000).

35. Robert Reich, *The Work of Nations* (New York: Vintage Books, 1991).

36. Ethan B. Kapstein, "We Are Us: The Myth of the Multinational," *National Interest* (winter 1991/92): 55–62. For a more recent scholarly defense of the same argument, see Paul N. Doremus, William W. Keller, Louis W. Pauly, and Simon Reich, *The Myth of the Global Corporation* (Princeton, N.J.: Princeton University Press, 1998).

37. Ethan B. Kapstein, *Governing the Global Economy* (Cambridge, Mass.: Harvard University Press, 1994).

38. Reich's recommendation, detailed in *The Work of Nations*, focused especially on the provision of retraining and adjustment assistance for workers displaced by global economic changes. Kapstein's proposals were more ambitious, in line with his more robust view of the degree of sovereignty and power still retained by the modern state. These proposals were laid out in Ethan B. Kapstein, "Workers and the World Economy," *Foreign Affairs* 75 (May/June1996): 16–37.

39. See the essays collected in Paul Krugman, *Pop Internationalism* (Cambridge, Mass.: MIT Press, 1996), and the essay "We Are Not the World," reprinted in Paul Krugman, *The Accidental Theorist* (New York: W.W. Norton & Co, 1998), 75–79.

40. Krugman, "We Are Not the World," 79.

41. Gary Burtless, Robert Z. Lawrence, Robert E. Litan, and Robert J. Shapiro, *Globaphobia* (Washington, D.C.: Brookings Institution, in association with Progressive Policy Institute and Twentieth Century Fund, 1998).

42. Burtless, et al., *Globaphobia*, 128–29.

43. Dani Rodrick, *Has Globalization Gone Too Far?* (Washington, D.C.: Institute for International Economics, 1997). See also Dani Rodrik, "Sense and Nonsense in the Globalization Debate," *Foreign Policy* 107 (summer 1997): 19–36.

44. The classic presentation of this framework can be found in Theodore J. Lowi, "American Business, Public Policy, Case Studies, and Political Theory," *World Politics* 16 (July, 1964): 677–715. For a contemporary discussion and application of this framework, see James E. Anderson, *Public Policymaking: An Introduction*, 4th ed. (Boston: Houghton Mifflin Co., 2000), 9–13.

Notes to Chapter 2

1. There are numerous excellent works on the history of the modern state system. My treatment is most influenced by the following: Hedley Bull and Adam Watson, *The Expansion of International Society* (Oxford: Clarendon Press, 1984); Gianfranco Poggi, *The Development of the Modern State* (Stanford, Calif.: Stanford University Press, 1978); Hendrik Spruyt, *The Sovereign State and Its Competitors* (Princeton, N.J.: Princeton University Press, 1994); and Charles Tilly, *Coercion, Capital, and European States, AD 990–1990* (Cambridge, Mass.: Basil Blackwell, 1990).

2. See Wolfgang Reinicke, *Global Public Policy* (Washington, D.C.: Brookings Institution Press, 1998), especially chap. 2. Reinicke's book is one of the best recent treatments of globalization and its impact on sovereignty, and I will rely upon it often in the following discussions.

3. F. H. Hinsley, *Sovereignty*, 2d ed. (Cambridge, UK: Cambridge University Press, 1986), 26 (emphasis in original). Hinsley's work remains the fundamental treatment of this concept and is the basis for much of my discussion. For more recent book-length reconsiderations of the concept and its relevance, see Joseph A. Camilleri and Jim Falk, *The End of Sovereignty?* (Aldershot, U.K.: Edward Elgar, 1992); Michael Ross Fowler and Julie Marie Bunck, *Law, Power, and the Sovereign State* (University Park: Pennsylvania State University Press, 1995); and Sohail S. Hashmi, ed., *State Sovereignty* (University Park: Pennsylvania State University Press, 1997).

4. Hinsley's definition expresses the same basic ideas as Max Weber's classic definition of the state as "a human community that (successfully) claims the *monopoly of the legitimate use of physical force* within a given territory." See Max Weber, "Politics as a Vocation," in *From Max Weber*, ed. H.H. Gerth and C. Wright Mills (New York: Oxford University Press, 1946), 78 (emphasis in original).

5. Janice E. Thomson, "State Sovereignty in International Relations: Bridging the Gap Between Theory and Empirical Research," *International Studies Quarterly* 39 (1995): 214. I have found Thomson's essay to be the most incisive and helpful of all the recent treatments of sovereignty.

6. Ibid., 216.

7. See Reinicke, *Global Public Policy*, especially chap. 2.

8. See the discussion in Gerhard von Glahn, *Law Among Nations*, 6th ed. (New York: Macmillan Publishing Co., 1992), chap. 5.

9. See Robert H. Jackson, *Quasi-States: Sovereignty, International Relations and the Third World* (Cambridge, UK: Cambridge University Press, 1990). Jackson is thinking especially about parts of west Africa.

10. For a systematic and powerful presentation of the argument that the meaning and practice of sovereignty are not stable over time and place, see Stephen D. Krasner, *Sovereignty: Organized Hypocrisy* (Princeton, NJ: Princeton University Press, 1999)

11. Hinsley, *Sovereignty*, 226.

12. These exceptions include such practices as recognizing the rights of diplomats in other countries and protecting citizens of other states traveling abroad. Interestingly enough, though, states often use the fiction of territoriality to deal with these exceptions. Thus, the territory on which one state's embassy is located in another state and the building itself are considered part of or extensions of the home state's territory and thus subject only to the sovereign control of the home state.

13. My use of the concept of boundaries owes much to Friedrich Kratochwil, "Of Systems, Boundaries, and Territoriality: An Inquiry into the Formation of the State System," *World Politics* 38 (October 1986): 27–52, and John Gerard Ruggie, "Territoriality and Beyond: Problematizing Modernity in International Relations," *International Organization* 47 (1993): 139–74.

14. See the cases discussed in Ethan A. Nadelmann, "Global Prohibition Regimes: The Evolution of Norms in International Society," *International Organization* 44 (Autumn 1990): 479–526.

15. My discussion of the modern state as an institution that creates and maintains boundaries closely parallels the argument and approach presented in Timothy Mitchell, "The Limits of the State: Beyond Statist Approaches and Their Critics," *American Political Science Review* 85 (March 1991): 77–96.

16. The key texts are Thomas Hobbes, *Leviathan*, ed. Richard Tuck (Cambridge, U.K.: Cambridge University Press, 1991), and Jean Bodin, *On Sovereignty*, ed. Julian Franklin (Cambridge, U.K.: Cambridge University Press, 1992).

17. For an excellent treatment of the emergence of the notion of popular sovereignty, see Edmund Morgan, *Inventing the People* (New York: W. W. Norton & Co., 1988).

18. John Locke, *Two Treatises of Government*, ed. Peter Laslett (Cambridge, U.K.: Cambridge University Press, 1991).

19. Benedict Anderson, *Imagined Communities*, rev. ed. (London: Verso, 1991).

20. My treatment of the spread of the sovereign state and the evolution of its meaning since the Second World War is based generally on Hedley Bull and Adam Watson, *The Expansion of International Society* (Oxford: Clarendon Press, 1984); Robert H. Jackson, *Quasi-States: Sovereignty, International Relations and the Third World* (Cambridge, U.K: Cambridge University Press, 1990); and (especially concerning international law) Gerhard von Glahn, *Law Among Nations*, 6th ed. (New York: Macmillan Publishing Co., 1992).

21. John Gerard Ruggie, "International Regimes, Transactions, and Change: Embedded Liberalism in the Postwar Economic Order," *International Organization* 36 (spring 1992): 379–415.

22. The analysis of the United States role in the post-World War II era as that of a "hegemonic power" is well presented in Robert Gilpin, *The Political Economy of International Relations* (Princeton, N.J.: Princeton University Press, 1987).

23. As scholars of the "hegemonic stability" approach emphasize, one of the responsibilities of a hegemonic power is to make short-term sacrifices of national interest to promote the longer-term survival of the global order it aims to support.

24. See Dani Rodrik, *Has Globalization Gone Too Far?* (Washington, D.C.: Institute for International Economics, 1997), especially chap. 4.

25. For more elaborate reflections on the importance of this relationship, see Michael Walzer, *Spheres of Justice* (New York: Basic Books, 1983), chap. 2.

26. For general background on migration over the past decades, see Myron Weiner, *The Global Migration Crisis* (New York: HarperCollins, 1995).

27. James McPherson, *Abraham Lincoln and the Second American Revolution* (New York: Oxford University Press, 1991).

28. Two useful accounts of the development of the American state during the Progressive Era are Stephen Skowronek, *Building a New American State* (Cambridge, U.K.: Cambridge University Press, 1982), and Robert H. Wiebe, *The Search for Order, 1877–1920* (New York: Hill and Wang, 1967).

29. For an excellent recent treatment of the New Deal, see Alan Brinkley, *The End of Reform* (New York, Alfred A. Knopf, 1995).

30. Walzer, *Sphere of Justice*, chap. 2.

31. A comprehensive overview of the elements of the post-1945 liberal order in the United States in presented in Steven Fraser and Gary Gerstle, *The Rise and Fall of the New Deal Order, 1930–1980* (Princeton, N.J.: Princeton University Press, 1989).

32. Robert Reich, *The Work of Nations* (New York: Vintage Books, 1991), chaps. 1–6.

33. The literature in this area is enormous. Four studies that have been particularly helpful to my analysis are Alan Brinkley, *The End of Reform* and *Liberalism and Its Discontents* (Cambridge, Mass.: Harvard University Press, 1998); Gosta Esping-Andersen, *Three Worlds of Welfare Capitalism* (Cambridge, U.K.: Cambridge University Press, 1990); and Fraser and Gerstle, *The Rise and Fall of the New Deal Order, 1930–1980*, especially the essays by Thomas Ferguson, Ira Katznelson, and Jonathan Reider.

34. See especially Alan Brinkley, "The Late New Deal and the Idea of the State," in *Liberalism and Its Discontents* (Cambridge, Mass.: Harvard University Press, 1998): 37–62.

35. Significantly, the major exception to this disappearance of "sovereignty" from political discourse was the claim of "state sovereignty" on the part of southern states to resist national laws aimed at the promotion of civil rights.

Notes to Chapter 3

1. For a solid presentation of this argument, see Joel Krieger, *Reagan, Thatcher and the Politics of Decline* (New York: Oxford University Press, 1986). Another good account of these developments, from a somewhat different perspective, is Charles S. Maier, ed., *Changing Boundaries of the Political* (Cambridge, U.K.: Cambridge University Press, 1987).

2. For an excellent exploration of the tensions in the relationship between business and the activist state, see Cathie Jo Martin, *Stuck in Neutral: Business and the Politics of Human Capital Investment Policy* (Princeton, N.J.: Princeton University Press, 2000).

3. Some of the best works on globalization, which will form the basis for my analysis, are the following: Barrie Axford, *The Global System* (New York: St. Martin's Press, 1995); Anthony Giddens, *The Consequences of Modernity* (Stanford, Calif.: Stanford University Press, 1990); Paul Q. Hirst and Grahame Thompson, *Globalization in Question*, 2d ed. (Cambridge, U.K.: Polity Press, 1999); Wolfgang Reinicke, *Global Public Policy* (Washington, D.C.: Brookings Institution Press, 1998); Roland Robertson, *Globalization* (London:

Sage Publications, 1992); Saskia Sassen, *Losing Control?* (New York: Columbia University Press, 1996); Susan Strange, *The Retreat of the State* (Cambridge, U.K.: Cambridge University Press, 1996); and Malcolm Waters, *Globalization* (London: Routledge, 1995).

4. David Harvey, *The Condition of Postmodernism* (Cambridge, Mass.: Blackwell Publishers, 1989); Anthony Giddens, *The Consequences of Modernity* (Stanford, Calif.: Stanford University Press, 1990); and Malcolm Waters, *Globalization* (London: Routledge, 1995).

5. This is the scholarly approach that is the basis of the accounts of globalization presented in the popular writings of Thomas Friedman and William Greider.

6. Robertson, *Globalization,* chaps. 6 and 11.

7. This is the basic insight that supports the view, presented especially in the writing of Benjamin Barber and Thomas Friedman, that the world today is driven by a conflict, or "dialectic," pitting the forces of deepening globalization against those trying to preserve or reinforce boundaries between groups and societies.

8. Reinicke, *Global Public Policy,* 11–12. The internal quotation is from Organization for Economic Cooperation and Development (OECD), *Globalization of Industry: Overview and Sector Reports* (Paris, 1996), 15.

9. Axford, *Global System,* 27.

10. See Hirst and Thompson, *Globalization in Question,* especially chap. 1. I will return to this argument in more detail during the discussion of the implications of globalization for sovereignty.

11. For the elaboration of the notion of an "ideal-type," see Max Weber, "'Objectivity' in Social Science and Social Policy," in Max Weber, *The Methodology of the Social Sciences,* ed. Edward A. Shils and Henry A. Finch (New York: Free Press, 1949), 49–112.

12. For an excellent theoretical discussion of this process, see Frederick Buell, *National Culture and the New Global System* (Baltimore: Johns Hopkins University Press, 1994).

13. A variety of tables and charts detailing these developments can be found in Hirst and Thompson, *Globalization in Question;* Joan E. Spero and Jeffrey A. Hart, *The Politics of International Economic Relations,* 5th ed. (New York: St. Martin's Press, 1997); and *The Economic Report of the President,* 1996 through 1999. However, it is important not to overemphasize the degree to which corporate identities and operations have been "denationalized." The best critique of this idea to date is provided by Paul N. Doremus, William W. Keller, Louis W. Pauly, and Simon Reich, *The Myth of the Global Corporation* (Princeton, N.J.: Princeton University Press, 1998).

14. For Friedman's discussion, see *The Lexus and the Olive Tree* (New York: Farrar, Straus, and Giroux, 1999), chap. 11.

15. For a review of the events leading up to the arrest, see Anthony Faiola, "Britain Arrests Pinochet at Spain's Request," *Washington Post,* 18 October 1998, p. A1. For a discussion of the outcome of this case, see Anthony Faiola, "Pinochet Returns to Chile: Flight from Britain Ends 16-Month Extradition Crusade," *Washington Post,* 3 March 2000, p. A1.

16. In both of these ways, globalization has worked to reinforce the kinds of relationships crucial to what Charles Lindblom called "the privileged position of business" in capitalist market societies. See Charles Lindblom, *Politics and Markets* (New York: Basic Books, 1977).

17. Of course, the United States acted globally throughout the Cold War. But its foreign and strategic policies were based on a relatively clear sense of the interests of the nation and a clear sense of the relationship between these interests and the other policy that might be pursued in the global arena. Today, my argument is suggesting, the line between domestic and "foreign" interests is much harder to draw, and thus the relationship between the goals of national security and other foreign policy aims is less clear. This may help explain the difficulty in coming up with a clear direction for national security policy in the aftermath of the Cold War.

18. Ethan Kapstein, *Sharing the Wealth* (New York: W.W. Norton & Co., 1999), 101–2. The internal quotation refers to the title of an essay by Richard Freeman, "Toward an Apartheid Economy," *Harvard Business Review* (September/October 1996): 114–21.

19. Dani Rodrik, *Has Globalization Gone Too Far?* (Washington, D.C.: Institute for International Economics, 1997), 4 (emphasis in original).

20. For good recent overviews of global environmental politics and the role of the United States in this area, see Norman J. Vig and Regina S. Axelrod, eds., *The Global Environment: Institutions, Law, and Policy* (Washington, DC: Congressional Quarterly Press, 1999), and Walter A. Rosenbaum, *Environmental Politics and Policy*, 4th ed. (Washington, D.C.: Congressional Quarterly Press, 1998).

21. The classic study of the immersion of law enforcement in an increasingly global context is Ethan Nadelmann, *Cops Across Borders: The Internationalization of U.S. Criminal Law Enforcement* (University Park: Pennsylvania State University Press, 1993).

22. For a comparison of capital flows in the beginning and end of the twentieth century, see Paul Bairoch and Richard Kozul-Wright, *Globalization Myths: Some Historical Reflections on Integration, Industrialization, and Growth in the World Economy*, United Nations Conference on Trade and Development (UNCTAD) Discussion Paper No. 113, March 1996; and Michael D. Bordo, Barry Eichengreen, and Douglas A. Irwin, *Is Globalization Today Really Different Than Globalization a Hundred Years Ago?* National Bureau of Economic Research, Working Paper 7195, June 1999.

23. It is sometimes forgotten that this movement went in both directions. Although the majority of persons never returned to their homeland, a significant proportion did, and played a relatively unexamined role in the process of turn of the century "globalization."

24. For an excellent review of the history of controls over human migration over the past two centuries, see John Torpey, *The Invention of the Passport* (New York: Cambridge University Press, 2000).

25. I will consider the relevance of these differences for the future of sovereignty later in this chapter. It should also be noted that some scholars believe the differences between the two periods can be exaggerated. For a good presentation of this argument, see Bairoch and Kozul-Wright, *Globalization Myths*.

26. For scholars following the lead of Immanuel Wallerstein, globalization is possible only in a world of separate sovereign states. The very division of territory into separate, mutually exclusive "sovereignties" creates the context for the kind of cross-border patterns of economic activity we are now discussing and the challenges they pose for political authority. For a recent statement of this perspective, with applications to the debate over globalization, see Immanuel Wallerstein, *Geopolitics and Geoculture: Essays on the Changing World-System* (Cambridge, UK: Cambridge University Press, 1991).

27. Of these discussions, perhaps the most eloquent was that of Karl Marx and Friedrich Engels presented in the opening sections of the *Manifesto of the Communist Party*. See

Karl Marx and Friedrich Engels, "The Communist Manifesto," in *Karl Marx: Selected Writings*, ed. Lawrence H. Simon (Indianapolis: Hackett Publishing Co., 1994), 157–86.

28. See Adam Smith, *An Inquiry into the Nature and Causes of the Wealth of Nations*, 2 vols. (Oxford: Oxford University Press, 1976), originally published 1776; Max Weber, *Economy and Society*, ed. Guenther Roth and Claus Wittich, 2 vols. (Berkeley: University of California Press, 1978); and Karl Polanyi, *The Great Transformation* (Boston: Beacon Press, 1957), originally published in 1944.

29. Here and in the rest of the book I use the term "Keynesianism" only in its broadest sense, to refer to the idea that governments could manage the level and direction of economic activity through manipulating the level of aggregate demand with the tools of fiscal and monetary policy. For a survey of the various meanings of Keynesianism and its impact on the post-World War II economy, see Peter A. Hall, ed. *The Political Power of Economic Ideas: Keynesianism Across Nations* (Princeton, N.J.: Princeton University Press, 1989).

30. For a balanced account of the successes and failures of these policies, see Orlando Patterson, *The Ordeal of Integration* (Washington, D.C.: Civitas/Counterpoint, 1997).

31. Perhaps the most representative expression of this mood was Lester C. Thurow, *The Zero-Sum Society* (New York: Basic Books, 1980).

32. For good examples of this kind of approach, see John H. Goldthorpe, ed. *Order and Conflict in Contemporary Capitalism* (Oxford: Clarendon Press, 1984), and Leon N. Lindberg and Charles S. Maier, eds., *The Politics of Inflation and Economic Stagnation* (Washington, D.C.: Brookings Institution Press, 1985).

33. See Martha Derthick and Paul J. Quirk, *The Politics of Deregulation* (Washington, DC: The Brookings Institution, 1985). Another useful account of the same developments, which also puts them in a longer historical perspective, is Marc Allen Eisner, *Regulatory Politics in Transition* (Baltimore: Johns Hopkins University Press, 1993), especially chap. 8.

34. For an excellent account of the failure of the attempt to reform the U.S. health care system and its implications for the polity as a whole, see Theda Skocpol, *Boomerang* (New York: W.W. Norton & Co., 1996).

35. Cerny's analysis is laid out best in two articles: P. Cerny, "Globalization and the Changing Logic of Collective Action," *International Organization* 49 (autumn 1995): 595–625, and P. Cerny, "Paradoxes of the Competition State," *Government and Opposition* 32 (spring 1997): 251–74.

36. Jay Mazur, "Labor's New Internationalism," *Foreign Affairs* 79 (January/February 2000): 79–93. In chapter 7 I will return to a discussion of this kind of response to globalization.

37. For a provocative recent presentation of this argument, see Robert Wright, "Continental Drift," *New Republic*, 17 January 2000, 18–23.

38. Susan Strange, *The Retreat of the State* (Cambridge, U.K.: Cambridge University Press, 1996).

39. Ibid., ix.

40. Ibid., 4.

41. It is important to emphasize that Strange is very careful to qualify her judgments in many ways unknown to the popular literature. For instance, she emphasizes that the United States is the one major exception to her argument, especially when one considers its power to shape the global economy as a whole. She is also far from those who would return to some golden age of the nation-state. But Strange's argument in the book comes closer to capturing the spirit of much of the popular "end of sovereignty" school than any other sophisticated scholarly analysis.

42. For a recent attempt to provide an overview of contemporary American political culture, which supports this characterization of citizens's views on the role of government, see Alan Wolfe, *One Nation, After All* (New York: Viking, 1998), especially chap. 6.

43. This argument is made forcefully by Helen Thompson in "The Modern State, Political Choice and An Open International Economy," *Government and Opposition* 34 (spring 1999): 203–25, and by Peter Evans in "The Eclipse of the State?: Reflections on Stateness in an Era of Globalization," *World Politics* 50 (1997): 62–87.

44. An excellent critique of the dangers of an overreliance on a "statist" approach is provided in Timothy Mitchell, "The Limits of the State: Beyond Statist Approaches and Their Critics," *American Political Science Review* 85 (March 1991): 77–96.

45. For an interesting attempt to explore the ways in which the distributive and symbolic aspects of policies are intertwined, see Dvora Yanow, *How Does a Policy Mean?* (Washington, D.C.: Georgetown University Press, 1996).

46. See chapter 1 for a more in-depth justification of this choice of policy areas.

Notes to Chapter 4

1. "The Politics of Trade: Despite the Boom, Globalisation Is One of the Hottest Issues Around. Why?" *The Economist* 353, no. 8142 (1999): 28.

2. An excellent short presentation and acknowledgment of the transformation in the politics of trade policy, cowritten by one of the leading scholars in the area, appeared just before the Seattle meetings. In hindsight, it provided good reasons to expect the kind of conflict that would emerge around the negotiations. See I. M. Destler and Peter J. Balint, *The New Politics of American Trade: Trade, Labor, and the Environment* (Washington, DC: Institute for International Economics, 1999).

3. E. E. Schattschneider, *Politics, Pressure, and the Tariff* (New York: Prentice-Hall, 1935).

4. The following account of postwar trade policy is based especially on Joan E. Spero and Jeffrey A. Hart, *The Politics of International Economic Relations,* 5th ed. (New York: St. Martin's Press, 1997).

5. Significantly enough, the defeat of the ITO was based on the fears of a newly elected Republican Congress that the treaty would threaten U.S. sovereignty.

6. For a clear tabular presentation of the trends in tariff protection during the post-World War II decades, see Richard B. Freeman, "Will Globalization Dominate U.S. Labor Market Outcomes?" in *Imports, Exports, and the American Worker,* ed. Susan M. Collins (Washington, D.C.: Brookings Institution Press, 1998), 107, table 3-1.

7. John Gerard Ruggie, "International Regimes, Transactions, and Change: Embedded Liberalism in the Postwar Economic Order," *International Organization* 36 (spring 1992): 379–415, and see the discussion of Ruggie's argument in chapter 2.

8. Raymond A. Bauer, Ithiel de Sola Pool, and Louis A. Dexler, *American Business and Public Policy* (Chicago: Atherton, 1963).

9. The classic elaboration of this approach was presented by Charles P. Kindleberger in a number of works; a good example is *The World in Depression, 1929–1939* (Berkeley: University of California Press, 1973). The most complete exposition and defense are provided in Robert Gilpin, *The Political Economy of International Relations* (Princeton, N.J.: Princeton University Press, 1987).

10. Two central works in this tradition are Robert O. Keohane and Joseph S. Nye, *Power and Interdependence* (Boston: Little, Brown and Co., 1977), and Robert O. Keohane, *After Hegemony* (Princeton, N.J.: Princeton University Press, 1984).

11. See Peter Gourevitch, *Politics in Hard Times* (Ithaca, N.Y.: Cornell University Press, 1986), and Ronald Rogowski, *Commerce and Coalitions* (Princeton, N.J.: Princeton University Press, 1989). There are important differences between these writers, especially concerning the importance of political institutions and ideas in shaping the process of coalition formation, and large literatures have grown up around each writer's approach. But for current purposes it is the shared kind of question they ask that is most important for understanding the different ways we can think about the politics of trade policy.

12. See Judith Goldstein, *Ideas, Interests, and American Trade Policy* (Ithaca, N.Y.: Cornell University Press, 1993). Earlier, scholars such as John Odell had begun to explore the role of ideas in the related area of U.S. international monetary policy. See John Odell, *U.S. International Monetary Policy: Markets, Power, and Ideas as Sources of Change* (Princeton, N.J.: Princeton University Press, 1982).

13. I. M. Destler, *American Trade Politics* (Washington, D.C.: Institute for International Economics and New York: Twentieth Century Fund). There have been three updated editions of this work in the intervening years, and I will draw upon these in the subsequent analysis.

14. See Destler, *American Trade Politics*, 3d ed., published in 1995; Goldstein, *Ideas, Interests*, and Graham Wilson, "American Trade Policy: System Withstands Pressure?" (paper presented at the 1997 annual meeting of the Midwest Political Science Association, Chicago, April 1997).

15. See Helen Milner, *Resisting Protectionism: Global Industries and the Politics of International Trade* (Princeton, N.J.: Princeton University Press, 1988).

16. My account of the Reagan administration's trade policies relies again on Spero and Hart, *The Politics of International Economic Relations*. An interesting and often polemical account of these years, written by a participant in the policymaking, is Henry R. Nau, *The Myth of America's Decline* (New York: Oxford University Press, 1990).

17. The notion of "unbundling" sovereignty has been explored by Friedrich Kratochwil, "Of Systems, Boundaries, and Territoriality: An Inquiry into the Formation of the State System," *World Politics* 38 (October 1986): 27–52, and by John Gerard Ruggie, "Territoriality and Beyond: Problematizing Modernity in International Relations," *International Organization* 47 (winter 1993): 139–74.

18. The literature on "two-level" games emerges from Robert Putnam's "Diplomacy and Domestic Politics: The Logic of Two-Level Games," *International Organization* 42 (summer 1998): 427–60. For two interesting explorations of this argument, one theoretical and one empirical, see Kenneth W. Abbott and Duncan Snidal, "Why States Act Through Formal International Organizations," *Journal of Conflict Resolution* 42 (February 1998): 3–32, and Robert Paarlberg, "Agricultural Policy Reform and the Uruguay Round: Synergistic Linkage in a Two-Level Game?" *International Organization* 51 (summer 1997): 413–44.

19. The single best study of the history and politics of NAFTA, written by a scholar who was working for Senator Bill Bradley during the ratification struggle, is Frederick W. Mayer, *Interpreting NAFTA* (New York: Columbia University Press, 1998). Mayer's book is the main source for my discussion of the politics of NAFTA. For an excellent short review of these events, see Stephen D. Cohen, Joel R. Paul, and Robert A. Blecker, *Fundamentals of U.S. Foreign Trade Policy* (Boulder, Colo.: Westview Press, 1996), chap. 12.

20. For a good analysis of the impact of the NAFTA ratification battle on the Clinton administration's larger agenda, see Theda Skocpol, *Boomerang* (New York: W.W. Norton & Co., 1996).

21. The best overviews and syntheses of this literature are found in William R. Cline, *Trade and Income Distribution* (Washington, D.C.: Institute for International Economics, 1997), and Susan M. Collins, ed., *Imports, Exports, and the American Worker* (Washington, DC: Brookings Institution Press, 1998). In addition, the works discussed in chapter 1 by Gary Burtless et al., *Globaphobia* (Washington, D.C.: Brookings Institution in association with Progressive Policy Institute and Twentieth Century Fund, 1998), and Dani Rodrik, *Has Globalization Gone Too Far?* (Washington, D.C.: Institute for International Economics, 1997), mark important contributions to the argument, and I will rely on them as well in the following discussion.

22. Collins, "Economic Integration and the American Worker: An Overview," in Collins, ed., *Imports, Exports*, 8.

23. For a good overview of the nature and sources of this decline, see Jeffrey E. Cohen, *Politics and Economic Policy in the United States*, 2d ed. (Boston: Houghton Mifflin Co., 2000), chap. 5. It is widely accepted among political scientists that American trade unions were always less able to control the distribution of income than were those in most of Western Europe. Again, we see how the particular, more "liberal" form of the post-World War II social compact in the United States facilitated the move toward globalization that began in the 1970s.

24. Michael J. Piore provides a thoughtful overview of these trends in "Trade and the Social Structure of Economic Activity," in Collins, ed., *Imports, Exports*, 257–303.

25. By 1998, of course, lower-wage workers finally began to see some improvement in their living standards, and we began to see some small reduction in the degree of income inequality in the U.S. economy. The causes of these trends seem quite clear: years of nearly full employment and sustained high levels of economic growth finally began to create some scarcity of lower-wage workers and a consequent rise in wages. But those families below the median of the income distribution have yet to recoup the losses of the previous decades, and the level of income inequality remains significantly greater than at the end of the 1970s. For a good recent review of these trends, see Sheldon Danziger and Deborah Reed, "Winners and Losers: The Era of Inequality Continues," *Brookings Review* 17 (September 1999): 14–17.

26. This is one of the major conclusions in William R. Cline, *Trade and Income Distribution* (Washington, D.C.: Institute for International Economics, 1997).

27. In addition to the work of Rodrik already cited, the same approach is offered in Robert C. Feenstra, "Integration of Trade and Disintegration of Production in the Global Economy," *Journal of Economic Perspectives* 12 (fall 1998): 31–50.

28. Rodrik, *Has Globalization Gone Too Far?* 26–27.

29. For a solid overview of the various policy options in this area, see Louis Jacobson, "Compensation Programs," in *Imports, Exports*, 473–537.

30. Krugman has been, indeed, one of the most influential scholars of the relationship between trade and the distribution of income.

31. See Cohen et al., *Fundamentals,* 238.

32. For good examples of the general consensus that NAFTA has not had a major impact on the U.S. economy, see Burtless et al., *Globaphobia,* and Nora Lustig, *NAFTA: Setting the Record Straight,* Brookings Institution Policy Brief #20, June 1997, at www.brook.edu/comm/PolicyBriefs/pb020/pb20.htm. For good examples of the argument that NAFTA has had a major impact, for good or ill, respectively, see Rebecca Reynolds Bannister, *NAFTA: A Progressive Look at a Landmark Agreement after Three Years,* Progressive Policy Institute "Backgrounder" at www.dlcppi.org/texts/trade/bannist.htm, and Jesse Rothstein and Robert Scott, *NAFTA's Casualties,* Economic Policy Institute Issue Brief #120, 19 September 1997, at www.epinet.org.

33. Mayer, *Interpreting NAFTA,* 257 (emphasis in original).

34. Patrick Buchanan, "GOP's NAFTA Divide," *Washington Times,* 23 August 1993.

35. Kim Moody and Michael McGinn, *Unions and Free Trade: Solidarity vs. Competition.* International Labor Rights Education and Research Fund, 1992, p. 1.

36. Paul Pierson, *Dismantling the Welfare State?* (Cambridge, U.K.: Cambridge University Press, 1994).

37. For an interesting analysis of the impact of the state system on the way we think about security and threats in contemporary politics, see R.B.J. Walker, *Inside/Outside: International Relations as Political Theory* (Cambridge, U.K.: Cambridge University Press, 1993).

Notes to Chapter 5

1. A good attempt to provide an overview of the political roots of the current immigration debate is Herbert Dittgen, "The American Debate About Immigration in the 1990's: A New Nationalism After the End of the Cold War?" *Stanford Humanities Review* 5 (1997): 256–86. See also David Reimers, *Unwelcome Strangers* (New York: Columbia University Press, 1998).

2. From this point on, I will refer to these by their more common titles, the "Immigration Reform" and "Welfare Reform" acts of 1996, respectively.

3. There are numerous excellent works that review immigration and immigration policy over the last three decades. My account draws from many of these sources; for the reader interested in good general reviews of the area, see the following treatments: Louis DeSipio and Rodolfo de la Garza, *Making Americans, Remaking America* (Boulder, Colo.: Westview Press, 1998); David Heer, *Immigration in America's Future* (Boulder, Colo.: Westview Press, 1996); John Isbister, *The Immigration Debate* (West Hartford, Conn.: Kumarian Press, 1996); Alejandro Portes and Ruben G. Rumbaut, *Immigrant America,* 2d ed. (Berkeley, Calif.: University of California Press, 1996); and Reimers, *Unwelcome Strangers.*

4. A reader interested in getting the full flavor of current anti-immigration sentiment should consult Reimers, *Unwelcome Strangers,* which contains the single best sampling of such opinion currently available.

5. Congressman Steve Chabot (R-OH), *Congressional Record*, 104th Cong., 2d Sess., 1996, 142, p. H2595, as cited in James G. Gimpel and James R. Edwards, Jr., *The Congressional Politics of Immigration Reform* (Boston: Allyn and Bacon, 1999), 3.

6. Gimpel and Edwards, *The Congressional Politics*, especially chaps. 1 and 2.

7. Gimpel and Edwards, *The Congressional Politics*, provides an unequaled analysis of the recent debates, legislation, and politics of immigration in Congress.

8. The classic study of American nativism is John Higham, *Strangers in the Land: Patterns of American Nativism, 1896–1925* (New Brunswick, N.J.: Rutgers University Press, 1955). For a recent study that explores the same tradition through a detailed analysis of the history of American citizenship law and policy, see Rogers M. Smith, *Civic Ideals* (New Haven, Conn.: Yale University Press, 1997).

9. Although most commentators recognize this to some degree, it is an especially important element of Isbister's argument. See Isbister, *The Immigration Debate*.

10. See Gimpel and Edwards, *The Congressional Politics*, and DeSipio and de la Garza, *Making Americans*, for these arguments.

11. My account of the history of U.S. immigration policy is based especially on DeSipio and de la Garza, *Making Americans*; Gerald Neuman, *Strangers to the Constitution* (Princeton, N.J.: Princeton University Press, 1996); Reimers, *Unwelcome Strangers*; and Smith, *Civic Ideals*.

12. Indeed, Michael Walzer has argued that relatively closed borders may be necessary to promote both the acceptance and integration of new populations into an established community. Without the sense of security derived from restriction on further entry, the dominant segment of the nation may be less willing to accept and adjust to ethnically or culturally distinct newcomers. See M. Walzer, *Spheres of Justice* (New York: Basic Books, 1983), especially chap. 2.

13. The best concise overviews of the growth of human migration since the 1960s are presented in Stephen Castles and Mark J. Miller, *The Age of Migration* (New York: Guilford Press, 1993), and Myron Weiner, *The Global Migration Crisis* (New York: HarperCollins, 1995).

14. The work of Saskia Sassen has been central in laying out many of these connections. See Saskia Sassen, *The Mobility of Labor and Capital: A Study in International Investment and Labor Flows* (Cambridge, U.K.: Cambridge University Press, 1988), and *Losing Control?: Sovereignty in an Age of Globalization* (New York: Columbia University Press, 1996).

15. Most of the sources cited in note 3 provide some overview of this policy record, but the treatment by Gimpel and Edwards, *The Congressional Politics*, is by far the most detailed and comprehensive.

16. This category of migrants, created at the insistence of Senator Edward M. Kennedy of Massachusetts, attempted to "diversify" the immigrant stream by increasing the percentage of migrants from Western Europe, especially Ireland.

17. See David Jacobson, *Rights Across Borders* (Baltimore: Johns Hopkins University Press, 1996). Jacobson has been justly criticized for overestimating the depth and impact of such changes, but his argument that these developments in the legal protections for migrants and immigrants in the United States can be seen as part of a larger movement in the 1970s and 1980s remains valid. It also provides an important element of the background for understanding the subsequent backlash against such changes, which will be the subject of the last parts of this chapter.

18. DeSipio and de la Garza, *Making Americans,* chaps. 4 and 5.

19. For general background on policy toward illegal immigrants, see the sources listed in note 3, as well as the chapters by Kitty Calavita and Philip Martin in *Controlling Immigration: A Global Perspective,* ed. Wayne A. Cornelius, Philip L. Martin, and James F. Hollifield (Stanford, Calif.: Stanford University Press, 1994), and Peter Andreas, "The Escalation of U.S. Immigration Control in the Post-NAFTA Era," *Political Science Quarterly* 113 (1998–99): 591–615.

20. Andreas, "The Escalation," 593.

21. For a more recent analysis of the same theme, see Louis Uchitelle, "I.N.S. Looks the Other Way on Illegal Immigration," *New York Times,* 9 March 2000, at http://www.nytimes.com/yr/mo/day/news/financial/unemployment-ins.html.

22. This argument is also presented by Wayne A. Cornelius, Philip L. Martin, and James F. Hollifield, eds., in "Introduction: The Ambivalent Quest for Immigration Control," in *Controlling Immigration: A Global Perspective,* 3–41.

23. Sassen's most complete presentation of this argument can be found in "The De Facto Transnationalizing of Immigration Policy," reprinted in *Globalization and Its Discontents* (New York: New Press, 1998), pp. 5–30.

24. See Jacobson, *Rights Across Borders,* and Yasemin Soysal, *The Limits of Citizenship* (Chicago: University of Chicago Press, 1994).

25. See Christian Joppke, "Why Liberal States Accept Unwanted Immigration," *World Politics* 50 (January 1998): 266–93, and James F. Hollifield, "Migration, Trade, and the Nation-State: The Myth of Globalization," *UCLA Journal of International Law and Foreign Affairs* 3 (1998): 595–636.

26. Jeanette Money, *The Political Geography of Immigration Control* (Ithaca, N.Y.: Cornell University Press, 1999).

27. The Schengen Accords, which took effect in March 1995, were signed by Germany, France, the Benelux countries (Belgium, the Netherlands, and Luxembourg), Spain, and Portugal. These accords established a system of free movement of persons among these states while committing the states to make greater efforts to prevent the entry of "illegal" persons across the borders of any of the signatories to the agreement. For good analyses of these accords and their impact, see Andrew Convey and Marek Kupiszewski, "Keeping Up with Schengen: Migration and Policy in the European Union," *International Migration Review* 29 (winter 1995): 939–63, and Gallya Lahav and Virginie Guiraudon, "A Reappraisal of the State Sovereignty Debate: The Case of Migration Control," *Comparative Political Studies* 33 (March 2000): 163–95.

28. For good reviews of the evolution of European immigration policies, see the contributions in Cornelius, Martin, and Hollifield, eds., *Controlling Immigration,* and Christian Joppke, ed., *Challenge to the Nation-State* (New York: Oxford University Press, 1998); see also Anthony M. Messina and Colleen V. Thouez, "Controlling Borders: The Logics and Politics of a European *Immigration Regime*" (paper delivered at the annual meeting of the American Political Science Association, Atlanta, 1999).

29. Sassen, *Losing Control?,* 60.

30. See Andreas, "The Escalation of U.S. Immigration Control."

31. See especially Peter H. Schuck, "The Politics of Rapid Legal Change: Immigration Policy in the 1980's," *Studies in American Political Development* 6 (spring 1992): 37–92, and "Membership in the Liberal Polity: The Devaluation of American Citizenship," in *Immigra-*

tion and the Politics of Citizenship in Europe and North America, ed. William Rogers Brubaker (Lanham, Md.: University Press of America, 1989), 51–65. Schuck presents a reevaluation of his argument, in light of policy and political developments in the 1990s, in "The Re-Evaluation of American Citizenship," in *Challenge to the Nation-State,* ed. Christian Joppke (New York: Oxford University Press, 1998), 191–230.

32. Schuck, "Membership in the Liberal Polity," 52.

33. For good examples of this kind of argument, presented by key figures in the immigration policy controversies of the 1990s, see Dan Stein, "Why America Needs a Moratorium on Immigration," and Patrick Buchanan, "America Needs a 'Time Out' on Immigration," both reprinted in Scott Barbour, *At Issue: Immigration Policy* (San Diego, Calif.: Greenhaven Press, 1995). Stein is the director of the Federation for American Immigration Reform (FAIR), a leading think tank promoting limits on further immigration.

34. Peter Brimelow, *Alien Nation* (New York: Random House, 1995).

35. For the evolution of immigration legislation in this period, see Gimpel and Edwards, *The Congressional Politics,* chap. 6.

36. The following account is based on Jan Austin, ed., *Congressional Quarterly 1996 Almanac* (Washington, D.C.: Congressional Quarterly, Inc., 1997). For the immigration reform legislation, see 5–3 to 5–17; for welfare reform, see 6–3 to 6–24.

37. The decision was *Reno v. American Arab Anti-Discrimination Committee,* 119 S. Ct. 936 (1997).

38. For a defense of the latter position, see Neuman, *Strangers to the Constitution.*

39. In addition to a variety of other sources, this argument has a solid pedigree in the scholarship on American constitutional law, having been most clearly and forcefully presented by Alexander M. Bickel in *The Morality of Consent* (New Haven, Conn.: Yale University Press, 1975), especially in chap. 2, "Citizen or Person? What Is Not Granted Cannot Be Taken Away." For some current arguments in the same vein, see Peter Spiro, "Dual Nationality and the Meaning of Citizenship," *Emory Law Journal* 46 (fall 1997): 1411–85, and Steven H. Legomsky, "Why Citizenship?" *Virginia Journal of International Law* 35 (fall 1994): 279–300.

Notes to Chapter 6

1. For an effective critique of this tendency and a defense of the importance of "symbolic politics," see Alison Brysk, "'Hearts and Minds': Bringing Symbolic Politics Back In," *Polity* 27 (summer 1995): 559–85.

2. I will pursue both directions of analysis at the same time, alternating between the politics of language and the role of symbolism along the way.

3. See David Easton, *The Political System* (New York: Alfred A. Knopf, 1953), especially chap. 5.

4. Edelman's classic work is *The Symbolic Uses of Politics* (Urbana: University of Illinois Press, 1964). His best recent work is embodied in *Constructing the Political Spectacle* (Chicago: University of Chicago Press, 1988), and *From Art to Politics* (Chicago: University of Chicago Press, 1995).

5. Ironically, perhaps, the emphasis on elite manipulation in Edelman's work has often served to reinforce the sharp distinction between "reality" and "symbolism" so prominent in political science. In his early work in particular, Edelman seemed always to work with the assumption of a political elite that could see its real interests and used its power to manipulate symbolism to protect these interests. His more recent work, which seems to move away from this assumption to some degree, fits better into the framework I am building.

   6. Benedict Anderson, *Imagined Communities*, rev. ed. (London: Verso, 1991), 6–7.

   7. The best single source on the history of language politics in the United States is Dennis Baron, *The English-Only Question* (New Haven, Conn.: Yale University Press, 1990). Two other good if less complete sources are the materials collected in James Crawford, ed., *Language Loyalties: A Source Book on the Official English Controversy* (Chicago: University of Chicago Press, 1992), and Raymond Tatalovich, *Nativism Reborn?: The Official English Language Movement and the American States* (Lexington: University Press of Kentucky, 1995).

   8. For a review of the history of alien suffrage in the nineteenth century and an evaluation of its significance for contemporary debates, see Neuman, *Strangers to the Constitution* (Princeton, N.J.: Princeton University Press, 1996), especially chaps. 4 and 8.

   9. See John Higham, *Strangers in the Land: Patterns of American Nativism, 1896–1925* (New Brunswick, N.J.: Rutgers University Press, 1955), for an overview and analysis of these movements.

   10. The political science literature on contemporary language politics is quite sparse, for reasons that should be clear by now. In addition to the sources cited in note 7, and occasional discussion in the literature on immigration policy, the most systematic studies have been conducted by Jack Citrin and his colleagues. See Jack Citrin, Beth Reingold, Evelyn Waters, and Donald P. Green, "The 'Official English' Movement and the Symbolic Politics of Language in the United States," *Western Political Quarterly* 43 (September 1990): 535–60, and Jack Citrin, "Language Politics and American Identity," *Public Interest* 99 (spring 1990): 96–109. An interesting critique of the work of Citrin et al. is presented in Deborah Schildkraut and Gregory Huber, "Symbolic Politics, Ideology, and Language Policy: Beyond Liberalism and 'Americanism'" (paper presented at the annual meeting of the Northeastern Political Science Association, Philadelphia, November 1997).

   11. Citrin, "Language Politics," 98.

   12. Ibid., 96.

   13. See the comprehensive listing of Official English amendments in appendix B of Tatalovich, *Nativism Reborn?*

   14. For good explorations of the English-Plus movement, see Crawford, ed., *Language Loyalties*, and Tatalovich, *Nativism Reborn?*

   15. Citrin et al., "The 'Official English' Movement," 536.

   16. See the data and analysis presented in Citrin et al., "The 'Official English' Movement," and Jack Citrin, Beth Reingold, and Donald P. Green, "American Identity and the Politics of Ethnic Change," *Journal of Politics* 52 (November 1990): 1124–54. To some degree, this analysis is challenged by Raymond Tatalovich, who emphasizes the role played by elites—whether representatives or interest group leaders—in stirring up the whole issue of language and using it to mobilize citizens for their own purposes. But the objection is not necessarily fatal to the Citrin et al. approach, for two reasons. First, as Tatalovich notes, his conclusions about the importance of elites applies more to the states where English-only laws were passed by legislators, as opposed to states such as California where the laws emerged out of referenda. Second, it seems to me that the two approaches need not be mutually exclusive for our purposes. Elites always play a central role in mobilizing publics or masses, but what I am particularly interested in is the factors that lead certain segments of a population to respond more willingly to these appeals. See Tatalovich, *Nativism Reborn?* especially 246–51.

17. This is clearly borne out by the data in Citrin et al., "The 'Official English' Movement."

18. In addition to the sources presented in note 7, the history and arguments concerning bilingual education are well analyzed in James Crawford, *Bilingual Education: History, Politics, Theory, and Practice* (Trenton, N.J.: Crane Publishing Co., 1989); Rosalie Pedalino Porter, *Forked Tongue: The Politics of Bilingual Education* (New York: Basic Books, 1990); and Richard Rothstein, "Bilingual Education," *Phi Delta Kappan* 79 (May 1998): 672–77.

19. This pattern exactly matches the periods of heightened interest, quiescence, and then reemergence of popular and legislative mobilization against immigration.

20. See Elizabeth A. Palmer, "Language Bill Passes House," *Congressional Quarterly Weekly Report*, 3 August 1996, 2205.

21. See Paul Van Slambrouck, "California Educators Struggle with End of Bilingual Education," *Christian Science Monitor*, 10 August 1998, p. 1.

22. See "Arizona Court Kills English-Only Law," *American Bar Association Journal* 84 (July 1998): 36. The decision was based on the law's restriction of First Amendment free speech rights, and the U.S. Supreme Court subsequently dismissed a challenge to this decision. It is important to remember that the Arizona law was the most far-reaching of its type, prohibiting any use of languages other than English by public employees performing public duties.

23. For some of the best syntheses of the literature, see Alejandro Portes and Ruben G. Rumbaut, *Immigrant America*, 2d ed.(Berkeley: University of California Press, 1996), and Gillian Stevens, "Immigration, Emigration, Language Acquisition and the English Language Proficiency of Immigrants in the United States," in *Immigration and Ethnicity*, ed. Barry Edmonston and Jeffrey S. Passel (Washington, DC: Urban Institute Press, 1994), 163–85. For a more general presentation of the same argument, see Robert D. King, "Should English Be the Law?" *Atlantic Monthly*, April 1997, 55–64.

24. Portes and Rumbaut, *Immigrant America*, p. 231.

25. Roland Robertson, *Globalization* (London: Sage Publications, 1992). See chapter 3.

26. See Barber, *Jihad v. McWorld*, and Friedman, *The Lexus and the Olive Tree.*

27. For an account of this pattern of change that comes to similar conclusions, though in a very different context and for different purposes, see Michael Sandel, *Democracy's Discontent.*

28. See Geoffrey Nunberg, "The Official English Movement: Reimagining America," in James Crawford, ed., *Language Loyalties*, 479–94.

29. No example is more classic than Louis Hartz, *The Liberal Tradition in America* (New York: Harcourt Brace, 1955).

30. Nunberg, "The Official English Movement," 484–85.

Notes to Chapter 7

1. For a relatively optimistic account of the possibilities for states finding ways to cooperate to govern this emerging global system, see Wolfgang H. Reinicke, *Global Public Policy* (Washington, D.C.: Brookings Institution Press, 1998).

2. For a more theoretical presentation of the same argument, see Ian Clark, *Globalization and International Relations Theory* (New York: Oxford University Press, 1999).

3. For an argument that such groups are likely to be increasingly frozen out of political power and influence in a globalized state, see Peter Evans's provocative essay "The Eclipse of the State?: Reflections on Stateness in an Era of Globalization," *World Politics* 50 (October 1997): 62–87.

4. Saskia Sassen, *Losing Control?: Sovereignty in an Age of Globalization* (New York: Columbia University Press, 1996), 38.

5. Even the "global financial markets" that Sassen discusses have specific territorial centers of operation; in the case of the United States, of course, this is New York City.

6. The single best presentation and elaboration of this thesis is presented by Wolfgang Reinicke, *Global Public Policy*, especially chap. 2.

7. Of course, globalization provides only one of a number of areas around which conflicts over the future of the polity are centering. In particular, dissatisfaction with the role of government and the operation of the political process has manifold sources, as the works discussed earlier trace in great detail. It is my contention, though, that the politics of globalization do and will provide a central axis around which these conflicts will play out.

8. I. M. Destler and Peter J. Balint, *The New Politics of American Trade: Trade, Labor, and the Environment* (Washington, D.C.: Institute for International Economics, 1999), 1.

9. For a defense of this approach, offered by three authors who held official positions in the Clinton Administration and were advisers to the presidential campaign of Al Gore, see W. Bowman Carter, Joan Spero, and Laura D'Andrea Tyson, "New World, New Deal: A Democratic Approach to Globalization," *Foreign Affairs* 79 (March/April 2000): 80–98.

10. See Helen Thompson, "The Modern State, Political Choice, and An Open International Economy," *Government and Opposition* 34 (spring 1999): 203–25, and "The Nation-State and International Capital Flows in Historical Perspective," *Government and Opposition* 32 (winter 1997): 84–113.

11. Stephen D. Krasner, *Sovereignty: Organized Hypocrisy* (Princeton, N.J.: Princeton University Press, 1999), 223.

12. Helen Thompson, "The Nation-State and International Capital Flows," 113.

13. Judith N. Shklar, *American Citizenship: The Quest for Inclusion* (Cambridge, Mass.: Harvard University Press, 1991).

Bibliography

Abbott, Kenneth W., and Duncan Snidal. "Why States Act Through Formal International Organizations." *Journal of Conflict Resolution* 42 (February 1998): 3–32.

Anderson, Benedict. *Imagined Communities.* Rev. ed. London: Verso, 1991.

Anderson, James E. *Public Policymaking: An Introduction.* 4th ed. Boston: Houghton Mifflin Co., 2000.

Andreas, Peter. "The Escalation of U.S. Immigration Control in the Post-NAFTA Era," *Political Science Quarterly* 113 (winter 1998–99): 591–615.

"Arizona Court Kills English-Only Law." *American Bar Association Journal* 84 (July 1998): 36.

Austin, Jan, ed. *Congressional Quarterly 1996 Almanac.* Washington, D.C.: Congressional Quarterly, Inc., 1997.

Axford, Barrie. *The Global System.* New York: St. Martin's Press, 1995.

Bairoch, Paul, and Richard Kozul-Wright. *Globalization Myths: Some Historical Reflections on Integration, Industrialization and Growth in the World Economy.* United Nations Conference on Trade and Development (UNCTAD) Discussion Paper no. 113, March 1996.

Bannister, Rebecca Reynolds. *NAFTA: A Progressive Look at a Landmark Agreement after Three Years.* Progressive Policy Institute Backgrounder, 1997, at www.dlcppi.org/texts/trade/bannist.htm.

Barber, Benjamin. *Jihad v. McWorld.* New York: Ballantine Books, 1996.

Barbour, Scott. *At Issue: Immigration Policy.* San Diego, Calif.: Greenhaven Press, 1995.

Baron, Dennis. *The English-Only Question.* New Haven, Conn.: Yale University Press, 1990.

Bauer, Raymond A., Ithiel de Sola Pool, and Lewis A. Dexter. *American Business and Public Policy.* Chicago: Atherton Press, 1963.

Bickel, Alexander. *The Morality of Consent.* New Haven, Conn.: Yale University Press, 1975.

Bodin, Jean. *On Sovereignty.* Edited by Julian Franklin. Cambridge, U.K.: Cambridge University Press, 1992.

Bordo, Michael D., Barry Eichengreen, and Douglas A. Irwin. *Is Globalization Today Really Different Than Globalization a Hundred Years Ago?* National Bureau of Economic Research, Working Paper 7195, June 1999.

Brimelow, Peter. *Alien Nation.* New York: Random House, 1995.

Brinkley, Alan. *The End of Reform.* New York: Alfred A. Knopf, 1995.

———. *Liberalism and Its Discontents.* Cambridge, Mass.: Harvard University Press, 1998.

Brysk, Alison. "'Hearts and Minds': Bringing Symbolic Politics Back In." *Polity* 27 (summer 1995): 559–85.

Buchanan, Patrick J. "America Needs a 'Time Out' on Immigration." *Conservative Chronicle,* 16 June 1993. Reprinted in *At Issue: Immigration Policy,* edited by Scott Barbour, San Diego, Calif.: Greenhaven Press, 1995, 31–33.

———. "GOP's NAFTA Divide." *Washington Times,* 23 August 1993.

———. *The Great Betrayal.* Boston: Little, Brown and Co., 1998.

Buell, Frederick. *National Culture and the New Global System.* Baltimore: Johns Hopkins University Press, 1994.

Bull, Hedley, and Adam Watson. *The Expansion of International Society.* Oxford: Clarendon Press, 1984.

Bureau of the Census. *Profile of the Foreign Born Population in the United States: 1997.* Current Population Reports, Special Studies P23-195, August 1999.

Burtless, Gary, Robert Z. Lawrence, Robert E. Litan, and Robert J. Shapiro. *Globaphobia.* Washington, D.C.: Brookings Institution, in association with Progressive Policy Institute and Twentieth Century Fund, 1998.

Camilleri, Joseph A., and Jim Falk. *The End of Sovereignty?* Aldershot, U.K.: Edward Elgar, 1992.

Carter, W. Bowman, Joan Spero, and Laura D'Andrea Tyson, "New World, New Deal: A Democratic Approach to Globalization." *Foreign Affairs* 79 (March/April 2000): 80–98.

Castles, Stephen, and Mark J. Miller. *The Age of Migration.* New York: Guilford Press, 1993.

Cerny, Philip. "Globalization and the Changing Logic of Collective Action." *International Organization* 49 (autumn 1995): 595-625.

———. "Paradoxes of the Competition State." *Government and Opposition* 32 (spring 1997): 251–74.

Citrin, Jack. "Language Politics and American Identity." *Public Interest* 99 (spring 1990): 96–109.

Citrin, Jack, Beth Reingold, and Donald P. Green. "American Identity and the Politics of Ethnic Change," *Journal of Politics* 52 (November 1990): 1124–54.

Citrin, Jack, Beth Reingold, Evelyn Waters, and Donald P. Green. "The 'Official English' Movement and the Symbolic Politics of Language in the United States." *Western Political Quarterly* 43 (September 1990): 535–60.

Clark, Ian. *Globalization and International Relations Theory.* New York: Oxford University Press, 1999.

Cline, William R. *Trade and Income Distribution.* Washington, DC: Institute for International Economics, 1997.

Clinton, William Jefferson. "Remarks by the President at the Annual Meeting of the IMF and the World Bank," White House Press Release, 11 October 1995, at www.pub.whitehouse.gov/uri-res/12R?unipdi://oma.eop.gov.us/1995/10/11/5.text.1

Cohen, Jeffrey E. *Politics and Economic Policy in the United States.* 2d ed. Boston: Houghton Mifflin Co., 2000.

Cohen, Stephen D., Joel R. Paul, and Robert A. Blecker. *Fundamentals of U.S. Foreign Trade Policy.* Boulder, Colo.: Westview Press, 1996.

Collins, Susan M., ed. *Imports, Exports, and the American Worker.* Washington, D.C.: Brookings Institution Press, 1998.

Convey, Andrew, and Marek Kupiszewski. "Keeping Up with Schengen: Migration and Policy in the European Union." *International Migration Review* 29 (winter 1995): 939–63.

Cornelius, Wayne A., Philip L. Martin, and James F. Hollifield, eds. *Controlling Immigration: A Global Perspective.* Stanford, Calif.: Stanford University Press, 1994.

Crawford, James. *Bilingual Education: History, Politics, Theory, and Practice.* Trenton, N.J.: Crane Publishing Co., 1989.

———, ed. *Language Loyalites: A Source Book on the Official English Controversy.* Chicago: University of Chicago Press, 1992.

Danziger, Sheldon, and Deborah Reed. "Winners and Losers: The Era of Inequality Continues," *Brookings Review* 17 (fall 1999): 14–17.

DeSipio, Louis, and Rodolfo de la Garza. *Making Americans, Remaking America.* Boulder, Colo.: Westview Press, 1996.

Destler, I. M. *American Trade Politics.* Washington, D.C.: Institute for International Economics, and New York: Twentieth Century Fund, 1986.

———. *American Trade Politics.* 3d ed. Washington, D.C.: Institute for Interntional Economics, and New York: Twentieth Century Fund, 1995.

Destler, I .M., and Peter J. Balint. *The New Politics of American Trade: Trade, Labor and the Environment.* Washington, DC: Institute for International Economics, 1999.

Derthick, Martha, and Paul J. Quirk. *The Politics of Deregulation.* Washington, D.C.: Brookings Institution Press, 1985.

Dittgen, Herbert. "The American Debate About Immigration in the 1990's: A New Nationalism After the End of the Cold War?" *Stanford Humanities Review* 5 (1997): 256–86.

Doremus, Paul N., William W. Keller, Louis W. Pauly, and Simon Reich. *The Myth of the Global Corporation.* Princeton, NJ: Princeton University Press, 1998.

Easton, David. *The Political System.* New York: Alfred A. Knopf, 1953.

Economic Report of the President. Washington, D.C.: U.S. Government Printing Office, various years.

Edelman, Murray. *The Symbolic Uses of Politics.* Urbana: University of Illinois Press, 1964.

———. *Constructing the Political Spectacle.* Chicago: University of Chicago Press, 1988.

———. *From Art to Politics.* Chicago: University of Chicago Press, 1995.

Edmonston, Barry, and Jeffrey S. Passel, eds. *Immigration and Ethnicity.* Washington, D.C.: Urban Institute Press, 1994.

Eisner, Mark Allen. *Regulatory Politics in Transition.* Baltimore: Johns Hopkins University Press, 1993.

Esping-Andersen, Gosta. *Three Worlds of Welfare Capitalism.* Cambridge, U.K.: Cambridge University Press, 1990.

Evans, Peter. "The Eclipse of the State?: Reflections on Stateness in an Era of Globalization." *World Politics* 50 (October 1997): 62–87.

Faiola, Anthony. "Britain Arrests Pinochet at Spain's Request." *Washington Post,* 18 October 1998, p. A1.

———. "Pinochet Returns to Chile: Flight from Britain Ends 16-Month Extradition Crusade." *Washington Post,* 3 March 2000, p. A1.

Feenstra, Robert C. "Integration of Trade and Disintegration of Production in the Global Economy." *Journal of Economic Perspectives* 12 (fall 1998): 31–50.

Fowler, Michael Ross, and Julie Marie Bunck. *Law, Power, and the Sovereign State.* University Park: Pennsylvania State University Press, 1995.

Fraser, Steven and Gary Gerstle. *The Rise and Fall of the New Deal Order, 1930–1980.* Princeton, N.J.: Princeton University Press, 1989.

Freeman, Richard. "Toward an Apartheid Economy." *Harvard Business Review* (September/October 1996) 114–21.

Frieden, Jeffry A., and David A. Lake, eds. *International Political Economy.* 4th ed. Boston: St. Martin's Press, 2000.

Friedman, Thomas L. *The Lexus and the Olive Tree.* New York: Farrar, Straus and Giroux, 1999.

Giddens, Anthony. *The Consequences of Modernity.* Stanford, Calif.: Stanford University Press, 1990.

Gilpin, Robert. *The Political Economy of International Relations.* Princeton, NJ: Princeton University Press, 1987.

Gimpel, James G., and James R. Edwards. *The Congressional Politics of Immigration Reform.* Boston: Allyn and Bacon, 1999.

Goldstein, Judith. *Ideas, Interests, and American Trade Policy.* Ithaca, N.Y.: Cornell University Press, 1993.

Goldthorpe, John H., ed. *Order and Conflict in Contemporary Capitalism.* Oxford: The Clarendon Press, 1984.

Gourevitch, Peter. *Politics in Hard Times.* Ithaca, NY: Cornell University Press, 1986.

Greider, William. *One World, Ready or Not.* New York: Simon & Schuster, 1997.

Hall, Peter A., ed. *The Political Power of Economic Ideas: Keynesianism Across Nations.* Princeton, N.J.: Princeton University Press, 1989.

Hartz, Louis. *The Liberal Tradition in America.* New York: Harcourt Brace, 1955.

Harvey, David. *The Condition of Postmodernism.* Cambridge, Mass.: Blackwell Publishers, 1989.

Hashmi, Sohail S., ed. *State Sovereignty.* University Park: Pennsylvania State University Press, 1997.

Heer, David. *Immigration in America's Future.* Boulder, Colo.: Westview Press, 1996.

Higham, John. *Strangers in the Land: Patterns of American Nativism, 1896–1925.* New Brunswick, N.J.: Rutgers University Press, 1955.

Hinsley, F. H. *Sovereignty.* 2d ed. Cambridge, U.K.: Cambridge University Press, 1986.

Hirst, Paul Q., and Grahame Thompson. *Globalization in Question.* 2d ed. Cambridge, U.K.: Polity Press, 1999.

Hobbes, Thomas. *Leviathan.* Edited by Richard Tuck. Cambridge, U.K.: Cambridge University Press, 1991 (originally published 1651).

Hollifield, James F. "Migration Trade, and the Nation-State: The Myth of Globalization," *UCLA Journal of International Law and Foreign Affairs* 3 (1998): 595–636.

Hunter, James Davison. *Culture Wars.* New York: Basic Books, 1991.

Isbister, John. *The Immigration Debate.* West Hartford, Conn.: Kumarian Press, 1996.

Jackson, Robert H. *Quasi-States: Sovereignty, International Relations and the Third World.* Cambridge, UK: Cambridge University Press, 1990.

Jacobson, David. *Rights Across Borders.* Baltimore: Johns Hopkins University Press, 1996.

Joppke, Christian. "Why Liberal States Accept Unwanted Immigration." *World Politics* 50 (January 1998): 266-93.

————, ed. *Challenge to the Nation-State*. New York: Oxford University Press, 1998.

Kapstein, Ethan. "We Are Us: The Myth of the Multinational." *National Interest* (winter 1991/92): 55–62.

————. *Governing the Global Economy*. Cambridge, Mass.: Harvard University Press, 1994.

————. "Workers and the World Economy," *Foreign Affairs* 75 (May/June 1996): 16–37.

————. *Sharing the Wealth*. New York: W.W. Norton & Co., 1999.

Keohane, Robert O. *After Hegemony*. Princeton, N.J.: Princeton University Press, 1984.

Keohane, Robert O., and Joseph S. Nye. *Power and Interdependence*. Boston: Little, Brown and Co., 1977.

Kindleberger, Charles P. *The World in Depression, 1929–1939*. Berkeley: University of California Press, 1973.

King, Robert D. "Should English Be the Law?" *Atlantic Monthly*, April 1997, 55–64.

Krasner, Stephen D. *Sovereignty: Organized Hypocrisy*. Princeton, N.J.: Princeton University Press, 1999.

Kratochwil, Friedrich. "Of Systems, Boundaries, and Territoriality: An Inquiry into the Formation of the State System." *World Politics* 38 (October 1986): 27–52.

Krieger, Joel. *Reagan, Thatcher, and the Politics of Decline*. New York: Oxford University Press, 1986.

Krugman, Paul. *Pop Internationalism*. Cambridge, Mass.: MIT Press, 1996.

————. "We Are Not the World." In *The Accidental Theorist*. New York: W.W. Norton & Co., 1998.

————. "Once and Again." *New York Times*, 2 January 2000, at www.nytimes.com/library/opinion/010200krug.html.

Kuttner, Robert. *Everything For Sale*. New York: Alfred A. Knopf, 1997.

Lahav, Gallya, and Virginie Guiraudon. "A Reappraisal of the State Sovereignty Debate: The Case of Migration Control." *Comparative Political Studies* 33 (March 2000): 163–95.

Lasch, Christopher. *The Revolt of the Elites and the Betrayal of Democracy*. New York: W.W. Norton & Co., 1995.

Legomsky, Steven. "Why Citizenship?" *Virginia Journal of International Law* 35 (fall 1994): 279–300.

Lindberg, Leon N., and Charles S. Maier, eds. *The Politics of Inflation and Economic Stagnation*. Washington, DC: Brookings Institution Press, 1985.

Lindblom, Charles. *Politics and Markets*. New York: Basic Books, 1977.

Locke, John. *Two Treatises of Government*. Edited by Peter Laslett. Cambridge: Cambridge University Press, 1991 (originally published 1689).

Lowi, Theodore J. "American Business, Public Policy, Case Studies, and Political Theory." *World Politics* (July 1964): 677–715.

Lustig, Nora. *NAFTA: Setting the Record Straight*. Brookings Institution Policy Brief, no. 20 (June 1997) at www.brook.edu/comm/PolicyBriefs/pb020/pb20.htm.

Maier, Charles S., ed. *Changing Boundaries of the Political*. Cambridge, U.K.: Cambridge University Press, 1987.

Mander, Jerry, and Edward Goldsmith, eds. *The Case Against the Global Economy*. San Francisco: Sierra Club Books, 1996.

Martin, Cathie Jo. *Stuck in Neutral: Business and the Politics of Human Capital Investment Policy*. Princeton, NJ: Princeton University Press, 2000.

Marx, Karl, and Friedrich Engels. "The Communist Manifesto." In *Karl Marx: Selected*

Writings, edited by Lawrence H. Simon, 157–86. Indianapolis: Hackett Publishing Co., Inc., 1994.

Mayer, Frederick W. *Interpreting NAFTA*. New York: Columbia University Press, 1998.

Mazur, Jay. "Labor's New Internationalism," *Foreign Affairs* 79 (January/February 2000): 79–93.

McPherson, James. *Abraham Lincoln and the Second American Revolution*. New York: Oxford University Press, 1991.

Messina, Anthony M., and Colleen V. Thouez. "Controlling Borders: The Logics and Politics of a European Immigration Regime." Paper presented at the annual meeting of the American Political Science Association, Atlanta, September 1999.

Milner, Helen V. *Resisting Protectionism: Global Industries and the Politics of International Trade*. Princeton, N.J.: Princeton University Press, 1988.

Mitchell, Timothy. "The Limits of the State: Beyond Statist Approaches and Their Critics," *American Political Science Review* 85 (March 1991): 77–96.

Money, Jeanette. *The Political Geography of Immigration Control*. Ithaca, N.Y.: Cornell University Press, 1999.

Moody, Kim, and Michael McGinn. "Unions and Free Trade: Solidarity vs. Competition." International Labor Rights Education and Research Fund (1992): 1.

Morgan, Edmund. *Inventing the People*. New York: W.W. Norton & Co., 1988.

Nadelman, Ethan. "Global Prohibition Regimes: The Evolution of Norms in International Society." *International Organization* 44 (fall 1990): 479–526.

———. *Cops Across Borders: The Internationalization of U.S. Criminal Law Enforcement*. University Park: Pennsylvania State University Press, 1993.

Nau, Henry R. *The Myth of America's Decline*. New York: Oxford University Press, 1990.

Neuman, Gerald. *Strangers to the Constitution*. Princeton, N.J.: Princeton University Press, 1996.

Odell, John. *U.S. International Monetary Policy: Markets, Power and Ideas as Sources of Change*. Princeton, N.J.: Princeton University Press, 1982.

Ohmae, Kenichi. *The End of the Nation State*. New York: Free Press, 1995.

Organization for Economic Cooperation and Development, *Globalization of Industry: Overview and Sector Reports*. Paris, 1996.

Paarlberg, Robert. "Agricultural Policy Reform and the Uruguay Round: Synergistic Linkage in a Two-Level Game?" *International Organization* 51 (summer 1997): 413–44.

Palmer, Elizabeth A. "Language Bill Passes House" *Congressional Quarterly Weekly Report*, 3 August 1996, 2205.

Patterson, Orlando. *The Ordeal of Integration*. Washington, D.C.: Civitas/Counterpoint, 1997.

Perot, H. Ross. "Keep Wealth in the North." *New Perspectives Quarterly* 10 (22 September 1993): 30–32.

Pierson, Paul. *Dismantling the Welfare State?* Cambridge, U.K.: Cambridge University Press, 1994.

Poggi, Gianfranco. *The Development of the Modern State*. Stanford, Calif.: Stanford University Press, 1978.

Polanyi, Karl. *The Great Transformation*. Boston: Beacon Press, 1957 (originally published 1944).

"The Politics of Trade: Despite the Boom, Globalisation Is One of the Hottest Issues Around. Why?" *The Economist,* 23 October 1999, 27–28.

Porter, Rosalie Pedalino. *Forked Tongue: The Politics of Bilingual Education.* New York: Basic Books, 1990.

Portes, Alejandro, and Ruben G. Rumbaut. *Immigrant America.* 2d ed. Berkeley, Calif.: University of California Press, 1996.

Putnam, Robert. "Diplomacy and Domestic Politics: The Logic of Two-Level Games," *International Organization* 42 (summer 1988): 427–60.

Reich, Robert B. *The Work of Nations.* New York: Vintage Books, 1991.

Reimers, David M. *Unwelcome Strangers.* New York: Columbia University Press, 1998.

Reinicke, Wolfgang H. *Global Public Policy.* Washington, DC: Brookings Institution Press, 1998.

Robertson, Roland. *Globalization.* London: Sage Publications, 1992.

Rodrik, Dani. *Has Globalization Gone Too Far?* Washington, D.C.: Institute for International Economics, 1997.

———. "Sense and Nonsense in the Globalization Debate," *Foreign Policy,* vol. 107 (summer 1997): 19–36.

Rogowski, Ronald. *Commerce and Coalitions.* Princeton, N.J.: Princeton University Press, 1989.

Rosenbaum, Walter A. *Environmental Politics and Policy.* 4th ed. Washington, DC: Congressional Quarterly Press, 1998.

Rothkopf, David. "In Praise of Cultural Imperialism?" *Foreign Policy* 107 (summer 1997): 38–53.

Rothstein, Jesse, and Robert Scott. *NAFTA's Casualties.* Economic Policy Institute Issue Brief no.120, 19 September 1997, at www.epinet.org.

Rothstein, Richard. "Bilingual Education." *Phi Delta Kappan* 79 (May 1998): 672–77.

Ruggie, John Gerard. "International Regimes, Transactions, and Change: Embedded Liberalism in the Postwar Economic Order." *International Organization* 36 (spring 1982): 379–415.

———. "Territoriality and Beyond: Problematizing Modernity in International Relations." *International Organization* 47 (winter 1993): 139–74.

———. "At Home Abroad, Abroad at Home: International Liberalization and Domestic Stability in the New World Economy." *Millennium* 24 (1994): 507–26.

Sandel, Michael J. *Democracy's Discontent.* Cambridge, Mass.: Harvard University Press, 1996.

Sassen, Saskia. *The Mobility of Labor and Capital: A Study in International Investment and Labor Flows.* Cambridge, U.K.: Cambridge University Press, 1988.

———. *Losing Control?: Sovereignty in an Age of Globalization.* New York: Columbia University Press, 1996.

———. *Globalization and Its Discontents.* New York: New Press, 1998.

Schattschneider, E. E. *Politics, Pressures, and the Tariff.* New York: Prentice-Hall, 1935.

Schildkraut, Deborah, and Gregory Huber. "Symbolic Politics, Ideology, and Language Policy: Beyond Liberalism and 'Americanism.'" Paper presented at annual meeting of the Northeastern Political Science Association, Philadelphia, November 1997.

Schuck, Peter H. "Membership in the Liberal Polity: The Devaluation of American Citizenship." In *Immigration and the Politics of Citizenship in Europe and North America,* edited by William Rogers Brubaker, 51–65. Lanham, Md.: University Press of America, 1989.

———. "The Politics of Rapid Legal Change: Immigration Policy in the 1980's," *Studies in American Political Development* 6 (spring 1992): 37–92.

———. "The Re-Evaluation of American Citizenship." In *Challenge to the Nation-State,* edited by Christian Joppke, 191–230. New York: Oxford University Press, 1998.

Shklar, Judith N. *American Citizenship: The Quest for Inclusion. Cambridge, Mass.: Harvard University Press, 1991.*

Skocpol, Theda. *Boomerang.* New York: W.W. Norton, 1996.

Skowronek, Stephen. *Building a New American State.* Cambridge, UK: Cambridge University Press, 1982.

Smith, Adam. *An Inquiry into the Nature and Causes of the Wealth of Nations.* 2 vols. Oxford: Oxford University Press, 1976 (originally published 1776).

Smith, Rogers M. *Civic Ideals.* New Haven, Conn.: Yale University Press, 1997.

Soysal, Yasemin. *The Limits of Citizenship.* Chicago: University of Chicago Press, 1994.

Spero, Joan E., and Jeffrey A. Hart. *The Politics of International Economic Relations.* 5th ed. New York: St. Martin's Press, 1997.

Spiro, Peter. "Dual Nationality and the Meaning of Citizenship." *Emory Law Journal* 46 (fall 1997): 1411–85.

Spruyt, Hendrik. *The Sovereign State and Its Competitors.* Princeton, N.J.: Princeton University Press, 1994.

Stein, Dan. "Why America Needs a Moratorium on Immigration." Reprinted in *At Issue: Immigration Policy,* edited by Scott Barbour. San Diego, Calif.: Greenhaven Press, 1995.

Stevens, Gillian. "Immigration, Emigration, Language Acquisition, and the English Language Proficiency of Immigrants in the United States." In *Immigration and Ethnicity,* edited by Barry Edmonston and Jeffrey S. Passel, 163–85. Washington, D.C.: Urban Institute Press.

Stock, Catherine McNicol. *Rural Radicals: Righteous Radicals in the American Grain.* Ithaca, N.Y.: Cornell University Press, 1996.

Strange, Susan. *The Retreat of the State.* Cambridge: Cambridge University Press, 1996.

Tatalovich, Raymond. *Nativism Reborn?: The Official English Language Movement and the American States.* Lexington: University Press of Kentucky, 1995.

Thompson, Helen. "The Nation-State and International Capital Flows in Historical Perspective." *Government and Opposition* 32, no. 1 (1997): 84–113.

———. "The Modern State, Political Choice and an Open International Economy." *Government and Opposition* 34, no. 2 (1999): 203–25.

Thomson, Janice E. "State Sovereignty in International Relations: Bridging the Gap Between Theory and Empirical Research." *International Studies Quarterly* 39 (1995): 213–33.

Thurow, Lester C. *The Zero-Sum Society.* New York: Basic Books, 1980.

Tilly, Charles. *Coercion, Capital, and European States, AD 990–1990.* Cambridge, Mass.: Basil Blackwell, 1990.

Tolchin, Susan. *The Angry American.* 2d ed. Boulder, Colo.: Westview Press, 1999.

Torpey, John. *The Invention of the Passport.* New York: Cambridge University Press, 2000.

Uchitelle, Louis. "I.N.S. Looks the Other Way on Illegal Immigration." *New York Times,*

9 March 2000, at http://www.nytimes.com/yr/mo/day/news/financial/unemployment-ins.html.

U.S. Immigration and Naturalization Service. *Fiscal Year 1998 Annual Report.* Washington, D.C.: I.N.S. Office of Policy and Planning, Statistical Branch, May 1999, at www.ins.usdoj.gov/graphics/publicaffairs/newsrels/98Legal.pdf.

———. *Statistical Yearbook of the Immigration and Naturalization Service,* 1997. Washington, D.C.: U.S. Government Printing Office, 1999.

Van Slambrouck, Paul. "California Educators Struggle with End of Bilingual Education." *Christian Science Monitor,* 10 August 1998, p.1.

Vig, Norman J., and Regina S. Axelrod, eds. *The Global Environment: Institutions, Law, and Policy.* Washington, D.C.: Congressional Quarterly Press, 1999.

Von Glahn, Gerhard. *Law Among Nations.* 6th ed. New York: Macmillan Publishing Co., 1992.

Walker, R.B.J. *Inside/Outside: International Relations as Political Theory.* Cambridge: Cambridge University Press, 1993.

Wallerstein, Immanuel. *Geopolitics and Geoculture: Essays on the Changing World-System.* Cambridge: Cambridge University Press, 1991.

Walzer, Michael. *Spheres of Justice.* New York: Basic Books, 1983.

Waters, Malcolm. *Globalization.* London: Routledge, 1995.

Weber, Max. "Politics as a Vocation." In *From Max Weber,* edited by H. H.Gerth and C. Wright Mills, 77–128. New York: Oxford University Press, 1946.

———. "'Objectivity' in Social Science and Social Policy." In *The Methodology of the Social Sciences,* edited by Edward A. Shils and Henry A. Finch, 49–112. New York: Free Press, 1949.

———. *Economy and Society.* Edited by Guenther Roth and Claus Wittich. 2 vols. Berkeley: University of California Press, 1978.

Wiebe, Robert H. *The Search for Order, 1877–1920.* New York: Hill and Wang, 1967.

Weiner, Myron. *The Global Migration Crisis.* New York: HarperCollins, 1995.

Wilson, Graham. "American Trade Policy: System Withstands Pressure?" Paper presented at the annual meeting of the Midwest Political Science Association, Chicago, April 1997.

Wolfe, Alan. *One Nation, After All.* New York: Viking, 1998.

Wright, Robert. "We're All One-Worlders Now." *Slate,* 24 April 1997.

———. "Continental Drift," *New Republic,* 17 January 2000, 18–23.

Yanow, Dvora, *How Does a Policy Mean?* Washington, D.C.: Georgetown University Press, 1996.

Index

American Civil Liberties Union, 155
Amnesty International, 62
Anderson, Benedict, 42, 148–49
Andreas, Peter, 133, 137
authority, and state sovereignty, 34–37. *See also* sovereignty
Axford, Barrie, 59

Balint, Peter, 175, 179
Barber, Benjamin, 5, 18, 160, 187n7
Bauer, Raymond, 90
bilingual education, 153, 156–57, 161
Bilingual Education Act of 1968, 153
Birmelow, Peter, 139
Bodin, Jean, 41
borders
    of the American state, 51
    and boundaries, 38–39
    defining and maintenance of the new social compact, 48
    immigration across (*see* immigration)
boundaries
    global and national economies, distinguishing, 61
    of the state, 38–40
Bretton Woods economic system, 8, 44, 181–82n17
Brinkley, Alan, 53
Brookings Institution, 22, 105
Buchanan, Patrick
    American sovereignty, concerns regarding, 3, 18
    globalization, costs of, 5, 10
    immigration reform, 119, 122, 139
    NAFTA, opposition to, 87, 102–03, 113, 115
    "nationalist" approach to trade, 173
    presidential campaign, early success in 1996, 105
    Reform Party, joining of, 174
Bush, George, 102
Bush, George, Jr., 123

California
    Proposition 187, 12, 120, 122–23
    Proposition 217, 13, 156–57
capital markets, 20-21, 63, 70–71
Cerny, Philip, 78
Chabot, Steve, 121
citizenship
    definition of and the Fourteenth Amendment, 125

devaluation of and immigration, 137–40
    economic, 172
    human rights of immigrants and, 135–36
    immigration and the politics of, 140–42
    inclusive vision of, need for, 179
    protecting the rights of, 118–19
    See also national identity
Citrin, Jack, 154–55, 158
Clinton, Bill, 9, 103
Collins, Susan, 107–08
competition state, 78, 113–14, 168
Congress, reform and trade policy, 95, 97–98
corporatism, American consideration of, 74
deregulation movement. *See* free-market politics
Derthick, Martha, 75
De Sipio, Louis, 124, 132
Destler, I. M., 92, 95–97, 175, 179
Dexter, Louis, 90

Easton, David, 147
Economist, The, 6
economy/economics
    capital markets, 20–21, 63, 70–71
    as cause of globalization, 8, 71–72
    economic interdependence, 61, 63
    income inequality (*see* income inequality)
Edelman, Murray, 147–48
education, bilingual, 153, 156–57
Edwards, James, 121, 124
embedded liberalism, 44, 90, 170
English, battle for as official language, 13, 152–59, 161–62
English Plus Information Clearinghouse (EPIC), 155
environmental policy, 61–62, 68
EPIC. *See* English Plus Information Clearinghouse
ethnic restrictionism, 141–42
European Union, 67, 136

fast-track authority
    congressional reauthorization, inability to obtain, 9–10, 105, 174
    creation of, 98
    and negotiating NAFTA, 102
Federal Reserve Board, 75
Federation for American Immigration Reform, 119
free-market politics
    as cause of globalization, 55–56

competition state, movement toward, 78,
113–14, 168
and globalization in the United States,
75–76, 96–97, 169–70
reaction to and concern with sovereignty,
114–17
Friedman, Thomas
American world dominance and globalization, 4
backlash against globalism, 160
capital markets, 61, 63
dialectic of globalization, 187n7
economic innovation and political transformation, 56, 71
environment and globalization, 62
sovereignty, loss of as a benefit, 15

de la Garza, Rodolfo, 124, 132
GATT. *See* General Agreement on Tariffs
and Trade
General Agreement on Tariffs and Trade
(GATT)
American policymaking and, 67, 90–91
contemporary state system, development
of, 45–46
Tokyo Round, 97
Uruguay Round, 9–10, 87–88, 99, 104
Giddens, Anthony, 57
Gimpel, James, 121, 124
Giuliani, Rudolph, 123
globalization
causes, scholarly explanations of, 55–56,
71–72
centrality of conflict over, 199n7
conceptual clarity, need for, 33–34
definitions of, 7, 24, 57–59, 168
early history of, 68–71
first steps toward, 45–46
as ideal-type, 59–60
and immigration (*see* immigration)
impact and significance of, 60–64, 77–79
and income inequality (*see* income inequality)
and language (*see* language policy)
and multilateral agencies, 100–101
and national identity (*see* national identity)
political dilemma of, 176–79
political explanation of, ix, 72–77, 167–68,
171–72
scholarly literature on, 18–24, 55–56,
71–72
social contract, breakdown of and, 163–64
and sovereignty (*see* sovereignty)
and trade policy (*see* trade policy)
and the United States (*see* United States)
Goldsmith, Edward, 5

Goldstein, Judith, 92, 96
Gore, Al, 104
Gourevitch, Peter, 91
Green Party, 174
Greider, William
economic interdependence, 61, 63
globalization, implications of, 5, 14–15, 71
globalization, opposition to, 105
nation-state, crisis of, 17
sovereignty, need to pool, 18
Grotius, Hugo, 41

Harvey, David, 57
Hayakawa, S. I., 154
Higham, John, 125
Hinsley, F. H., 35, 37–38, 40
Hirst, Paul, 59
Hobbes, Thomas, 41
Hollifield, James, 135
Hull, Cordell, 89
human rights, 62–63, 135–36
Human Rights Watch, 62
Hunter, James Davison, 5

identity, national. *See* national identity
ideology, and American trade policy, 92
Illegal Immigration Reform and Immigrant
Responsibility Act of 1996, 118, 123,
139–40
IMF. *See* International Monetary Fund
immigration
backlash against, 119–24
citizenship and, 118–19, 137–40, 140–42
conflict over globalization, arena for,
134–37
contemporary wave of, 127–30
and culture, 66–67
English as the official language, battle for,
153–57
globalization and recent American policy,
11–12, 130–31
history of American policy, 124–27
impact of American policy, 132–34
literacy tests, 151–52
and national identity, 123 (*see also* national identity)
pre-contemporary, 70
restriction movement, 118–19, 141–42
reverse, 188n23
and the welfare state, 132
Immigration Act of 1990, 130–31
Immigration Reform and Control Act of
1986 (IRCA), 121, 129–30
income inequality
globalization, contribution of, 65–66,
108–12

income inequality (*continued*)
  growth in and fears of free trade, 105–06
  improvements, recent, 192n25
  institutional change, contribution of, 108–10
  policy responses, 111–12
  scholarship on trade and incomes, emergence of, 106–08
  technology, contribution of, 108–10
International Monetary Fund (IMF)
  creation of, 89, 182n17
  and development of the contemporary state system, 45
  as element of American hegemonic trade regime, 91
  as institution of the world economy, 67
  markets and globalization, 63
international political economy, and trade policy, 91–92
international trade, 69–71
International Trade Organization, 89
Internet, 60
IRCA. *See* Immigration Reform and Control Act of 1986

Jackson, Jesse, 3, 87, 103
Jackson, Robert, 37
Jacobson, David, 131, 135–36, 194n17
Joppke, Christian, 135

Kapstein, Ethan, 20–21, 65–66, 111, 171
Katzenbach v. Morgan, 152–53
Kennedy, Edward, 194n16
Keynesianism, 189n29
Krasner, Stephen, 178
Krugman, Paul, 4, 21–22, 112
Kuttner, Robert, 5

labor, movement across national boundaries, 135 (*see also* immigration)
labor, organized
  decline in power of, 108–09
  demands for protection, 98
  limited powers of American, 192n23
language policy
  English, battle for as official language, 152–58
  history of American, 150–52
  national identity, and globalization, 13, 144–45, 162–63
  national identity, and the Official English movement, 158–62
  social compact, breakdown of and, 163–64
Lasch, Christopher, 5
Lau v. Nichols, 153
Lincoln, Abraham, 49

Lind, Michael, 126
Lindblom, Charles, 187n16
Locke, John, 42
Lowi, Theodore, 26

Machiavelli, Niccolo, 41
Mander, Jerry, 5
manufacturing industries, demands for protection, 98
Mayer, Frederick, 112–13
Mazur, Jay, 78
McGinn, Michael, 115
McPherson, James, 49
method and approach, 82–83
Mexican American Legal Defense and Education Fund, 155
Milner, Helen, 98
modern state. *See* state, the
Money, Jeanette, 135
Moody, Kim, 115
multilateral institutions, 100–101
multinational corporations, 69, 134–35

Nader, Ralph, 3, 87, 115, 173–74
NAFTA. *See* North American Free Trade Agreement
National Education Association, 155
national identity
  globalization, threat posed by, 159–61
  historical development of, 49–54
  language and, 155–57, 162–63, 175–76
  Official English as an assertion of, 158–59, 161–62
  state's role in promoting, 48
  and symbolic politics, 148–50
  See also citizenship
nationalism, 42–43, 48
nation-state. *See* state, the
Nixon, Richard, 94
nontariff barriers to trade, 97
North American Free Trade Agreement (NAFTA)
  and American policymaking, 67
  domestic political conflict over, vii, 9–10, 102–04
  failure of contemporary model to predict conflict over, 93
  immigration, fears of and, 122–23
  and income, fears of loss of, 105–06
  negotiation of, 101–03
  and symbolic politics, 112–17
  trade and sovereignty, impact on, 112–13
  and the transformation of trade policy, 87–88
Nunberg, Geoffrey, 162–63

Office of the Trade Representative (OTR), 95, 98
Official English movement, 152–59, 161–62
Ohmae, Kenichi, 4, 56, 71
Omnibus Trade and Competitiveness Act of 1988, 99
OTR. *See* Office of the Trade Representative

Perot, H. Ross
    American sovereignty, loss of, 3
    immigration reform, 119, 122, 139
    NAFTA, opposition to, 10, 87, 102–06, 113
    presidential candidacy of, vii
    Reform Party, creation of, 173
Personal Responsibility and Work Opportunity Reconciliation Act of 1996, 118, 123, 39–40
Pierson, Paul, 115–16
Pinochet, Augusto, 62–63
Plyer v. Doe, 132
Polanyi, Karl, 23, 72
political identity. *See* national identity
Pool, Ithiel de Sola, 90
popular sovereignty, emergence of, 41–43
Portes, Alejandro, 159
privatization. *See* free-market politics
Proposition 187, 12, 120, 122–23
Proposition 217, 13, 156–57
protectionism
    historical tradition of, 89
    and income inequality, 111
    and the Office of the Trade Representative, 98
    reemergence of, 94–95, 98
Pufendorf, Samuel von, 41

Quirk, Paul, 75

race, and restrictionist sentiments, 141–42
Reagan, Ronald, 108
Reform Party, vii, 173
Refugee Act of 1980, 129
Reich, Robert
    economic inequality and globalization, 65
    globalization, implications of, 19–21
    multinational corporations, 61
    national community, undermining of and globalization, 171
    nation-state and national economy, development of, 53
Reinicke, Wolfgang
    globalization, new institutional and legal framework for, 179
    globalization, origins of, 58
    multinational corporations, 61
    sovereignty, defining, 34, 36

Robertson, Pat, 3
Robertson, Roland, 57–59, 60–61, 160
Rodrik, Dani
    globalization, implications of, 23
    labor markets and globalization, 110–11
    national community and globalization, 171
    popular expectations and the limits of globalization, 179
    welfare state, 47
Rogowski, Ronald, 91
Rothkopf, David, 16
Ruggie, John Gerald, 44, 90, 170
Rumbaut, Ruben, 159

Sandel, Michael, 5
Sassen, Saskia, 134, 136–37, 172
Schattschneider, E. E., 89
Schengen Accords of 1995, 136, 195n27
Schuck, Peter, 138
Shklar, Judith, 179
Smith, Adam, 72
Smith, Lamar, 123, 139
Smoot-Hawley tariff, 89
Soros, George, 105
sovereign state. *See* state, the
sovereignty
    and American political development, 52–54
    authority v. state capacity, distinction between, 35–37
    conceptual clarity, need for, 33–34
    definition of, 34–38
    and globalization, issue of, vii–ix, 21, 79–81
    historical evolution of the concept, 41–43
    and immigration, 134–37, 140–42
    and international relations, 37–38, 40, 44–46
    legal v. operational, distinction between, 36
    loss of, benefits regarding, 15
    loss of, fears regarding, viii, 102, 104–05
    and multilateral institutions, 100–101
    new social compact, emergence of, 47–49
    popular, emergence of, 41–43
    and state boundaries, 38–40
    threat to as symbolic politics, 113–17, 174
    and the welfare state, 44–45
Soysal, Yasemin, 135
state, the
    American (*see* United States)
    boundaries of, 38–40
    capacity v. authority, distinction between, 35–37
    competition, 78, 113–14, 168
    historical development of, 41–43

state, the (*continued*)
 historical development since World War
 II, 43–46
 mobilization of to promote globalization,
 100–101
 and the new social compact, 47–49
 political identity within, 148–50
 sovereignty and globalization, 79–81
 sovereignty and the origins of, 34–36
 weak and globalization, 64
Stock, Catherine McNicol, 5–6
Strange, Susan, 79–80
symbolic politics
 and immigration policy, 141
 and language policy, 144–47
 scholarship on, 147–50
 and trade policy, 113
Tatalovich, Raymond, 158
technology
 as cause of globalization, 56, 58, 71–72
 impact of globalization, 60
 and income inequality, 108–10
Thompson, Grahame, 59
Thompson, Helen, 177–79
Thomson, Janice, 35–36, 39
Tolchin, Susan, 5
trade, international, 69–71
trade policy
 and congressional reform, 95
 and domestic politics, 90, 92
 free trade policy and politics of the
 1980s–1990s, 96–101
 globalization, commitment to and domestic political conflict, 8–11, 104–05
 history of American, 88–90
 and ideology, 92
 and income inequality (*see* income inequality)
 international context of, 91–92
 North American Free Trade Agreement
 (*see* North American Free Trade Agreement)
 protectionism, reemergence in the 1970s,
 93–96
 scholarly explanations of, 90–93
 sovereignty, concern with as symbolic politics, 112–17

unions. *See* labor, organized
United Nations, creation and function of, 44
United States
 contemporary state system, role in developing, 46
 and corporatism, 74
 global action during the Cold War,
 187–88n17

globalization, and competing visions of
 American culture, 176–79
globalization, debate over the impact of,
 3–6
globalization, impact on politics and policymaking, viii, 6–7, 13–14, 64–68,
 172–76
globalization, political framework for explaining, 72–77
globalization, promotion of, 17, 168–70
globalization, significance of contemporary, 77–79
as hegemon, 3, 76–77, 91, 94, 169, 185n23
immigration to (*see* immigration)
language, policy and conflict over (*see* language policy)
modern state and new social compact,
 emergence of, 50–54
national purpose, globalization and the, 7
origins of the state and sovereignty in,
 49–50
political rhetoric over globalization, 14–18
sovereignty and globalization, 79–81
trade policy (*see* trade policy)
U.S. Border Patrol, 119, 121, 123, 133
U.S.–Canada Free Trade Agreement, 87, 100
U.S. English, 154

voluntary restraint agreements, 96, 99

Wallerstein, Immanuel, 188n26
Walzer, Michael, 52, 194n12
Waters, Malcolm, 57
weak states, and globalization, 64
Weber, Max, 72, 184n4
Webster, Noah, 151
welfare state
 American, 51, 53–54
 globalization and, 114–17
 and immigration, 124, 132
 social compact of the mid-twentieth cen-
 tury, 44–45, 47–48
Wilson, Graham, 96
Wilson, Pete, 122
Wilson, Woodrow, 43
World Bank, 91, 182n17
World Trade Organization (WTO)
 creation of, 9, 76, 88, 100, 104
 as institution in the world economy, 67
 Seattle protests, viii, 4, 9–10, 78, 88, 174,
 183n32
World War I, and development of the nation-
 state, 42–43
Wright, Robert, 15–16
WTO. *See* World Trade Organization